Experiences of Death:
An Anthropological Account

To David Brooks, in gratitude for the gifts
he has offered to each one of his students

Experiences of Death:
An Anthropological Account

Jennifer Lorna Hockey

EDINBURGH UNIVERSITY PRESS

© Jennifer Lorna Hockey 1990

Edinburgh University Press
22 George Square, Edinburgh

Distributed in North America
by Columbia University Press
New York

Set in Linotron Plantin
by Koinonia Ltd, Bury and
Printed in Great Britain by
Page Bros Ltd, Norwich

British Library Cataloguing
    in Publication Data
Hockey, Jennifer
    Experiences of death : an anthropological account.
    1. Death. Attitudes of society
    306.9

ISBN 0 7486 0221 6

Contents

Preface   1
  An Anthropology of Death?

Chapter One. An Approach to the Field   8
  Approaching Old Age   10
  Doing Fieldwork   15
  Interpretation and the Emergence of Meaning   21

Chapter Two. Boundaries Between Life and Death   27
  Historical Perspectives   44
  Professional Interventions   46
  Privacy and the Control of Social Space   46
  Contemporary Ammendments to Practice   49
  Problematic Experiences of Bereavement   50
  The Counsellor as an Agent of Change   52

Chapter Three. Death Past and Present   56
  Life, Death and Health: The Medical Model   63
  Cancer and the Myth of Medical Infallibility   69
  Malignant Growths and Metaphoric Expansion   77

Chapter Four. Setting the Stage for Death   81
  Dying and the Construction of Non-ordinary
    Times and Spaces   90
  Highfield House   91
  The Matron as Sentinel   94
  Controlling the care   96
  Metaphoric Scene-shifting: The Homely
    'Here-and-Now'   97
  Passage Through Residential Care   98

Chapter Five. Keeping Them Going: The Work of Care Staff   107
  Keeping Them Going   115

Chapter Six. One-way Journeys: Residents' Experience   124
  Two Lives   128
  Gender and the Experience of Admission to
    Residential Care   132
  Self-Sustaining Strategies   138
  Just a Song at Twilight   142

Chapter Seven. The Hospice Alternative   155
  Setting the Stage   159

Chapter Eight. Living with Death   167
  Strathcarron Hospice: Entry to Exit   167

Chapter Nine. Ageing and Death: The Continuing
    Challenge   178
  The Commitment to Care   182
  The Power of the Weak   183
  Powerholders   186
  Implicit Structures of Control:
  Strathcarron's Revealing Masquerade   190

Notes   202

References   206

Index   211

FIGURES

1: The Structuring of Space at the periphery of Highfield
  House   95
2: Hospice Care, the temporal, spatial and conceptual
  breaching of the prevailing life/death continuum   165

Preface

In 1955 my 74 year old grandfather was admitted to hospital from the tiny family home where I had always lived with him, my mother and my father. Suffering from heart trouble, he remained in hospital for more than a week. Though I sent in cards and presents for him, as a 9 year old child I was excluded from visiting. Within ten days of his admission, whilst lying awake in the living room where I slept, I overheard my father anwering the front door. His 'Oh Lor!' and my mother's unusually firm squeeze as they left the house evoked no conscious suspicion on my part – but I remember them still. The following morning, seated on either side of the kitchen fireplace, my parents announced my grandfather's death. Straight-away I began crying. Then, being told 'Don't cry. Grandad wouldn't want you to', I stopped, permanently. Soon after I spent the day with family friends, a special treat. Everyone else went to his funeral. A barely used toothpaste tube, the cards and the presents made a slightly disturbing re-appearance in the house. For nine years my grand-father had been by the kitchen fire, my sometimes frightening story teller and my solid climbing frame. Closer and more consistently accessible than either parent, he made a rapid, invisible and emo-tionally unremarked departure.

In October 1966 my mother, apparently healthy in her very early fifties, announced that she had to go to hospital, 'just for tests'. Her concern that I might be worried surprised me – I wasn't. Within a fortnight my father appeared in the library where I worked to pass on the doctor's announcement that she had ovarian cancer, that there was no hope, that she would die within nine months. Our decision to withhold the diagnosis from her was easily reached. Her un-changed manner and appearance gave a lie to the shocking inform-ation we were concealing. Its impact remained but was oddly dulled. We assimilated it privately as she, slowly, deteriorated. Our long held expectations were fulfilled the following March. When my father woke me to announce, 'She's just gone', my emotional response was minimal. Whilst the sound of her coffin bumping on the narrow stairwell walls remains in my memory I can recall no powerful feelings. In so small a house I somehow managed to see neither her body nor her coffin. It appeared later, from the back of a hearse, but as the focal point of a minimal crematorium service it evoked little more than an odd feeling of headiness.

In May 1977 a phone call brought news of the sudden death of one member of a recently acquired circle of friends. In his mid-thirties, the friend had died with the impact of a head-on car crash. In the weeks that followed a lack of appropriate experience became evident among many members of his social circle. While some were able to approach his widow, many failed and very few were familiar with the range of emotions she experienced. Similarly the offering of funeral wreaths was a gesture fraught with uncertainty about what to give and where and when to give it. Letters of condolence too were attempted, re-attempted and then abandoned.

A crowded country church and a winding procession to a hillside graveyard provided an evocative, traditional setting for such an encounter with death. Yet the young man's widow made a more personal choice in following his coffin to the grave in white linen rather than sombre black. Afterwards friends and family met at a sunlit funeral tea which in many ways resembled a long preceding sequence of night-time parties. In his physical absence benumbed mourners recreated the context of the young man's social life. Food and drink were laid out just as before and embraces were exchanged on all sides. The pattern was disrupted merely by the timing, the sunshine rather than darkness, the children rather than adults party-dressed, and now bicycling on the lawn. Only through such incongruities could the still unbelievable nature of the young man's absence be grasped.

At this point I was a mature student, engaged in a degree course in Anthropology. On many levels I was perplexed by the lack of death-related knowledge and experience among those who survived this young man. Other people in other places operated through systems which apparently provided more expansive answers to the questions raised. At this point in my personal history I had already begun to acquire the anthropological perspective through which I have since sought to approach and unravel such an enigma. These three bereavements lie at the heart of what is to follow – an account of the journey through which my unravelling was undertaken.

Initially, in an undergraduate dissertation (Hockey 1978), I moved from my own experience into the similar histories of others.

Conversations, largely with members of my own generation and social class, yielded material which corresponded closely with the details of my own past. A setting out of numerous 'death histories' established a pattern of childhood exclusions, adult silences and prevailing uncertainty, if not uneasiness, with respect to the anticipated death-related experience of the future.

The material was absorbing, but ultimately limited. Permeated by gaps and silences, it gave insufficient insight into dying itself. The full impact of the deaths which had approached me and others of my generation had, in many cases, been deflected. I needed to seek out areas of experience more intimately associated with death. In electing to make this approach to death, I sought it in its well-ordered context of old age. Later reflection tells me that in choosing this direction I was attempting to minimise my own exposure to the unpredictability of human mortality. I approached very elderly people whose timely dying was managed through the practised care of a residential home. Significantly I made choices in keeping with the prevailing assumption that mortality, when postponed sufficiently, becomes acceptable. Those who had avoided 'tragic', 'premature' or 'wasteful' death were, I assumed, the informants who, at that more appropriate stage of life, lay beyond the strategy of avoidance through which younger people managed their own untimely brushes with mortality.

Only with time did I become aware of the veiled structures of separation and control which, in the condensed living/dying spaces of a residential home, allowed staff and residents to keep death at a distance. Living closest to death and dying, residents' experience was among the most telling in that the minimal spatial and temporal boundary between life and death was given maximal cultural and social emphasis.

The three bereavements I have presented took place within the twenty years between the mid fifties and the mid seventies. Richard Hillier (1983: 320) cites the very early 1960's as the time of 'a rash of outstanding publications' about death and dying. Sociologists Glaser and Strauss (1965; 1968), and Feifel (1959) were publishing alongside doctors and psychiatrists such as Saunders (1959; 1965; 1967), Murray Parkes (1964a; 1964b; 1972) and Hinton (1963; 1967). Their work was the first indication of the innovations of the late sixties onwards when numerous hospices and bereavement support organisations were to emerge. When my mother died in 1967 I was living in a family context where religious and close social networks were lacking – and where my very traditional post 11+

Grammar school education was highly valued. Rather than a relative
or clergyman, I turned to a book, *Dying*, published that year in
Pelican edition by a psychiatrist John Hinton. Thus, as I emerged,
confused, from a secretive six months culminating in the unseen
removal of my mother's body from my home I found, in popular
edition, a book addressed to '... defining the known boundaries of
acceptance and distress'(cover notes). Hinton, it asserts, '... sets out
to give a balanced, truthful picture of how people approach death in
our post-war society'(1967:9).

Five years later, in 1972, another psychiatrist, Colin Murray
Parkes, published *Bereavement*, a book addressed to '... unravelling
the problems of grief and mourning', '... furthering our scientific
understanding of grieving', and '...trying to develop means whereby
bereaved people can be helped'(1972:Foreword). Further involved
in an academic education, I turned to this book in 1977 on the
sudden death of my friend.

In the material which had been proliferating around me since the
mid fifties there was an acknowledgement that death, one of the few
certainties of human life, had become a mystery. Through books
written by doctors and psychiatrists, readers sought a 'picture' of
how death was being approached, they needed to have the boundaries of grief 'defined'. Grief and mourning had become a 'problem'
to be 'unravelled' in order that 'scientific understanding' might be
'furthered'. Thus, those medical professionals who had made the
management of death their business were now identifying its everyday occurrence as a mystery and a problem. Their work confirmed
that my own experiences of confusion and uneasiness were an aspect
of 'our post-war society'.

This literature told of the human need to know, to articulate and
to grieve. And it told of new ways in which these needs were being
met, through counselling and through Hospice care for dying
people. In beginning research among elderly people living and dying
in residential care I gained not only an appreciation of the dehumanising aspects of existing systems of care, but also an understanding of the underlying set of beliefs expressed in this system. I
moved on to explore the new ways in which human needs were being
met. The contemporary bereavement support organisation, Cruse-
Bereavement Care, was founded as recently as 1959. I worked from
within this organisation as a voluntary befriender/counsellor to
bereaved people, thereby finding out at first hand about the experience of grief, and the challenges facing individuals who volunteered
their help. In addition, I worked as a volunteer in a hospice for dying

people where a relatively similar approach was being used in the care it offered.

AN ANTHROPOLOGY OF DEATH?

Having recognised that some very fundamental and intriguing questions lay behind my uneasy feelings over three personal bereavements, I found my preoccupation to be a far-from-isolated activity. I became part of a strong current of academic interest, yet I was using research methods developed in the study of either non-Western societies or small communities within our own society. Before looking at the details of how I saw deaths being managed, it is important to discuss the specific approach to this area which I used.

Those early anthropologists, such as Malinowski and Radcliffe-Brown, who moved out of the armchair school of social theorising, went into societies about which they had very little prior knowledge.[1] Such a venture inevitably brings a sharp encounter with the self. That is to say the anthropologist is made forcibly aware of the society and the cultural system which they have left behind. In addition they are subject to the scrutiny of others whose beliefs and way of life may be vastly different. An anthropological understanding stems from that initial encounter between self and other; that is, the self as re-experienced by the anthropologist, and as experienced for the first time by members of another society. Traditionally, anthropological monographs have given little insight into this source of understanding. In keeping with the methods of the natural sciences, the self is erased in the interests of objectivity and scientific rigour. Field diaries tell a different story.[2] Indeed since the mid-fifties anthropologists such as Smith Bowen (1954) have slowly begun to declare themselves and their experiences within the field as the source of anthropological knowledge.

This preface opens with accounts of three bereavements I have experienced. I have located my emotional and intellectual responses to each one within the context of a growing recognition of quite specific difficulties currently being felt in this area. As stated, my personal experiences lie at the heart of the project described in this book. Moreover that project, and the knowledge which it offers, arises out of interactions between myself and others. Though the question of the relationship between self and other as a source of knowledge will be explored fully in the next chapter, the process begins here in the preface and it is important that this is noted.

What I have written arises out of an extended dialogue between myself and individuals who aged, died and/or were bereaved in the course of my work; between myself and a 'supporting cast' of care assistants, counsellors, nurses, doctors, friends and family. At times the dialogue took the form of explicit exchanges or conversations. Essentially, though, it is an implicit process of negotiating a shared encounter with the idea and the event of death.

My field methods were entirely traditional. I chose field locations – a residential home for elderly people; a hospice for dying people; a bereavement support organisation. I sought entry, a role and a modus vivendi within each location. Predominantly, I bathed and fed people who were very elderly, I provided transport for people who were dying, and I counselled people who were bereaved. And, in the established manner, I wrote fieldnotes of as extensive, detailed and descriptive a kind as possible.

However, it was within, rather than as a result of, the flow of such visible activities that knowledge about our shared encounter with death was constructed. Rather than a series of findings which, if the quality and quantity of field material is good and sufficient, can be extracted from the final sum, this book offers the outcome of a protracted, intersubjective process. It was my entry into the imminent, immediate or remembered experience of others which opened up the range of ways in which members of British society manage death. Limited by the boundaries of what is seen within this society as a coherent set of responses, individuals nonetheless sought to manage their own suffering, loss and bewilderment in a variety of ways. I am distinguished among them not as an observer or a self-elected participant. I am distinguished from them primarily through my additional commitment to recording, exploring and elucidating what we were all doing.

The pursuit of an academic study of death lead me into a way of life in which the intellectual, emotional and practical issues of human mortality predominated. On more than one occasion a phone call from a widow seeking support through a particularly painful day interrupted highly theoretical reading addressed nonetheless to the cultural and social management of change and loss. Circularities of this kind pervaded the period through which I was working.

During this time I received invaluable support from a wide variety of sources. In the summer of 1977, death was the topic of an initial, extended conversation which I sought with David Brooks in the Anthropology Department at Durham University. His responses opened up an astonishing vista which I am still exploring. The enthusiasm and the insightfulness which he offered on that occasion were available to me continuously throughout the entire period of my later research. Those years were a turning point and I will always be indebted to him.

Judith Okely, Allison James, Marie Johnson, Malcolm Young, Bob Simpson, Peter Fillemore, Joan Knowles, John Malley and Ian Edgar provided me with an intellectual and social context which is special and enduring. To Judith Okely I am particularly grateful for an irresistible invitation into the fields of personal anthropology and research within my own society. Peter Fillemore has given me generous help in preparing Chapter Three of the book.

Bel Wilson at the Newcastle branch of the Cruse Organisation for Bereaved People, and Inge Samwell at Strathcarron Hospice, Stirling, readily gave me critical points of entry into fieldwork. During unnerving and lonely field experiences Bel Wilson and Inge Samwell watched closely and helped me to discover the necessary personal resources. Tom Scott, administrator of Strathcarron Hospice, offered very useful editorial comments on the final draft of material which discusses the hospice. Similarly the tireless patience and good humour of the care staff who guided me into and through the disorienting environment of a residential home for elderly people has been invaluable.

Central to the project was the trust offered me by individuals who were suffering both physical and emotional pain. Very few of them remain alive today. Their capacity to be both open and vulnerable is an important legacy for younger adults often culturally constrained by an excluding sense of privacy, a narrow commitment to autonomy and a concept of growth which disallows decline.

My most constant sources of support were the friends and family who accompanied me through an otherwise lonely period of study. In particular Carole Seheult and Dorothy Neave have actively shared in my enthusiasm, offered me companionship, and left me alone to get on with it. Bob, Joanna and Gareth Hockey, my immediate family, provide me with the safe place from which I set out and to which I return. I count myself very fortunate in this respect.

This book is dedicated to the memories of Meredith Watling, Lorna Manning, Bill Bennett, Eileen Carr and Bill Davison. Their lives provided the inspiration and the deaths the challenge which have made its completion possible.

Jennifer Lorna Hockey
Sheffield, April 1989

Chapter One

An Approach to the Field

In taking the human encounter with death as its focus, this book sets out to expand existing understanding of how death may be thought about. To gain such an understanding, our society's ritual and symbolic acts or events associated with death must be explored. It is through action or talk, in the present, that the human encounter with death comes into being.

In other words, our conceptions of 'death', and its relationship to 'life', are not only expressed in, but also generated through, the culturally-specific forms or institutions through which we manage death. For example, the Hospice Movement represents a set of ideas which challenge the medical approach developed in the West over the last three centuries. However these ideas take on their full meaning only in the current 'performance' of Hospice care. That is to say, a 'performance' which involves the slow persuasive process of bringing home an awareness of the imminence of death.

I will show that an appreciation of how a process such as Hospice care operates, and how a particular quality of experience is brought about for dying people, requires the active participation of the researcher within the process. It is through actions, events or utterances taking place within the here-and-now that meaning is generated.

What are the implications of these statements for research ? What kinds of methods allow one to find out what death means to people in British society, how they make death meaningful, and how they seek to come to terms with it? In the preface I suggested that the relationship between the anthropologist and the informants was the initial source of knowledge about the society within which the researcher is working. This suggestion has not only been found by anthropologists to be the case in practice – it also reflects a quite specific theoretical understanding of the way in which human thought, and therefore human action, comes into being.

Traditional research methods, as used within the natural sciences and, to an extent, the social sciences, are grounded in the separation of the researcher and their field of study. If used within the social sciences, this approach creates a relationship of observer to object between the researcher and the informant or respondent. Such methods reflect a specifically Western set of assumptions about the nature of reality and how we perceive it. Lakoff and Johnson (1980) have identified two 'myths' which prevail in our society, the 'objectivist' and the 'subjectivist' myths. Both myths reflect the idea that '... the world is made up of distinct objects with inherent pro-perties and fixed relations among them at any instance'(1980:210).

According to these myths, human thought and language is a fixed and immediate reponse to the world about us. The variety of responses to the world which different human beings quite evidently display is understood as their own 'subjectivity', that is a product of individual intuition, emotion or the imagination. Lakoff and Johnson counter this view with the assertion that human beings do not experience and understand the world in which they live in a fixed or immediate fashion, but rather through an inherited system of culturally-specific constructs or metaphors. They argue that individual experience can better be understood in terms of the rational, structured and creative metaphoric concepts though which we think and act within the world. 'Experientialist' is the term Lakoff and Johnson use to describe the properties of such concepts. By this they mean that a conceptual system is a society's hypotheses about the nature of the world, tested through experience within the world, and abandoned or elaborated according to their aptness, richness or usefulness. Hypotheses or metaphors of this kind describe some dimensions of a phenomenon in the world – love, work, death, time – highlighting certain of its aspects, downplaying others. Time, for example, although now understood to be amenable to measurement and therefore to have fixed qualities, is nonetheless open to a whole range of alternative metaphoric frames. This, of course, is reflected in the very different ways in which individuals may experience time. Rather than being a reflection of individual mood or idiosyncracy, that experience stems from the particular, systematic metaphors which inform the thought of that individual. Compare the quality of time for the businessman for whom 'time is money' with the prisoner who is 'doing time'.

When it comes to death, a potentially painful and in many ways intangible process, societies throughout the world have encountered it through a whole range of metaphors, or conceptual constructs. For example, death can be understood and experienced as a deliver-

ance from 'the burden of the flesh'; 1 as a punishment to which the
individual is sentenced; as a misfortune resulting from a curse; 2 as
matrydom; or as a necessary aspect of the regeneration of life; 3 In
order to come to some understanding of the management of death
within our own society, it is important to recognise those metaphors
as the primary focus of research.

Tambiah has argued '... in the human sciences, the pretence that
the observer is divorced from the thing observed does not accord
with the fact that human consciousness and social representations
are their ultimate subject matter, and the realities they deal with are
the products of intersubjective interactions and conventions created
in an open-ended historical process'(1985:352-353). Tambiah
therefore identifies social discourse as the primary field of study.
Only within the flow of events, speech and behaviour which constitute social discourse is meaning generated, and it is there that the
task of research must be pursued.

APPROACHING OLD AGE

Using research among elderly people as an example I will demonstrate the practical implications of these methods for fieldwork.
There is a joke which often turns up in the back pages of magazines
or on matchbox sleeves:

> Three old ladies were sitting on a park bench. One of them said
> 'It's windy today, isn't it'. 'No, I think it's Thursday', her
> friend replied. 'Well so am I', added the third old lady. 'Let's
> go and have a cup of tea'.

That elderly ladies might scramble distinctions of time, weather
and bodily needs is taken for granted. And we are prepared to be
amused by the apparently mild humour of this joke. Less apparent
is the joke's ageist implication that incompetence may unthinkingly
be assumed as an attribute of elderly women. Racist and sexist jokes
usually refer to individuals who are permanently separate and
different from the teller. Ageist jokes evoke fearful possibilities
which may constitute the future of the teller.

Research among elderly people must involve a recognition of
such jokes as one of the means by which fears about a future old age
are metaphorically distanced and set to one side by younger adults.
They call to mind a whole network of jokes and stereotypes through
which a conceptual separation is made between adulthood and old
age, between present and future. Prior to any research I stand, as an
adult, in this relationship to elderly people. The quality of research
therefore rests quite critically upon an ability to unravel and be

conscious of that relationship and of the cultural metaphors through which it is constituted.

Issues of methodology and ethics are raised from the outset in work among elderly people. It involves a particularly strange and pressing configuration of questions concerning the study of human beings by their fellows. For example, whilst the bodily experience of elderly people may be barely conceivable to the adult researcher, their bodies do suggest what might lie ahead in old age. Furthermore, on social, economic, political, as well as personal levels, much anxiety and apprehension is currently being aroused by the approaching spectre of an evergrowing body of infirm and unproductive elderly people. Such images lend an increasing urgency to the problem and policy oriented studies which predominate in the field of gerontological research. A literature review reveals this orientation in titles such as *The Social Challenge of Ageing* (Hobman, 1978), *The Measure of Need in Old People* (Isaacs & Neville, 1976), *The Social Medicine of Old Age* (Sheldon, 1948), 'and *The Care of the Elderly in the Community* (Williams, 1979). More emotively, there are titles such as *Sans Everything* (Robb, 1967), *Old and Alone* (Tunstall, 1966), *The Last Refuge* (Townsend, 1964) and *Old and Cold* (Wicks, 1978).

Thus, gerontological research can involve experiences which prompt the researcher to speculate upon the possibly disturbing nature of their own future – and, simultaneously, involves contact with members of a social category perceived to be a challenge or even a threat to society as a whole. It must be borne in mind that this perception of elderly people has been shown to have emerged as recently as the late nineteenth century. Thane (1983) argues that only with the advent of increasing trade pressure from abroad during the final decades of that century was pressure for retirement introduced. Employers' needs for a smaller but fitter workforce were met by shedding older, less productive workers. For the first time elderly people came to be perceived as a large, separate category, dependent upon society in general rather than upon their own families. As was the case with the social category, 'child', the gradual bureaucratising of the system of wage labour led to the creation of marginal, economically dependent social categories.

When set within the broader context of changing patterns of labour in the post-industrialised West, the orientation of much gerontological research begins to take on a particular significance. A parallel can be seen between the emergence of the 'social problem of the elderly' as an outcome of intensified trade pressure under industrialised capitalism, and the use of control-oriented measuring instruments through which to ascertain the extent of need among elderly people. Both are grounded in principles of scientific rationality without which the process of industrialisation could not have taken place. In the case of research within the social sciences, methods developed within the natural sciences were appropriated at the beginning of this century in order to lend status and credibility to less established forms of academic enterprise such as sociology. Gerontological research currently encompasses a variety of research methods, yet the social survey continues to be prominent among them. Moreover, given that increasing dependency is countered primarily through support of a practical kind, it is the extent and nature of material needs among elderly people which predominates as the focus of research. Tinker notes that '...the social surveys of the late 1950's, the 1960's and the 1970's were concerned first with the relationship between need and provision and secondly with the importance of taking into account informal networks as well as state provision'(1981:18-19).

She goes on to note that 'the medical aspect still continues to take a central place in the literature', pointing out that the authors of a number of standard works on social aspects of ageing are doctors rather than sociologists (1981:20).

Thus the main body of gerontological research is couched in problem and policy oriented terms. Its credibility arises from accurate assessment and measurement of what might be called 'the facts of the matter' – that is, provision for need and resource allocation.

Nonetheless, despite a strong commitment to identifying, quantifying and remedying problems of a practical kind, the emotional dimension of this work, for both researched and researcher, does make itself felt. For those involved in survey work through questionnaire and interviewing it is an often unwieldy dimension, both in collecting and interpreting material. For example, 'Life Satisfaction' tests were administered in geriatric wards by Evers,[4] and in a residential home for elderly people by Clough (1981:34). Once put into practice, Evers found their use to be not only inappropriate but distressing and abandoned them completely. She also abandoned plans for interviewing, finding that replies tended to be monosyllabic. Clough draws attention to the ethnocentric concept of 'life satisfaction' through which younger adults have formulated such tests. While he did make some use of such tests, he points out that they are a better measure of life dissatisfaction, in that elderly people cannot be expected to be happy in situations which are 'demonstrably miserable and unsatisfactory'.

Similarly, Willcocks, in the synopsis of a paper entitled 'Evaluating the consumer view of residential care', reports that 'We discovered at the pilot stage that residents tend to be acquiescent and passive; they are reluctant or unable to provide critical comment on a residential setting, and they found it difficult to express preferences'(1981).

Material was finally acquired by compiling a cartoon card pack containing twenty-seven items depicting various aspects of residential care provision. Residents then arranged the cards in order of preference. Willcocks writes 'With these cards we played our "ideal home" game in one hundred homes with some one thousand elderly residents' (1981). In this way the need for extensive sampling demanded by quantitative research was satisfied.

The difficulties encountered in these three examples are not uncommon. They can be seen to arise from a pressing need for 'objectivity'. Wenger, investigating the experience of loneliness among elderly people, writes in the abstract of her paper of '...a new scale which attempts to overcome problems of stigma and denial in data collection'(1983). She notes that 'The definition of loneliness has, however, remained problematic and it is therefore difficult to assess just what is being measured when the subject is discussed'(1983:160).

Wenger points out that it is large sample studies which convince central government funding bodies of the representativeness of results. She suggests that in-depth, time-consuming studies might be more fruitful. I suggest that were she able to pursue a study of this kind the apparently 'problematic' issues of definition, denial and stigma might offer critical and indeed very fruitful avenues into the quality of experience of elderly people.

Thus, although the emotional dimension of gerontological research makes itself felt repeatedly, it is the perception of elderly people as members of a needy social category which consistently reinforces the hegemony of 'objective' research. In order to allocate resources appropriately, research must provide an 'objective' assessment of the true nature of their condition. As Okely notes, the traditional means of ensuring 'objectivity' is to eradicate the link between researcher and researched (1975:171-188). This can be achieved through the use of pre-determined sets of questions such as 'Life Satisfaction' tests. Extensive sampling is similarly effective in that confrontation between researcher and researched is mediated by large groups of assistants who generally do not design or modify

the questionnaires, or analyse the data. As an alternative to preclud-
ing the possibility of a subjective response on the part of the
researcher through the use of such distancing techniques, Okely
advocates that the researcher cultivate an awareness of their own
particularity as a cultural and social being. In this way the significance and the implications of their personal responses can be
properly understood and made use of in subsequent interpretation.

In the field of gerontological research the traditional objectifying
techniques of separation and distancing are not only of dubious
merit, but also indicative of the deeply problematic nature of the
relationship between these particular categories of researcher and
researched. In a sociological thesis Fairhurst describes the use of
participant observation in a rehabilitation unit for geriatric patients.
She writes explicitly of '...the results of declining physical functioning such as incontinence, brain damage and ulcerated legs
(which) are unpleasant for one human being to witness in another'(1981:95). She goes on to say that:

> It is precisely because unpleasant aspects of doing research
> on the elderly, particularly those in hospitals, are inextricably
> linked with the notion of personal experience that arguably
> accounts, at least in part, for the relatively few ethnographies
> on old age. The concern with resource allocation, be it in terms
> of medical or social services, in many studies of old age is an
> example of what Roth (1962) has termed 'management bias'
> on the part of social scientists. (1981:97)

Thus in contexts such as geriatric homes and hospitals the
personal feelings of the researcher can be brought powerfully into
play. The quantification of survey material can be understood not
only in terms of a spurious search for 'objectivity', but also as an
important self-protecting strategy used by those whose sensibilities
are inevitably assailed by their informants. The 'humourously'
aggressive titles given to conference papers such as Ford's (1982),
'Dissecting the Elderly: Forging a new Sociological Tool', indicate
the researcher's very personal need to arm themselves against the
emotional onslaught of material of this kind. As I will show, personal
responses such as these have a weight and a significance which is
often overlooked. They are intrinsic to the relationship between
younger adults and elderly, and represent a fruitful starting point for
those who seek to explore that relationship. Without such an
awareness a fluid social world created and re-created through the
participation of its individual members can be subsumed within the
static depersonalising categories of power holders – those who seek

to control and to create order among the unproductive members of politically and economically competitive Western societies. As a result distances are induced within the shared experience of human growth and decline in such a way that the identity of both researcher and researched can become depersonalised. As in the parallel examples of ethnic minorities such as gypsies, or deviant social categories such as criminals, their 'awkward' individuality is threatened by control-oriented research methods. In consequence deviousness or silence may be their only defence.

DOING FIELDWORK

Participant observation, the extended involvement of a researcher within the world of the researched, is grounded in the assumption that individual experience can be understood in terms of the rational, structured and creative metaphoric concepts through which human beings think and act within the world. In the case of frail elderly people, they are often seen by younger adults to represent an undesirable or frightening future condition – and also to constitute a social category which for historical reasons[5] has come to be dependent upon that category of younger, working adults. Thus the metaphoric concepts through which younger adults perceive elderly people are likely to be associated with both fear and with a sense of superior power and independence.

Lakoff and Johnson have demonstrated the potency of metaphoric concepts in giving shape to what we experience as 'reality'. They further elaborate upon this idea, pointing out that '...whether in national politics or in everyday interaction, people in power get to impose their metaphors'(1980:157).

Thus metaphoric concepts are not only powerful in themselves, but, in addition, can be potent vehicles through which 'people in power' can shape the 'reality' experienced by those who stand in a weaker position in relation to them. It follows therefore that to understand the dependency of today's category of elderly people (and institutionalised elderly people) in purely material terms is to ignore their more profound vulnerability to the potency of the metaphoric concepts of the younger adult. Given that those engaged in gerontological research are members of that more powerful social category, it is critical that work pursued in this area should arise out of and take full account of the nature of that relationship.

Although a relationship of some kind links all researchers and the social categories or groups among whom they work, that relationship requires careful scrutiny when the field lies close at hand, where a shared language is in use, and where an asymetrical relationship of power pertains between researcher and researched. In such a setting the fieldworker is very much an 'insider', a circumstance which can be problematic and confusing. As noted, the jokes, and indeed the entire metaphoric system through which a less powerful social category such as 'the elderly' are perceived, may be a far from obvious aspect of the fieldworker's personal world view. Thus the language used unthinkingly by the fieldworker may take on a whole new set of meanings to the ears of those who appear to share the same world, yet whose experienced reality is significantly different – for example, if an informant's freedom is curtailed through imprisonment; or if their sense of self is deteriorating rapidly through an advancing illness. While the fieldworker makes free metaphoric use of bodily experience such as health, mobility, or sight – for example 'I'm sick to death of this wet weather', 'I'd better run along now', 'I see what you mean' – the elderly or criminal person may be acutely aware of the literal rather than figurative meaning of such a turn of phrase.

An example from personal fieldwork experience in a hospice illustrates this point. A hospice volunteer, wrestling with a badly-tangled bundle of cane, sought to encourage persistence among a group of would-be basket makers/dying patients through the inspirational metaphor, 'Never say die!' Her unthinking choice of metaphor resonated awkwardly, taking on at least three disturbing literal meanings which were quite specific to the context of the hospice. First, the Hospice Movement is committed to finding acceptable ways of actually 'saying die'. Second, the bald 'saying of die' is nonetheless inappropriate in that the Movement seeks to facilitate acceptance rather than cause fear among patients. Third, to be able 'never to say die' and to escape mortality may, at least at times, be the heartfelt desire of many patients.

It is often remarked that the English and the Americans are divided by a shared language. In other words, the meaning of that shared language is not fixed, but is embedded within, and arises out of, two very different lived contexts. Similarly, for those whose life within a specific context is dwindling rapidly the meaning of a hitherto 'shared' language can be dramatically transformed.

The problem of mis-understanding the meaning of language, owing to the false assumption that words have fixed meanings, leads on to the related problem of discovering the meaning of language, and indeed events and actions, which appear to be entirely familiar to the researcher.

Just takes up this point (1978:81–97), suggesting that for those

who work within their own society '...the task is to take the accepted
and common-sensical and, by some (other) process of 'translation',
to render it momentarily strange and bizarre so that we might seek
to understand it'(1978:85).

Just goes on to say that for those who work within more remote
'foreign' societies '...the task was to encounter the seemingly strange
and bizarre and, by a process of 'cultural translation' render it
acceptable to 'common sense' so that we might understand
it'(1978:85).

Just's choice of the word 'encounter' is apt. For the anthropologist working abroad, the strange and the bizarre are encountered
with a force which is impossible for someone working among groups
already 'known' and 'classified' according to their own values and
assumptions. If a very familiar social group or category is the focus
of study, participation observation becomes invaluable in that it can
allow a genuinely anthropological account of that group's metaphoric system to be produced. The richer and more extensive one's
own cultural perspectives with respect to a particular social group or
category, the more necessary an experiential approach, such as
participant observation, becomes in gaining access to both our own
and their conceptual systems. The use of role play in teaching or
therapeutic situations is an acknowledgement of this principle,
where the aim is limited to the discovery of 'what it actually feels like'
to be the other, too well-known individual. The anthropologist's
aim, however, is to question or explore the pre-conceptions of
familiar social categories, to engage in a learning process which is
essentially incomplete. That is to say, 'immersion', as a venture,
hinges critically upon an ability to do so in a partial and self-
conscious manner. In this way the 'critical lack of fit', from which
Ardener describes the anthropological experience as deriving
(1971:xvii), can deliberately be constructed by those working
among more familiar social groups. In the case of fieldwork within a
residential home for elderly people the decision to participate can
raise further questions.

Of relevance here is the term 'practical mastery', used by
Bourdieu (1977) to describe the competence of an individual to
pursue their own intentions by negotiating the rules, roles and values
of their own culture. Above all, it is a mode of operating which stems
from a learned ignorance, or lack of awareness, within the individual
as to the generative principles, or sources, from which their cultural
style derives. For the following reasons, I sought to discover the
generative principles from which cultural style within the residential

home derives through a partial and self-conscious attempt to assume the 'practical mastery' of a care aid.

First, there is the question of familiarity. From my own point of view, that of a member of the same society, a residential home for elderly people appears to fall very much into the category of 'the accepted and the commonsensical'. Many of the values and assumptions which hold sway in such an institution have echoed through the schools and the hospitals which make up my own personal history. Similarly, child-care and housework have been the occupations through which I have defined myself throughout an extended period of my early life. Nonetheless, I was aware that the apparent 'ordinariness' of institutional life represented a very particular mode of managing the 'non-ordinary' processes of deterioration and death. It seemed clear that an understanding of such a mode could be acquired only through extensive participation in the fine grain of that 'ordinariness'.

Through learning the skills and taking on the tasks of a care aid for a period of nine months, I encountered the confusions and the pitfalls of performing hitherto familiar tasks such as bedmaking and bathing, table-laying and toileting, in an unfamiliar role, responsible for elderly and often incapable strangers rather than youthful relatives. These experiences were common to each novice care worker, uncomfortable but fleeting. For the fieldworker these experiences are material to be grasped, stored and sifted through. With every blunder and hesitation the gap between personal assumptions and the priorities of the institution widens. Through careful reflection each can be made to stand and be known in sharp contrast to the other. In this way a critical lack of fit comes to arise, by virtue of the fieldworker's deliberate and self-conscious cultivation of a sense of personal disorientation.

Through this method the conditions of old age, from immobility and incontinence to depression and confusion became the pressing focus of all my energy and attention – physical, emotional and intellectual. Deeply familiar tasks of cleaning and bathing, conversing and coercing, were no longer framed and defined by the personal, the private and the domestic world of family. The movement back and forth between the home and my home effectively reoriented my understanding of the significance of these aspects of life for a very different category of dependents.

Second, there is the question of how I was perceived within the institution. Through negotiating a role with the Matron I gained insights into the nature and range of the institution's categories.

Certain of my characteristics – gender, age, parental experience – were perceived by her to be in keeping with the role of voluntary care aid. That I was accepted in this role by other care staff, and by residents, suggests that its tasks and requirements are comfortably in keeping with my past experience as a professionally untrained wife and mother. The management of death in old age emerged as a process for which my role as female parent qualified me. Had I been male, had I been medically qualified, had I been employed by the local social services research department, I might have chosen or been placed in a quite different role. As it was, the perceived appropriateness of my gender and parental experience for the job of caring for elderly people gives immediate insights into the way in which this task is understood within British society.

In contrast with an anthropologist working outside Western society I crossed only the most subtle of boundaries in my role as care-aid. The ease with which I could accept a lowly status, menial tasks, and a minimum of responsibility – and the readiness of staff and residents to accept a woman who displayed both warmth and willingness – are aspects of fieldwork which reveal much about the system within which I worked.

By contrast, hospice staff offered me the role not of domestic or orderly, but of voluntary driver and 'companion' to less ailing patients. Pervaded throughout by a middle-class ethos, the hospice made ready use of middle-aged, middle-class women such as myself, placing them at its periphery as 'front women' whose presence promoted an atmosphere which was both warm yet dignified. While the residential home made use of my domestic experience and was wary of my social class, the hospice made use of my social class, whilst offering me little menial work. Both made use of my gender.

Third, there is the question of the kind of knowledge I sought to acquire. In certain contexts interviewing and direct questioning are appropriate, particularly if implicit metaphoric systems have been transformed and objectified in an explicit form such as a folk ideology. In a residential home for elderly people practical mastery prevails. Its 'ordinariness' is the product of a culturally contrived, socially maintained ignorance of the home's 'non-ordinary' function – the channelling of deteriorating human beings towards their deaths. If we can learn something from the difficulties involved in administering formal tests, it is that much of what goes on and much that is critical within a residential home for elderly people cannot be articulated. Thus the problems encountered in eliciting verbal statements give vital insights into how a culture of care is constructed.

For example, Clough observes that those who care for elderly people are unique among health and welfare employees in their lack of formal training and instruction. He notes the ambiguous and vague terms in which even senior staff describe the aims of residential care workers – for example, 'keeping the residents happy' and 'giving them care' (1981:141). Often there is no external structure or programme to chart the process through which each worker acquires the skills intrinsic to the carer's role. By remaining largely inaccessible to the conscious mind, the constraints and the paradoxes of the 'care staff' role are managed, if not overcome.

In addition to the ambiguities of the care staff role, the structural dependency and physical weakness of elderly people admitted to care must be taken into account when making choices about research methods. Their circumstances mitigate against their being able to express or even conceptualise alternatives to their present circumstances. In their frailty, residents perceive the authority represented by capable staff as a necessity rather than an imposition. Nonetheless residents retain some scope for power in their own infirmities. The partial immobility, deafness or incontinence brought about by the ageing process can become a resource to be deployed sporadically when dependency irks most. A slumped body or a deaf ear are effective and direct statements which mutely assert that which rarely finds form in thought or word. Bodily as well as verbal statements have an important place in the anthropologist's fieldnotes.

In summary, my participation in a culture of care involved none of the distancing techniques of structured interviewing or survey administration. Instead I involved myself, often through action rather than words, with staff and residents. It was in this way that I became part of the human encounter with death – that is, the conceptual, social, spatial and temporal boundary between life and death, where my informants, ageing, dying and bereaved, discovered themselves. My approach represents a process of conscious decision-making, a particular interpretation of the cluster of ideas and approaches known as participant observation. In a context such as the residential home, that which Bourdieu describes as 'symbolic and cultural capital' (1977) is objectified primarily within the body as it moves through the confined and carefully structured space which is the home. In order to apprehend that which is learned only in practice, and reaches the level of discourse only in humour and allusion, I made use of my own body. By intercepting otherwise imperceptible processes of transmission I was able to transform my pre-existing understanding of ageing.

INTERPRETATION AND THE EMERGENCE OF MEANING

To explore the encounter with death within the residential home for elderly people I worked as a care aid. In the hospice I worked as a volunteer, and within the bereavement support organisation I worked as a voluntary counsellor. This approach allowed me to locate myself within the flow of social discourse taking place within each setting. It is in keeping with the idea that human experience arises out of, or is shaped by, a society's fluid yet structured metaphors. In that such metaphors or constructs are lived, and recreated within social discourse, it is there that meaning can begin to be approached. There remains, however, the question of interpretation. How can meaning emerge from the experience of fieldwork?

It is important to recognise that on some level, either explicitly or implicitly, the anthropologist is asking questions of their own experience as they have recorded it in fieldnotes. Indeed the very process of recording reflects the queries and the curiosity of the researcher in that they have made all kinds of choices about what to include and in what degree of detail.

With the cross-cultural perspective of the anthropologist I brought to my field material questions about variation in the way in which death is conceptualised and managed. In particular I wanted to find out how concepts of death, and their associated ritual or institutional forms, actually work to produce a particular quality of experience in people who are ageing, dying or bereaved. Close involvement with individuals undergoing such experiences makes for the possibility of accurate description, the writing of ethnography. There remains the question of interpretation, of drawing out sets of hidden, culturally-specific metaphors, and showing their role as frames or mediators of human experience. Discussing the nature of anthropological understanding, Geertz argues that immersing oneself within the experience of others, becoming 'a walking miracle of empathy, tact, patience and cosmopolitanism' may not, of itself, allow insights into the metaphoric system through which the experience of others is being produced. Geertz asserts that 'The ethnographer does not, and in my opinion, largely cannot, perceive what his informants perceive. What he perceives – and that uncertainly enough – is what they perceive "with", or "by means of", or "through", or whatever word one may choose. In the country of the blind, who are not as unobservant as they appear, the one-eyed is not king but spectator'(1977:482).

He goes on to address the question of how the ethnographer/ spectator may unravel the metaphors which make their informant's experience possible. He points out that '... ideas and the realities they disclose are naturally and indissolubly bound up together'(1977:482). As a way of beginning to separate out key ideas or metaphors he suggests a 'tacking back and forth' between everyday immediacies and the over-arching concepts which frame them.

To illustrate the way in which my decision to locate myself the flow of discourse produced material which I could interpret through a process of 'tacking back and forth', I offer accounts of three events which involved me closely with elderly people. It is significant that only one of the three actually took place within the old people's home. Each event was enacted at a different time and in a separate space. Each one involved physical and emotional participation on my part. It was participation of this kind which allowed me to perceive the shared system of cultural metaphors embodied within each one. My subsequent intellectual juxtaposing of the events was possible only because I had decided to assume a degree of 'practical mastery' by consciously immersing myself in the role of care aid within the residential home.

(1) Travelling north on a long distance coach I shared a double seat with an elderly woman. Close by the window, she slept deeply for a large part of the journey. Without warning an attack of sickness disrupted her sleep and she struggled in confusion to recover her dentures amidst the vomit. Lacking both social skills and a cloth of any kind, I looked immediately to my fellow passengers along the aisle. All stared intently towards their own windows. My proximity to the event was taken to indicate that responsibility for its management remained with me. Somehow the woman and I recovered ourselves with a few mumbles and a small handful of tissues.

(2) (from fieldnotes made on the eleventh day of fieldwork in the residential home) After lunch the new care aid and I had to get a resident, Winnie,[6] now in sick bay, up and into a chair. Winnie appeared fast asleep and, on awakening, resolutely insisted that she wasn't getting up. Attempts to persuade her, uncover her, were countered by Winnie going limp and apparently going back to sleep. I felt at a loss and went out to get advice or help. I came back in, finding no-one around, and the care aid laughed, saying that Winnie had woken up as soon as she heard the door close, thinking we both had left. The care aid suddenly became assertive, refusing Winnie's insistence on staying in bed. Her deep-voiced, North Eastern

'Howay Winnie, howay !' surprised me as the rather silent girl, only sixteen years old, had given no warning of her confidence in dealing with these matters. I followed her lead and we heaved the inert, soaking-wet Winnie into a sitting position and forced her clothes onto her limp body.

(3) Shortly after completing fieldwork in the residential home I spent time staying with a relative. Late one evening her elderly neighbour sought our help as his companion, a woman in her eighties, had been brought home distressed after a heavy fall in the street. My relative asked if I would go in with her and I found the woman on the neighbour's settee in considerable pain, crying, vomiting and urinating. Though my relative and her neighbour were familiar with, and therefore closer to the woman, I moved into the situation unhesitatingly, making tea, finding and holding a bucket for vomit and organising an ambulance. Meanwhile my relative, an able and forceful mother of five, and her neighbour, a constant companion to the woman, did very little. Unlike the event on the coach this was a situation in which I was in no way the obvious member of the group to assume responsibility. Nonetheless the entire trio ceded control to me, commenting as they watched on how well I coped.

How can meaning be read out of the accounts of these three events? Written in the first person they demonstrate a changing personal response to very similar situations. To show how such experiences illuminate a sphere far wider than the purely personal and introspective I will explore their relationship to one another in time and space. If the second event is assumed to be the only true field experience, then the residential home itself is being mistakenly perceived as an object of study. This assumption implies an 'objectivist' stance in that the institution is being seen as a discrete entity, amenable to direct study. While the home's spatial boundary is indeed important, it is not as a limit to the sphere of study, but rather as an embodiment of conceptual boundaries which divide up the biological continuum of human life, creating widely separated social categories. If the anthropologist works with this kind of perspective, they can develop a new awareness of their own, previously unquestioned, cultural and social categories.

For example, in the second account, my involvement in the role of care aid was total in that, unreservedly, I assumed responsibility for getting Winnie up. Nonetheless I approached her in a polite and distant style of my own. It cut very little ice. Winnie successfully outmaneouvred me and the care aid, a member of my daughter's generation, was prompted to demonstrate the appropriate and effective cultural style of the institution. Through physically assisting the girl, I absorbed directly a little of this style myself. The anthropological value of the incident is, however, discovered retrospectively. It lies in the deliberate, if uncomfortable, opposing of two styles, one being an elaboration of working class style within the inner world of the institution, and one being an example of the middle class world of the university outside. Though the opposition occurred in the 'field', it was about the relationship between inner and outer worlds and the boundaries which separate them. By allowing the mismatch between my assumed role and my personal style as a member of an educated middle class to become evident, and to take its course, I was able to explore this relationship.

My polite and distant style would have been unremarkable in any middle class woman finding herself in unfamiliar promimity to a urine-soaked and decrepit stranger. It demonstrates a considerable cultural investment in concepts such as privacy, freedom and social equality, these being expressed in direct confrontation with a member of a social category customarily contained and set apart from the world of healthy and affluent adults. Thus I am polite, but keep my distance.

As for the care aid, she was new to the home, but six months voluntary work with elderly patients in the nearby hospital had been sufficient for her to absorb the assertively familiar style of low-ranking NHS employees when dealing with less-esteemed categories of patients. For those employed in this way, making people do what is required of them is frequently understood through metaphors such as 'its for your own good', 'sometimes you have to be cruel to be kind' and 'we all have to go through it'. Such metaphors highlight areas of the experience such as bodily welfare and the inevitability of pain or discomfort. They also conceal or downplay other areas such as loss of privacy and loss of adult status. The power of these metaphors is reflected in the effectively assertive style of the care aid. They preclude any hesitancy or diffidence which might diffuse her authority or complicate the maneouvre she was attempting.

Some days after the event described, I was again involved in getting Winnie up. This time I worked with Jan, a slightly older and more experienced staff member. In speech and gesture Jan gave still more subtle and effective form to metaphors of this kind. She approached Winnie, gently patting her cheek and telling her we were getting her up. Then came a swift, rhetorical 'Any objections ?'

Having thus established that Winnie's getting up would take place, she left to find stockings. It was then possible for me to sit Winnie up without difficulty. As we worked, Winnie's odd remarks, 'I'm fed up', 'I'm no good at all', were countered by the reply, 'Well that makes two of us Winnie', from Jan who had overslept that morning.

In summary this preliminary reading of the second event shows how my participation produces an interaction which is more fruitful than mere observation might be. The narrowness and the particularity of the care aid's metaphors are revealed when set in contrast, through action, with my own. The reverse is also true. My own metaphors or cultural categories, which otherwise might distance or distort my understanding, are not only made evident, but can also be recognised as an aspect of the total social situation which has given rise to institutions such as the residential home.

As my familiarity with the field increased I, like other novices, absorbed the embodied metaphors of residential care. Though my style was lacking in the authenticity of those committed to the role of carer, events such as the third one described reveal that much had been internalised. Reflection upon the details of this event, particularly in comparison with the first event, throw yet more light upon what can be called the meaning of residential care for elderly people. It was clear that the physical and emotional condition of the elderly woman in the third example was perceived by her companion and my relative to be chaotic and disordered. It was something which they felt hesitant about dealing with, despite their relationship with her, and their competence in other areas of life. In this respect their behaviour resembled my own, and that of my fellow passengers, in the first event. Had I not recently been working in the residential home, I too would undoubtedly have extended the chaos by deferring to my already muddled relative and her neighbour before offering help or advice. As it was, I not only shared their perception of the woman as disordered, but also had access, within myself, to the metaphoric systems through which such disorder is categorised and contained within our society. In other words, in so far as the woman's particular distress would have been perceived as an entirely 'ordinary' event on the inside of the institution, so the institutional mode of speech and behaviour through which I took control of the situation was accepted as entirely authentic by these three members of the wider society.

In summary, the three case studies show the heuristic possibilities of immersing oneself, quite consciously, within the field of study. For example, the contrasts and oppositions which occur within and between each event give insights into the way in which some areas of human experience come to be perceived as culturally and socially disordering. Among the three women, the third was undoubtedly suffering the most acute physical and emotional distress. Yet my reordering of the situation involved possibly less in terms of gross physical intervention than either of the two preceding events. It was through my use of a particular cultural style of speech and movement that all those present came to feel that incipient chaos was now controlled. Rather than diagnosing or relieving the pain in the woman's shoulder, the apparently immediate problem, I was primarily giving shape to an unscripted situation, directing or guiding this trio of individuals through an experience which lay well beyond the bounds of their everyday relationships with one another. Indeed without the performance of embodied metaphors of the kind I have described, the chaos described in the first event holds uncomfortable sway.

This chapter introduces the theoretical perspective through which I approached and made sense of the encounter with death experienced by people ageing, dying and being bereaved in Britain during the early 1980's. I have argued that human experience, and the ways in which that experience is made meaningful, arise out of the constructs or metaphors which are particular to the individual's own society, or social context. This point has crucial implications for the methods of social research, in that the fieldworker too can experience and interpret what she observes only through recourse to her own set of metaphors. Using a specific example – of research among elderly people living in care – I have argued that an underlying metaphoric system can be approached only as it manifests itself in action, event or utterance in the here-and-now. As a result, fieldwork requires the conscious immersion of the researcher within the unfolding daily lives and deaths of informants. Three case studies exemplified the process through which the metaphoric systems of both informant and researcher can be made to come to the surface, in this case through the uncomfortable opposing of their cultural styles.

Chapter Two

Boundaries Between Life and Death

Death can appear at close quarters in contemporary British society
– in graphic news-reporting; in drama and documentary; in the
publications of professional 'carers'; in the jokes and metaphors of
everyday life; and in the domestic sequences of short-lived family
pets. Yet, like the marginalised and diminished 'world of nature'
made accessible in zoos, safari parks and wildlife films (see Berger
1980:1-26), it is a similarly transformed death which is currently
experienced through the flow of news coverage, dramas or docu-
mentaries into the home via the letter-box and the television set.

Writing in 1965, Gorer assserted that '... the majority of British
people are today without adequate guidance as to how to treat death
and bereavement and without social help in living through and
coming to terms with the grief and mourning which are the inevitable responses in human beings to the death of someone they have
loved'(1965:110).

Ten years later, in 1975, Illich argued that in the case of terminal
illness 'Today, the man best protected against setting the stage for
his own dying is the sick person in critical condition. Society, acting
through the medical system, decides when and after what indignities
and mutilations he shall die. The medicalisation of society has
brought the epoch of natural death to an end'(1975:149).

Both Gorer and Illich perceive an inability on the part of individual members of British society to manage their own encounter
with death – whether in bereavement or terminal illness. Gorer
relates their difficulties to a lack of 'social help'. Illich decries the
overdetermined intervention of 'society' in the form of the medical
system. In both cases the living are seen to have no direct relationship with death. It stands apart, separated off by boundaries of all
kinds, whether medical, social or conceptual. Gorer and Illich are
writing within the context of a growing literature addressed to what
has been described as 'the social invisibility of death' in the West
(Martins, 1983:xi-xv). The examples of 'social invisibility' cited by

Martins include a cultural ideal of a discrete and emotionally low-key death; cremation as practised in Great Britain; and a diminishing of outward social forms for the expression of grief. Once these examples are brought together, a common pattern, or strategy, of disguising and distancing death becomes apparent.

Martins also points out that the literature which offers a critique of Western approaches to death often sets them in unflattering contrast with death ritual at other times and in other places. Historical and anthropological material is seen to yield the possibility of more meaningful, therapeutic and dignified modes of disposing of the dead. What Martins describes as 'death utopias' are discovered in non-Western societies, often in social contexts where a broader examination would reveal underprivilege and punitive social control.

Anthropological monographs have frequently been plundered in the search for such images, spatially and temporally distant from the here-and-now of the contemporary Western reader, closer to a lost world of nature.

Cannadine, a social historian, notes that within his own discipline there have been similar utopian or nostalgic interpretations of the death ritual of previous periods in Western history (1981). Victorian death ritual has been a particular focus in the work of Aries (1974) and Stannard (1977:188-94) where, Cannadine notes '... if grieving in the nineteenth century was successful, death was almost pleasurable'(1981:188).

Such attempts to evaluate the ritual forms of other societies are valid endeavours. While Martins is appropriately sceptical about the breadth of perspective of some writers, there is, nonetheless, variation in the extent to which a society's cultural forms can be said to offer an expansive set of metaphors through which death may be encountered.

Writing in 1907, Hertz observed that '... when a man dies, society loses in him much more than a unit; it is stricken in the very principle of its life, in the faith it has in itself' (orig. 1907; 1960:78).

Hertz's essay demonstrates that death is a social rather than merely biological event. He argues that there is a requirement, particularly at times such as a death, that the central values and belief system of the society as a whole be experienced by its members as given, unquestionable and enduring. As a result, a funeral is often a critical event for the anthropologist in that what it expresses can give clues as to the meaning of material gathered from quite different spheres within a specific society. If the 'success' of death ritual can be discussed at all usefully, it is with respect to its power to express and to recreate a society's central values or issues in a covincingly authentic fashion. Current dissatisfaction in the West with death and mourning ritual, coupled with nostalgic sideways or backwards glances towards exotic or bygone forms, reflects the persistence of this requirement. Given that religious belief in Great Britain today is in many senses partial, the couching of all death ritual, at least minimally, within a religious aesthetic readily evokes the major issues to which religious experience addresses itself but now, no longer, provides a universal resolution. Indeed, while ritual associated with birth and marriage is frequently dispensed with, or enjoyed merely as tradition or colourful ceremony, the quality and character of ritual associated with death continues to be a focus for powerful emotion. When priest and liturgy, deceased and bereaved, are meeting for the first time, the resulting lack of personal significance felt by survivors may cause their grief to deepen into a more pervasive sense of loss as 'meaning' itself becomes questionable.

At this point I wish to introduce three anthropological accounts of death ritual within societies which are located geographically within the West, but which represent quite distinctive and different social systems. I have argued that, at the time of death, members of British society may discover themselves to be excluded from, or confused by, that experience as a result of divisive boundaries which keep death at a distance from life. The following ethnographic material exemplifies other ways in which the relationship between life and death can be conceptualised, and describes varying metaphoric forms or images through which it is managed.

In rural Greece both death and marriage ritual involve similar cyclic symbolism. Du Boulay (1982), has described not only the way in which dying is conceptualised, but also the ritual forms brought into play by a death. In this society the moment of death is understood through the image of the slashing of the dying person's throat by Charos, the angel of death. In this way, with the last breath, the soul leaves the body. Blood, violently released by Charos, pollutes the body, house and household and is purged only through washing, changing of clothes and, formerly, whitewashing of walls. Once cleansed the body is transformed into a state of precarious holiness which is maintained only through the care of mourners. On the body's navel a flat spiral candle made up of coiled threads, each one the length of the body, burns from the centre in an anti-clockwise direction during the three nights of the wake. Stringent care is taken to avoid the passage of anything (cups, cushions, a child

or an animal) across the body. All are passed, hand to hand, around
the body. Failure to observe this precaution brings about the
demonic possession of the soul. The body is then re-animated in the
form of a vampire which returns, seeking the blood of its own family,
and is defeated only through the irrevocable destruction of the
deceased's soul.

The meaning of these beliefs and practices can be understood
when they are set within the context of village life past and present.
Blood and the right-handed spiral are key symbols which resonate
throughout many other areas of life. In death ritual they are central.
Failure to maintain a continuity of thought and imagery at the
moment of death precipitates the embodiment of terror, the vampire
lying gleaming-eyed in its grave, emerging to penetrate the noses of
its kin and drink their blood. Du Boulay shows in detail how cyclic
imagery, the ordering principle of marriage patterns and of dance, is
used in the structuring of the relationship between the cultural
categories 'life' and 'death'.

Thus the separation of the body and blood of physical life from
the soul of spiritual existence is precipitated by Charos' bloodletting.
Ritual acts of purging, candle-lighting and encircling rather than
crossing the body are the ways in which such a separation must be
actively created and maintained. Only burial assures it. Only then
can the equivalence of blood with life be opposed to the bloodless-
ness of death. Full-blooded village life involves 'vivid and vital face-
to-face relationships'. In the shadowy 'other world' the bloodless
dead drift in endless motion, right hands stretched out behind them
in unseeing encounters with their half-forgotten fellows. The possibility of such an opposition rests upon the careful separation of the
conceptual categories 'life' and 'death'. Failure to maintain the
separation brings about the blurring of the two categories in the
terrifying, ambiguous form of the vampire, a devil-possessed soul
which re-animates its own undecaying corpse. The principle of an
auspicious spiral flow of blood, also expressed in the movement of
women out of their own homes to marriage among 'strange' kindred, is suddenly, dangerously, reversed. When women marry back
into the kin group from which their male kin have already taken a
wife, this 'turning back' or 'returning of blood' precipitates misfortune; when passage across a body breaks the encircling ritual
movements of mourners the living dead vampire returns to prey on
the blood of its kindred.

Du Boulay sums up her discussion by pointing out that while
Greek rural death ritual is firmly oriented towards the maintenance

of a separation between the cultural categories 'life' and 'death', it is through the careful structuring of that separation that the possibility of transcendence is created. Charos' blood-letting separates body and blood from soul, but in so doing sets the progression of the soul in motion. The cyclic imagery of marriage patterns and of the dance is recreated in the spiral candle and in the encircling of the body which ensure the safe passage of the soul to the 'other world' where the dead drift in an endless sequence of right-handed encounters. As Du Boulay states '...a continuity of understanding...informs the processes both of life and death'(1982:236). She concludes '...the spiral dance of life, while it divides irrevocably blood from non-blood and the living from the dead, at the same time permeates the opposed worlds of life and death, and transcends, though it does not reconcile, their opposition' (1982:236).

Du Boulay's material shows that human emotion can be engaged and focussed through the performance of death ritual. The threat of the vampire is far more than a nightmare folk-tale in that the exorcising of 'a great heavy woolly apparition' is remembered in disturbing detail by all the older villagers. This raises the question of how death ritual such as this actually works to produce a sense of meaning which can be felt by a society's members at the time of a death. Du Boulay's ethnography describes ritual acts and gestures, but it is through their performance that such formuli take on meaning-in-the-world. By including marriage patterns and dance within her interpretation, she shows how the symbolic forms which constitute death ritual in rural Greece resonate throughout the entire cultural and social context of participants. As a result a single, quite specific death may be encountered through a fixed ritual process which addresses the universal life cycle event, death. Both the event and the idea of death become simultaneously meaningful, on both a cosmic and a personal level. This is something which is often felt to be lacking with respect to death ritual within our own society.

Gypsy death ritual lends an important dimension to Okely's ethnographic account of gypsy culture (1983:215-230). As in Du Boulay's work, this material shows how a particular quality of experience is produced at the time of death, in that it is framed by a set of culturally-specific metaphors. Okely too identifies the creation of a separation between the cultural categories 'life' and 'death'. Here the management of death is organised through ideas about the nature of gypsy identity and gypsy/non-gypsy relations.

At the time of death, identity is a critical area of social life, one likely to be given maximal ritual expression. Indeed the inverse of this assertion is manifestly true, demonstrated in recent events throughout the world where ethnic identity is the cause par excellence for which individuals are prepared to give their lives.[1]

For a social group such as gypsies, living on the margins of other more dominant groups and dependent upon them as an economic resource, the maintenance of ethnic identity is culturally elaborated as a key organising principle within cultural and social life. Gypsies are a nomadic as well as marginal group and for them the body is an important focus for symbolic expression. Through bodily conceptions and bodily techniques the boundary which separates the social categories 'gypsy' and 'gorgio' (non-gypsy) is given cultural and social form. Thus the outer body, polluted through necessary contact with gorgio society, and the inner body, expressive of pure gypsy identity, are maintained in strict opposition to one another through a separation which permeates many areas of life. These include eating, washing, and animal classification.

At death, as at birth, the inner body can no longer be kept separate from and contained within the outer body. The dead body in its entirety and the spirit (mulo) thus become dangerously polluting, the objects of intense fear. Once the gypsy/gorgio separation can no longer be expressed through bodily boundaries, emphasis shifts to the boundary between the deceased and their cognates, between the dead and the living. As Okely says 'The boundary between life and death is used to make symbolic statements about another ethnic boundary'(1983:230).

Almost every aspect of death ritual, from the place of death to the care of the grave, can be seen as expressive and affirming of the boundary between the survivors and the dangerous mulo. Intense fear of the dead is the emotion which prevails at this time and which has been noted by gypsiologists. What Okely's work shows is the structured significance of this emotion. Only by bringing together all aspects of gypsy culture and, particularly, of the crucial gypsy/gorgio boundary, can the intense fear associated with the boundary between life and death be appreciated and understood as a socially meaningful response to death.

Crying is one example of emotional expression often thought of as a universal, individual response. Okely describes how gypsy dead are buried, at a safe distance, in gorgio churchyards. To the gorgio parson who conducted one such gypsy funeral, the uninhibited, even hysterical, wailing and sobbing of the congregation appeared 'very sad'. To authors of critiques of contemporary Western death ritual, active emotional discharge of this kind is often perceived as a desirable and therapeutic release of individual feelings. Using an anthropological perspective, Okely shows such displays of emotion to be culturally and socially generated, part of a necessary process of appeasing and distancing an imminently polluting spirit.

The relationship between the cultural categories 'life' and 'death' among gypsies can therefore be described as tense. There is no gypsy afterlife, no transcendent relationship between these two categories. The biological process of dying involves a fusion of the inner and outer body which is entirely inconsistent with gypsy identity. In that the dead are made immobile in the gorgio space of the churchyard, they can be said to have been dispatched for all time from a nomadic gypsy society and assimilated into the sedentary world of the gorgio. Cultural continuity is achieved not by an extension of the society of the living into the world of the dead, but rather through the social death of those whose bodily condition cannot be seen as anything other than an inversion of gypsy ethnic identity. Continuity lies in the future, in the biological and cultural regeneration of the group through its children.

Parallels to gypsy death ritual can be found in Faris's work on Cat Harbour, a small Newfoundland fishing community (1973:45-59). Faris argues that a metaphoric system can be understood only by setting it within the past or present circumstances within which it has been generated. His starting point is the system through which collective social events are classified in Cat Harbour.

Certain gatherings are recognised indigenously as 'occasions'. These include weddings, scoffs, funerals, birthdays, times and mummers. In trying to understand why 'occasions' are seen to be different from other social events such as church services, banquets, union meetings (which Faris terms 'non-occasions'), he explores Cat Harbour's history as a precarious settlement, illegally founded on the very periphery of the Newfoundland mainland. In the world view of its inhabitants, those who stand outside the local community are traditionally strangers of the most threatening kind. Local identity has been established in opposition to a harsh outside world of both mainland and sea-borne enemies.

Just as the maintenance of ethnic purity has been elaborated as a central organising principle among gypsies, so an insider/outsider opposition permeates the cultural and social frameworks through which life in Cat Harbour is conceived and experienced. Outsiderhood provides the metaphoric concept through which all socially unacceptable behaviour is made sense of and controlled. Blackness is the image/colour through which outsiderhood is evoked. Open, volatile emotionality, whether precipitated by alcohol or by grief, whether displayed in sexually licentious behaviour or close peer-group friendships, is an example of behaviour perceived to be dangerously unpredictable and unguarded. Theft is a similarly deviant behaviour.

Having established the present role of a historical opposition between insiderhood and outsiderhood, Faris shows the common elements shared by social events referred to as 'occasions'. These include the metaphoric or symbolic use of blackness, and the presence of behaviour such as theft, sexual licentiousness and uncontrolled emotionality, customarily thought of as deviant. 'Occasions', Faris argues, are a context for sanctioned deviance. Given the breadth of this very detailed material, which takes account of historical as well as contemporary perspectives, the full cultural and social significance of the behaviour of bereaved individuals in Cat Harbour can be appreciated. Of mourners, Faris says '...their role is considered potentially a very emotional expression, and any overt emotional exposure is regarded as potentially dangerous and avoided in Cat Harbour' (1973:56). It is thus that the exclusion of mourners from contact with the deceased, and indeed with all everyday activities, can be understood. At funerals they are spatially set apart from the rest of the congregation and from the 'helpers' (close outsiders who manage the corpse, the grave and the burial). With black ribboned lapels, mourners sit inside black ribboned-off space in the church. Helpers sit in a corresponding white ribboned-off space.

Faris limits the material presented in this paper to the structuring of immediate death ritual and its implications for the significance of emotional expression. Though cosmological considerations are not addressed, it is clear that the relationship between the culturally constrained emotionality of life and the emotional exposure thought inevitably to be precipitated by death is one of opposition. Such is the expected nature of grief that it cannot be encompassed within the category of experience 'life' but, along with other examples of sanctioned deviance, is set apart and framed within the times and spaces known as 'occasions'. Through imagistic or metaphoric references to blackness the concept of outsiderhood is evoked at all such 'occasions', thereby distancing and setting them in opposition to the acceptable sociality of the insider.

Questioning the way in which the biological events of life and death are culturally elaborated in different societies is central to an anthropological approach to the management of death. Death ritual as a way of framing the boundary between life and death is exemplified in the ethnographic material presented above. An appropriate movement across this boundary is critical within rural Greek society where one of its key concepts, the idea of life-giving energy or vitality, is understood through images of an irreversible right-handed movement or flow. By contrast material from isolated or marginal social groups such as a Newfoundland fishing community and gypsies shows ethnicity to be a central issue. In these contexts, where social continuity involves maintaining a clear boundary between insiderhood and the surrounding world, the biological boundary between life and death becomes a focus for elaborate symbolic expression.

Thus, to return to Hertz's assertion that society is 'stricken in the very principle of its life' (orig.1907; 1960:78) at the time of a death, these examples show how death ritual can encapsulate those very 'principles' or beliefs and values which are most under threat at this time. The particular way in which the boundary between life and death is managed can therefore be seen as a critical means of fostering a sense of cultural continuity in the face of the loss of society's individual members. These ethnographic examples are the wider context within which I am setting material from British society. What I will demonstrate is that within this society too the boundary between the categories 'life' and 'death' is critical. While that boundary may be so elaborated in other societies as to generate and affirm meaning, for members of Western societies it may raise disturbing questions about the very existence of meaning itself.

Aries has identified certain developments within Western society over the last three centuries which have given the boundary between life and death a very particular shape and quality (1981:559-601). He describes the intensifying of affectivity within smaller, more independent family groups during the eighteenth and early nine-teenth centuries. For the first time the loss of a family member gave rise to the kind of intense distress which we now think of as a 'natural' response to loss. Its culmination is the emotional death-bed farewell to a dying paterfamilias during the mid nineteenth century. So disruptive to the notion of the stable, patriarchal family was the death of a father that the entire household was immobilised through the symbolism of black. By the second half of the nineteenth century such intense emotion had begun to be managed through the 'loving lie', a protective strategy which robbed the dying person of their hitherto weighty personal responsibility for preparing for their own death. The success of this strategy rested upon increasing domestic privacy at the time of death. However this period was also marked by the stigmatising of visible dirt within the home, particularly the organic substances associated with bodily processes. The medicalisation of sickness and decay during the first half of the twentieth century can be seen as crucial to the final separation of the private, unclean and emotionally distressing event of death from the everyday domestic world of the home.

The maintenance of a boundary of this kind between life and death as a prevailing strategy for the management of death within Western society is the primary theme to be explored in this book. This strategy manifests itself in, for example, the way spatial separations are introduced between living and dying; in the way that temporally distant old age is seen to be the proper time for dying; in the way that medical control of this boundary has become critical; in the way death has been made the province of distinct, often marginal social categories such as 'the elderly', 'the bereaved', 'the mortuary attendant', 'the funeral director'; and in the way language of a euphemistic or humourous kind is used to assert the nature of a life/death separation, to distance the future process of dying. The following examples amplify these points.

(1) Spatial Boundary

In 1985, as Table 1 shows, only about 26% of all deaths occured in the person's own home. Nearly 69% of deaths took place in institutions. Thus home, the space within which living takes place, is seen to be inappropriate as a space for dying.

Table 1. Place of Death in England and Wales, 1985.[2]

	M	F
Total number of deaths	292,327	298,407
Place of Death		
NHS psychiatric hospitals	4,892	6,427
Other psychiatric hospitals	134	237
NHS hospitals & institutions		
for the sick	165,018	168,438
Other hospitals & institutions	10,029	17,020
Other institutions	9,190	26,602
At home	83,249	67,446
Other homes/places	19,815	12,237
Summary		
Death in institution	189,263	218,724
Death in other homes/places	19,815	12,237
Death at home	83,249	67,446

Thus, when the North East Co-operative Society sought to convert its Washington store into a funeral parlour, local residents, councillors and the town's MP campaigned to block the plan. *The Durham Advertiser*[3] explained:

An 80-year-old widow's ground floor flat on the Coach Road Estate, Washington is less than 20 yards from a newly-converted funeral parlour which is due to go into operation soon. From her kitchen she will be able to see hearses carrying coffins to the parlour's chapel of rest – formerly a Co-op store.

Every time Ivy Stearman washes the dishes or cooks a meal she comes face to face with death.

Twenty yards was thus deemed an insufficient spatial separation between the business of living and the prospect of dying.

(2) Temporal Boundary

The perception of death prior to old age as an abberrant happening is revealed in the language – 'tragic', 'untimely', 'wasteful', 'premature' – used to describe such deaths. Death in childhood can provoke condolence in the form of the words such as:

In Loving Memory of Ann, a beautiful flower who came
to bud on earth and to bloom in heaven.

The cycle of plant life is the metaphor through which life comes to be seen as something which involves all stages, from early growth through to complete blossoming. The biological reality that death can precede maturity is contrary to this perception of life – and the expected 'blooming' then takes place in another dimension.

By contrast, the idea that old age is the expected and appropriate time of death is expressed in language used to describe the death of an elderly person. Thus, they 'were getting on a bit', 'had a good innings', 'lived to a ripe/ grand old age', 'died in the fulness of time'.

(3) Medical Control of Life/Death Boundary

An example from field material illustrates the pervasiveness of medical control at the time of death. When I visited a widow who had sought support from Cruse-Bereavement Care, a national organisation which suports people who have been bereaved, her first, brief description of her husband's sudden death included a relatively extensive account of the dialogue which took place between herself and the doctor of the day of his death.

'Is it serious ?' she asked the doctor
'I'm afraid it is. He seems to have had a heart
attack', he replied.

'Will he get better ?' she asked.
'I'm afraid he won't. I've taken his blood pressure
and he has almost none', came the reply.

As her husband dies she experiences the event through the
medically authentic descriptions which she seeks from the doctor.
His are the words she repeats when she re-describes what happened.
Thus it is not only the event of death itself which is subject to medical
control, but also the very way in which the event is subsequently
understood by surviving relatives.

(4) Social Boundaries – the Marginalising of
Social Categories Associated with Death

Widows are one example of a social category which is seen to occupy
a marginal position within society. Thus, a widow who came to the
Cruse Organisation for help described how her family found her
open expression of grief unacceptable. She told me that although her
sister invited her for weekends, the proviso was 'Now, no tears
mind'. She told me 'Nobody wants you in your grief'.

While this woman's family had been unusually open about their
unwillingness to accommodate her grief, many bereaved people
sensed the same feelings among friends and relatives and sought to
hide their distress. Women felt uneasy about knocking on neighbours doors for company – and one woman compared her position
unfavourably with that of men who, she felt, could go to the pub or
'walk the lanes' (narrow access roads behind terraced houses in the
North East).

Alongside the experiences of bereaved people can be set those of
members of social categories professionally associated with death.
For example, in the North East certain district nurses, Twilight
nurses, take special responsibility for the care of terminally ill
patients. Discussing the 'taboo' on talk of death evident among the
families of her patients, one such nurse told me that she herself felt
stigmatised through working with dying people. When acquaintances discovered the nature of her work they would turn away,
saying, 'Oh, how morbid'.

(5) Linguistic Boundaries

While death, as a topic, is becoming an acceptable focus in academic
and more popular publishing, and a theme to be explored in
broadcasting, social discourse concerning death at a personal level is
impoverished. Euphemisms range from the coy – 'when my time
comes' – to the humourous – 'when I snuff it'. Those involved

professionally in the care of dying people have other euphemisms such as, 'terminal', 'going downhill fast', 'likely to pop off soon'. Language of this kind effectively keeps death at a distance, so maintaining a divisive boundary between life and death.

Similarly, when we make metaphoric use of death to impute an ultimate or extreme quality to the events or emotions of life, we reaffirm that boundary. For example, we are tickled or frightened 'to death'. We are 'dead' pleased, 'dead' certain, and 'dead' on time. In each case 'death' is the metaphor through which we suggest that our fear, our pleasure or our punctuality has reached some kind of limit or boundary, that it cannot be surpassed. By contrast, in societies where images of transcendance and continuity are stressed at the time of death, we find a corresponding metaphoric use of death to suggest transition. 'Deaths' are enacted in many rites of passage, particularly initiation.[4]

In the course of the last twenty-five years there has been a growing awareness within British society that death is being managed by keeping it at a distance from life. The examples set out above indicate the multiple forms which that distance or boundary can take and reveal the consistency of such a strategy for managing death. An anthropological account of life within a residential home for elderly people, to be presented in later chapters, shows this strategy being put into practice. It is through performances of this kind that death comes to take on sets of culturally-specific meanings – meanings which are reflected in the quality of life lived in close proximity to death.

While a divisive boundary between life and death may continue to be recreated in the provision of residential care for elderly people, debate about the dehumanising implications of such practices is well advanced. Indeed organisations such as Cruse, which supports bereaved people, and the Hospice Movement, which cares for dying people, are material representations of a felt need for alternative strategies.

These points are illuminated by glimpses into a selection of material from the Western popular literature and the press during the late 1970's and early 1980's. Particularly in newspapers produced for a 'serious' middle class readership, questions about the positioning and the nature of the boundary between life and death are raised for discussion, both in feature articles and in readers' letters. Local newspapers produced for a wider readership carry reports, one of which is exemplified here, of court cases where that boundary is open to legal contest. As a source of dominant mythologies, the following material therefore reveals fundamental categories of experience, 'life', 'death', 'dying', and 'health' being publicly held up for vehement questioning or criticism. The nature of life and of death, and their relationship to one another is being challenged. The examples encompass 'deaths' of many kinds.

(1) A blurred boundary at the beginning of life

Material from the popular press shows a lack of consensus as to when a human being can begin to be described as 'alive' – for example, in the sense of having an inalienable right to survive. Prior to birth the idea that the needs of the child's mother/parents have priority still retains some weight. After birth full membership of the category 'living' is still not assumed. Hence 'reforms' in the treatment of stillborn children which carry the innovative implication that it is the dead body of a former 'living' person which is being disposed of. Should a handicapped infant survive birth, its right to go on living is however not assumed. For example:

What's wrong with Abortion ? (Scarisbrook, 1980:2) Life Publication.

The question 'What's wrong with abortion ?' can be answered quickly. Fundamentally, abortion is wrong because it kills innocent human life. Abortion is death before birth. How can we be so sure ? Because human life begins at conception. That is not an opinion, a subject for debate or a matter of religious faith. It is a scientific fact.

For Ourselves. (Meulenbelt, 1981:223) Sheba Feminist Publishers: London.

The right to self-determination is still a political issue.In Britain we still have to be on our guard so that our still limited right to a safe legal abortion isn't taken away. In many countries the 'protectors of the unborn child' force women back to the back streets for abortions which often kill them, or make women suffer unwanted pregnancies and constant dread of pregnancy. The legislation of birth control today has a lot to do with population politics ... In America, for example, clinics were set up in the black ghettos to give advice on birth   control, while in the rest of the country there were hardly any clinics, and there are many known cases of Indian, black and poor women being forcibly sterilised, against their will.

Mourning by the Family after a Stillbirth or Neonatal Death. (Lewis, 1979:303) Archives of Disease in Childhood.

It is the nature of stillbirth that leads us all to avoid the subject. Bourne (1968) described stillbirth as a nonevent in which there is guilt and shame with no tangible person to mourn. A stillborn is someone who did not exist, a nonperson with no name. It is an empty tragedy and a painful emptiness is difficult to talk about ... To facilitate mourning I recommend that a stillbirth be managed by making the most of what is available and can be remembered Bereaved parents should be encouraged to help lay out their dead baby. A post-mortem photograph, examination and x-ray will assist genetic counselling. Parents should also be persuaded to take an active part in the certification of stillbirth, to name the baby, and to make the funeral memorable. The practice of burial in a common and nameless grave should be avoided. The family should be encouraged to attend the funeral or cremation and to know of a marked place or grave.

The 69-hour Life of John Pearson. (Gillie, 1981). The Times Health Supplement.

Dr Arthur wrote out instructions for the nursing staff: 'Parents do not wish baby to survive. Nursing care only'.He prescribed a drug, DFl18, up to 5 mg every four hours to be given if necessary, to relieve distress at the nurses discretion. He told the police that he had prescribed a sedative to stop the child seeking sustenance but the significance of this phrase was strongly disputed by the defence. Dr Arthur later explained ... that the purpose of the drug was solely to reduce suffering and not to cause the death of the child.

A Suitable Case for Treatment. (Carey, 1981). The Times Health Supplement.

'You are faced with the awesome responsibility of a verdict. Are you to condemn a doctor as a criminal because he cared ? Are you to condemn him as a criminal because he helped two people in their tragedy at the time of their greatest need ?' With those words to the jury in Leicester Crown Court Mr George Carman QC laid the basis for his successful defence of Dr Leonard Arthur against the charge of the attempted murder of a mongol baby. They reflect the unanimous view of doctors throughout the country and especially of paediatricians ...

(2) Medical intervention and the quality of life

This material shows a strong commitment to the idea that being alive confers the right to go on being alive. It implies a moral imperative to actively maintain 'life' using whatever means available. For example:

Cash Shortages Limits Heart Transplants. (Gillie, 1984). The Sunday Times.

400 heart transplants a year could be performed in Britain if all

available donor hearts were used. But fewer than 100 will be done this year and patients are regularly dying on the waiting list because of a shortage of money ... The demand for heart transplants is increasing steadily as doctors see the success of the operation and become more willing to refer patients – and as patients themselves become less fearful of it.

Kidney Patients Dying Untreated. The Times, 27.9.84. A transplant surgeon disclosed today that 1,500 kidney patients die in Britain each year because they do not receive treatment. Mr Michael Bewick, a consultant at Dulwich Hospital, South London, said 'that, statistically about 3,500 people between the ages of one and seventy suffered 'end stage' renal failure each year. Fewer than 2,000 were treated on kidney machines, placed on some other form of dialysis, or given a transplant'.

(3) Medical intervention and the quality of death

This material is addressed to dilemmas being introduced within the transition from life to death through the possibility of medical intervention. Each of these four extracts describes the bodily deterioration associated with ageing being 'treated' in terms of a medical model – that is, as an experience to be eradicated rather than managed and made sense of. As in the fourth example, by Toynbee, death itself is put forward as a preferred alternative to that part of life which, otherwise, must be managed prior to dying. Thus the meanings associated with the category 'life' do not extend to the deterioration of the ageing process. Should medical intervention fail to transform this process in such a way that it can be encompassed within the limitations of the category 'life', then extreme ageing is perceived to be little more than a 'living death', one perhaps more appropriately transmuted to a biological death. For example:

When Medical Treatment Becomes an Assault. The Guardian, 28.12.82, (letter).

I share Ann Corbett's sense of despair (Dec 17) over the bulldozing approach of hospital care to dying patients...(my father) was near the end of his life due to progressive heart failure, but was quite content and alert at home being looked after by my mother and the district nurse. After some random and inappropriate treatment from his GP he was eventually admitted to hospital for 'investigations'. The next few weeks were unmitigated hell for him and deeply upsetting for my mother. The medical treatment he received was no less than an assault, reducing him in a few days to a frightened hallucinating, physical and mental wreck – he was too frail to cope with the abuse he was being subjected to. He developed infections in direct response to hospital 'care' and for the first time in his life became violent and angry with those he blamed for his suffering. My mother and I watched helplessly ...

Why Dope the Old into Tranquillity ? The Guardian, 14.2.79, (letter).

My mother died in March after some 12 years of worsening rheumatoid arthritis, and... I got the strong impression...that nurses and doctors caring for the old commonly harm their patients by the too-free use of tranquillising drugs. Almost totally paralysed but mentally herself, my mother was asked to be admitted to the local cottage hospital for three weeks' 'experiment'... (five days later)... On entering the day-room I had to scan the line of patients more than once before recognising my mother – her condition being quite different from any any I had seen her in before; collapsed, and only able to drawl single words. The explanation for this drugging was that her groans of pain had kept other patients awake at night. At the end of her three weeks it was a question, no longer of whether life would be easier in or out of hospital, but of how many days life would go on.

The Death Kit in a Carrier Bag. The Northern Echo, 15.4.81

Death came in a carrier bag for the willing victims of Mark Lyons, 69, a court was told yesterday. Inside was a suicide kit – a quarter bottle of brandy, two plastic bags, elastic bands and tablets. The shabby man in the woolly hat, a member of EXIT, the voluntary euthanasia society... faces one count of murder and nine charges of assisting suicides... The murder charge involved Mrs Isabella Ward, a chronic back pain sufferer, who had twice tried to kill herself. Mrs Ward... joined EXIT in 1979 and was told by Reed that a man called Victor – one of a number of Lyons' alleged aliases – would call on her. When Victor arrived – he described himself as a doctor – he told Mrs Ward he would give her sleeping drugs to make her unconscious and then place a plastic bag over her head with an elastic band round her throat.

What Arthur Koestler could do with Dignity, the Law Forced James Haig to do Brutishly and Cruelly. (Toynbee, 1981) The Guardian.

Only a few weeks ago I visited a long-term geriatric ward. It was lunch time and rows of senile, incapable old women were being fed, spoonful by weary spoonful. One woman whose head lolled and tongue protruded, rocked and moaned without stopping, 'No, oh no. No, oh no!' She said it all the time, every day, all day. Whatever went on in her mind, it was constant misery. The time for decisions has passed these poor old people by. How many of them would have chosen to die had they been given the choice at an earlier stage? For the rest of us, what would we not give to save us from ending up like that ?

The examples selected reveal individuals contesting their society's most fundamental, 'given' categories of experience, 'life' and 'death'. From birth through to life-threatening illness and ageing, the categories of British society are found wanting and alternatives are being sought after. Within this range of currently problematic human experience lies bereavement and I now turn to a more exhaustive appraisal of the difficulties which are perceived to arise out of its present day management. Beginning with a discussion of historical perspectives, I will move on to consider current amendments to practice in this area.

HISTORICAL PERSPECTIVES

Gorer introduces his survey of the management of death in modern Britain with a description of 'the full panoply of widow's weeds and unrelieved black' worn by his mother, bereaved of his father in the sinking of the Lusitania in 1915. So visible a form of mourning was to vanish before the end of the First World War. Gorer writes:

> One can see the point, of course. The holocausts of young men had created such an army of widows; it was no longer socially realistic for them all to act as though their emotional and sexual life were over for good, which was the underlying message of the ritual mourning. And with the underlying message, the ritual too went into discard. There was too, almost certainly, a question of public morale; one should not show the face of grief to the boys home on leave from the trenches. (1965:6)

Gorer argues that, in the succeeding years of the twentieth century, bereavement received increasingly little public expression, becoming an evermore carefully hidden and private experience. The social historian, Cannadine, offers an alternative perspective on the years following the mass bereavements of World War One (1981). He argues that the very visible elaboration of mourning during the nineteenth century had already been questioned during the last years of that century. The celebration of death which prevailed up until the 1880's began to wane, giving way to the glorification of death in active (military) service for one's country. In response to the bereavements ensuing from World War One, the 'celebratory' ostentation of the nineteenth century was no longer found to be an appropriate form. Describing this period, Cannadine writes 'Two responses in particular merit attention: the one official, public and ceremonial; the other private, spontaneous and individualistic. The first was the construction throughout the country of war memorials, and the gradual evolution of the ritual of Armistice Day. The second was the massive proliferation of interest in spiritualism'(1981:219).

Both responses, he argues, were widespread and spontaneous – external social forms popularly appropriated for the expression of individual emotion. Cannadine sums up his discussion of this period as follows:

> In private seance, as in public ceremony, inter-war Britain was obsessed with death. The easy transition, so often depicted, from a death-dominated, sex-denying nineteenth century to a death-denying, sex-dominated twentieth century completely ignores this massive, all-pervasive pall of death which hung over Britain in the years between 1914 and 1939, and also the inventiveness with which the grief-stricken responded to their bereavement. (1981:230)

After the second world war such rituals lost something of their intensity – for example, Remembrance Day was held on a Sunday when public immobilisation was less visible, and war memorials erected after World War One were pressed into further service to bear the additional names of those who died in World War Two. In Cannadine's view the management of death since World War Two is not necessarily 'worse' than at previous times during history. The perception of nineteenth century death ritual as therapeutically superior is, he feels, not only misplaced but also misleading, in that resolutions to contemporary evils such as the threatened nuclear holocaust, the deprivations of the geriatric ward and the possibility of euthanasia, must be sought from within contemporary practice.

Cannadine's work has been taken up by Richardson who has looked again at the lack of public expression of grief since World War Two.[5] In her view, the pall of death which prevailed during the childhood and young adulthood of today's 'young' elderly people (fifty, sixty and seventy year olds) has lead to a current reluctance within this generation to dwell extensively upon the emotional experience of bereavement. It is their immediate successors, the post-war 'boom' generation of the 1940's, brought up to withhold or contain expressiveness of this kind, who have questioned and, in part, overcome such hesitancy.

In summary the role of two world wars, though variously viewed in terms of their implications, is nevertheless critical in any appraisal of the experience of bereavement today. They must be set alongside the growing importance of professionals at the time of death.

PROFESSIONAL INTERVENTIONS

Professional appropriation of the passage from life to death intrudes, to some degree, upon the emotional, social and practical relationship existing between the patient and their close relations and friends. As already noted, the emotional death-bed farewells of the mid nineteenth century were given extended expression in the immobilising of entire households through the symbolism of black. Such practices lent to the bereaved or soon-to-be-bereaved individual a clearly defined social role vis-a-vis both their deceased or dying relative, and also the outside world within which they found themselves. By contrast the 'loving lie', the protective strategy of the twentieth century cited by Aries (1981:559-601), diffuses emotional closeness between the dying individual and their family. Similarly lack of medical expertise on the part of family precludes ultimate responsibility for the management of the death falling to either the patient themselves or to their relatives.

Distances of this kind, established during the period leading up to a death, are extended in the appropriation of the corpse by a member of yet another social category of professional expert, the funeral director. Former practices, such as the preparation of the body for burial by a familiar member of the neighbourhood, and the subsequent care of the prepared body by the family in their own home, are no longer assumed within much of Western society.

Unfamiliarity not only with funerary ritual but, indeed, with religious ritual in general may further blunt or confuse the senses of a surviving relative whose 'management' of their bereavement has so far consisted largely in complying with sets of procedures imposed upon them by professionals. Whilst these possibilities prevail to very varying degrees within Western society, they can be seen, at whatever level they exist, to help seal off the bereaved person from their social and their physical environment. This raises another important issue – the nature of social relationships within British society as expressed at the time of a death.

PRIVACY AND THE CONTROL OF SOCIAL SPACE

Describing 'the death of the other' in nineteenth century Europe, Aries mentions the concept of privacy as being central to the confining of affectivity within the nuclear family. Elaborating upon this idea, he asserts that 'Privacy is distinguished both from individualism and from the sense of community, and expresses a mode of relating to others that is quite specific and original'(1981:609-

610). The concept Aries is seeking to elucidate is, he feels, best described by the English word 'privacy' – from the latin 'privare' meaning to deprive.

By contrast, Sudnow, exploring the (medical) management of death in American culture, describes very different forms of social behaviour displayed by newly-bereaved individuals in his own society. Using Goffman's term, he suggests that they are 'open persons', receiving both close relatives and distant acquaintances into their home without prior invitation. Thus he writes:

> It is apparently a custom in sectors of our society for the immediately bereaved's house to be open in the days immediately following a death...the door is left open and all comers are free to walk in and pay their respects. One finds, in such circumstances, an admixture of close relatives, close friends, and mere acquaintances. (1967:156-157)

With regard to social relationships between bereaved and non-bereaved members of British society, an implicit sense of privacy is often transformed into what may appear to the bereaved person to be a deliberate avoidance. In some cases the bereaved person reports having developed strategies for initiating conversation, particularly with respect to the dead person. Some are thus able to overcome the boundary. In other cases acquaintance or friendships come to an end as feelings of mutual embarrassment and betrayal take hold.

Avoidance of the bereaved individual by other non-bereaved individuals is matched by an emphasising, in death-associated ritual, of the private nature of grief itself. In the 'In Memoriam' verses published in the columns of local newspapers, secrecy is stressed in this apparently public expression of grief, directed ostensibly towards the dead. Whilst newspaper offices often carry pamphlets of set-piece verses, staff report that bereaved people usually bring in verses culled from previous months' selections, modified or restructured according to their personal preference. Though such verses are one of the very few public expressions of intense emotion, they are usually couched in highly stylised language. For example:

> Missed with a love beyond all telling
> Missed with a heartache beyond all tears
> Too dearly loved ever to be forgotten by granddaughter Dorothy.[6]

Public though they may be, these stylised expressions of overwhelming grief frequently include reference to the private nature of the emotional experience of bereavement. For example:

(from a man bereaved of his wife)

No-one knows my sorrow
Few have seen me weep
I cry from a broken heart
While others are asleep.[7]

Silent thoughts, tears unseen
Keep their memories evergreen.[6]

A secret longing, a silent tear
Always wishing you were here.[8]

Thus feelings of grief, expressed publicly by bereaved people towards the dead, contain frequent references to the silent, hidden, barely articulated nature of the experience. It is only from within the formalised style and content of these verses that personal choices are made and private feelings declared openly.

Thus, those whose close social relationships have been dislocated rather than intensified through the the constraints of the medical model of dying, and the professionalising of disposal, may go on to experience bereavement within the confines of a culturally prescribed privacy. In some cases, all but the immediate family are excluded from death ritual. In other cases, close human contact of any kind is avoided. Again newspaper announcements of death prescribe a privacy at the time of disposal which, thus established, re-asserts itself through successive annual 'In Memoriam' notices. For example:

Friends please meet at chapel. Afterwards private.

Funeral service on ... followed by private cremation. Family flowers only please.

Funeral private from residence. Friends please meet at church.[9]

Thus, at the time of a death, customary social separations which prevail in the form of 'privacy', are asserted yet more forcibly in the confining of the experience of grief to within the immediate family, or to within the bereaved individual. The possibility of a barrier of some kind between the bereaved individual and their surrounding world is thus established. In this way the extended, disorienting process of grief takes place, in many cases, in isolation from the outside world.

CONTEMPORARY AMENDMENTS TO PRACTICE

During the late 1950's, a small group of doctors and psychiatrists began to address themselves to some of the problems encountered by individuals who suffered a bereavement within the cultural and social context described above. Given that grief had come to be seen as a very private experience, a felt need for more public models of that experience arose. Dora Black, a consultant psychiatrist, describes grief as predominantly a healthy form of depression.[10] She suggests that numbness, followed by violent physical and emotional surges of protest, marks the beginning of grief. However, it is through a period of withdrawal into depression that the process of recovery may eventually be accomplished.

She describes the process in the following terms. In depression the individual withdraws from everyday life, and loses touch with customary daily habits or rhythms of eating and sleeping, becoming absorbed in obsessive, repetitive thoughts. Through behaviour of this kind, the past may be examined repeatedly. The reliving and summing up of both pleasant and regretted aspects of the past allows the bereaved person eventually to relinquish it, to put it into the past. It is the more elusive or ambiguous aspects of the lost relationship which are less easy to relive, and to let go of. Nonetheless a compulsive and repetitive mode of thought is not only characteristic of depression, but also instrumental in affirming and re-affirming the changes brought about by the death of a loved one. It is evident, from this model, that attempts, either by bereaved people or their helpers, to maintain superficial daily rhythms of life in an artifically dominant position may exclude and hinder the bereaved person's involvement with the deeper processes of change which are occuring. A de-structuring of external reality is necessary for the internal re-structuring of the emergent future self.

Models of bereavement such as this began to emerge in popular form from the early 1970's onwards, in the work of authors such as Murray Parkes (1972), Kubler Ross (1970, 1975) and Worden (1982). Their work is part of a movement stemming from the late 1950's, when articles such as those by Cicely Saunders on the care of dying people (1959) were published. In 1959, Margaret Torrie, a social worker, initiated what she described as 'a quiet experiment in social care'. She invited a small group of widows to drink tea with her, at home in Richmond. Within a few weeks the News Chronicle published an article about the venture. It stimulated widows to write, describing their personal experiences of bereavement. In this way an awareness of the lack of 'adequate guidance' and 'social help', identified by Gorer, became more widespread, and the contemporary organisation, Cruse-Bereavement Care, stems from Margaret Torrie's 'quiet experiment'. Now a national organisation, it has branches in one hundred and forty-five cities and towns throughout Great Britain. Support is offered to bereaved people in the form of social clubs, drop-in centres, information packs, and group and individual counselling. Almost all those offering support are volunteers, many of whom have suffered a major personal bereavement in the past.

PROBLEMATIC EXPERIENCES OF BEREAVEMENT

The broad cultural and historical context within which bereavement is currently being encountered is outlined above. Within that context, some individuals discover the prevailing boundaries between life and death to be particularly divisive and insurmountable. For example, individuals in their sixties and seventies may have been partners in very 'private' marriages; others may have experienced a relationship where illness or disability provided a powerful focus for an exclusive intimacy; they may lack a supportive social network, particularly within the extended family; they may have been bereaved in particularly painful circumstances, such as the sudden death of a child; or they may be people who have maintained a very rigid control of emotional experience throughout their entire lives.

The following material, recorded from my own experience of counselling, illustrates the varying circumstances described above:

Mrs Crawford was widowed very suddenly during her early fifties. Living alone, she was materially very well off, but considerably handicapped by chronic arthritis. During counselling visits she talked about her marriage. She and Ian had always been 'very close', they'd done everything together. Now she wonders if they shouldn't have lived more separate lives. She has only one daughter – no other family. She was married for thirty-four years and felt that her life really began when she met Ian.

Mr Dawlish was in his early seventies, living alone, and had cared for his wife, at home, during the six years of illness which lead up to her recent death. During visits he talked over all Majorie's illnesses, repeating the words they said to each other, imitating the voices they used. Her 'coo-ees' when she wanted something had become deeply familiar to him. He talked of his awareness of her every movement through the night – how watchful he was in case she should try to get out of bed.

Mrs Jackson was widowed in her mid sixties, lived alone, and felt unsupported by her family who lived locally. Following the rift with her son and daughter-in-law, Mrs Jackson had turned her hopes towards her own family again and they'd made no move towards her. Her sister in a nearby town said she was having no visitors until after Christmas. Mrs Jackson said 'But I'm not visitors. I'm family'. However the ban has been aimed very clearly at her.

Mrs Patterson was in her thirties, divorced, and living with her three children at the time of the sudden death of the youngest from a congenital neurological complaint. She described how the police had come to tell her to phone the hospital where her small daughter, Helen, was on a ventilator.In her panic, she locked herself out of the house – had to get the police again to let her in. Eventually she set off for the hospital but Helen was already dead when she arrived. She died suddenly and peacefully, Mrs Patterson was told. She described fragments of what happened afterwards. She was amazed at how physical the shock was – she felt as if a storm had broken out all around her. Her legs wouldn't hold her up – the hospital refused to let her drive – she had a sudden kidney infection over the weekend.

Mrs Kirby was in her early forties, childless, and recently bereaved of her husband, who was also her boss at work. Before seeking counselling, she had frenziedly pursued driving lessons and heavy gardening, in addition to a demanding fulltime job. Severe weightloss and deeply depressed lethargy ensued within months.

Mrs Thompson was in her sixties, an ex-nurse, living alone after the death of her husband. She had long committed herself to the role of a 'tower of strength' – this both within her village and throughout the long terminal illnesses of her sister-in-law and her husband. Though Mrs Thompson accepted a minimum of counselling visits, she begrudged herself the possibility of support and fought on in an effort to overcome her grief.

In different ways, the individuals described above have found themselves unable to enter into the grief ensuing from a particularly far-reaching loss. A barrier or boundary of some kind lies between the bereaved person and their entry into, and relinquishing of grief. These circumstances can conspire to maintain them betwixt and between the life that is lost and the life that lies ahead. With difficulty, and over time, separating boundaries of this kind can be so transformed as to become mediating links. Thus, for example, past events can be progressively reappraised in such a way that they take on new and more sufferable meanings. Should a bereaved person seek counselling help, then her counsellor is an agent through which this kind of transformation may take place. Mrs Crawford provides an example of this process, showing how new meanings can be attached to previously painful memories as four months of counselling pass by:

12th July, 1981

Mrs Crawford talked about the garden. She has all the equipment for a pool which Ian planned to make. She's not really interested in getting it done now – she just wants the terrace finished off and tidied up. She feels that so many of the things she cared about and enjoyed with Ian are now empty and meaningless – all the large ornaments in the house which they brought back from holidays, the Wedgewood dinner service. She can't see herself using it again – it will just sit there. She never sits in the lounge on her own (only when I'm there). She spends her time in the little dining-room. She feels she should make the effort but at the moment it just emphasises her loneliness.

8th November, 1981

Mrs Crawford said she feels Ian's presence in the house more and more strongly. She now has a happy feeling when she comes back into it after she's been out.Previously it just felt desparately empty. She feels she would never leave it now – all the ornaments are full of significance as she and Ian chose them together. They are very much a point of contact with him. Ian seems close at hand now and she knows they will never be parted – she looks forward to being with him again after death – a communion of souls.

THE COUNSELLOR AS AN AGENT OF CHANGE

Time spent together by a Cruse counsellor and a bereaved person can be extensive, often continuing into the second year after a death. Weekly visits of at least an hour, becoming less frequent only after some months, are not uncommon. For very isolated, or indeed very determinedly 'busy' bereaved individuals, an intervention of this extent is not insignificant. The counsellor becomes that part of the bereaved person's social context through which a loss may be realised and made sense of. Rather than participating in the bereaved person's grief, the counsellor is an intermediary vehicle through which grief comes to take place. One of the most significant aspects of this process is the entry of the counsellor into the private space of the bereaved person's home.

Entry of this kind is a powerful gesture on the part of the counsellor. Not only the bereaved person, but also the counsellor, are made forcibly aware of the empty space which now fills the home. The attention of the bereaved person is focussed upon the reality of their loss and also their consequent appeal for help. An example from field material illustrates this point:

> Mr Dawlish, an elderly widower, said that his wife had had her bed downstairs in the front room where he had taken me – he pointed out the mark of its foot on the carpet, just in front of me. Obviously I had sat down just where she had lain.

Thus the barrier which, to a varying extent, lies between the individual and their wider social context has been bridged through the visit. While relief from isolation may be felt, the bridging of the gulf again involves the focussing attention upon the loss. Movement across this space, and into the empty space, is therefore invariably a powerful initial act on the part of the counsellor. Responses to it vary.

For those committed to independence and a sense of control over their own circumstances, such visits signal helplessness and as such may not be tolerated beyond a minimum of occasions. Furthermore the raising of painful issues by the counsellor may lead such individuals into area of emotion over which they have little control – and again extensive visiting may not be tolerated.

By contrast, there are others for whom the incursions of another individual into the space which they now occupy alone is an opportunity for the physical re-enactment of the final scenes shared with the dead person in that space. The shared life of the past may be performed yet one more time. For example:

> Mrs Jackson, a widow in her sixties, recalled the day her husband got up from his chair and went to look at himself in the mirror above the fire. As she told me this she got up, re-enacting the event, taking his part. She told me that she herself was sitting on the settee, exactly where I was at that moment. 'By, I've got an awful look' he'd said, brushing back his hair. Turning, he put his arms around her neck, saying, 'Tell me its not so dreadful to leave this evil world'.All this she acted out,

crying as she did so. 'So he knew' she said, returning to her seat. Mr Dawlish said he found he had so much time on his hands – after being so totally occupied with his wife's needs. He described in detail all the care he'd given her, getting up to act out having to lift her from one place to another, coming over to almost grasp my shoulders, demonstrating what he'd done.

Most commonly the visit is accepted as relief of some kind from isolation. Nonetheless, whilst entry into the empty space has occurred, the bereaved person may not necessarily make use of the counsellor in order to openly express, and therefore enter into, their own experience. In very many cases, the bereaved person negotiates a path back and forth between 'safer' topics and the more painful areas associated with their loss. It is often only during an extended visit that the many routes back out of painful areas are relinquished and, often in a darkening room, the reality of the loss is encountered. For example:

(during a visit to Mrs Crawford).

The room darkened towards the end of the three hours, and Mrs Crawford began to speak more and more freely, and in more detail, of the events and feelings surrounding her husband's death.

Thus, through the entry and subsequent re-entries of the counsellor the social and emotional process of bereavement may be fostered and managed. In responding to the needs of those who discover themselves to be unable to pass through this process, the bereavement counsellor is confronted by the spatial, social and conceptual boundaries through which death has come to distanced from life. As the representative of an organisation which has sprung from a growing social awareness of the dehumanising effects of these boundaries, the counsellor embodies contemporary ammendments to practice in the management of death.

This chapter has taken up the now widely acknowledged notion that in our society death has become 'taboo', and is no longer a part of life. It asks questions about the nature of the boundary through which we manage to keep death at a distance from life. As exemplified, that boundary can be found to operate in terms of where we die, when we die, who controls our dying, what happens to our social identity when death comes into our lives, and how we talk about our own deaths. By contrast, ethnographic examples from other societies showed how the boundary between life and death, in being acknowledged, is transformed through death ritual into a mediating link with future life, either in this world or the next. The use of metaphors, and images, rooted in the most fundamental assumptions and values of a particular society, serves to maintain a sense of cultural and social continuity among survivors.

Later chapters will explore in more detail the nature of the boundaries which currently separate death from life in our own society, showing them in operation within a residential home for elderly people. However, the present chapter has gone on to introduce some of the contemporary responses to the de-humanising effects of such an approach to the management of death. Cruse-Bereavement Care represents one attempt to overcome the boundaries which otherwise separate bereaved people from the events, and emotions, surrounding the death of someone they love. It marks a shift away from a stoical, distancing approach to the management of death, and towards a shared and more emotionally unconstrained response. Here there is a clear parallel with the critique of dehumanising research methods which require the strictly controlled separation of researcher and informant. In Chapter One I have questioned the predominant use of such methods, calling for an appreciation of the fruits of an intersubjective, self-aware dialogue within the field. The final chapters of this book contain a more exhaustive appraisal of the Hospice Movement, as expressed in the care of terminally ill people in one specific hospice.

The last twenty years have seen a turning point in the management of death in British society. Fieldwork gives insight into the process of change, revealing the persistence of divisive boundaries between life and death, and the challenges confronting those who question, and seek to amend, prevailing practice.

Chapter Three

Death Past and Present

Taking as its focus an organisation addressed to the special difficulties now facing many bereaved people, the last chapter used a historical starting point to explore the impact of two world wars, the professional appropriation of care of dying people, and the pervasiveness of privacy within social relations in Britain. This chapter builds upon Aries' awareness of the de-humanising isolation of dying people, drawing key points from Capra's account of the dangerous fragmentation of knowledge in the West today (1982). As historian and physicist, both Aries and Capra offer interpretations of developments in ways of thinking about the managment of death and the management of life from the Middle Ages through to the present day. Alongside the very broad perspectives offered by these writers will be set the work of social critics or theorists Illich (1975), Berger (1976, 1980), and Sontag (1983). Grounded in a variety of disciplines, theology, history, fine art, literary criticism, they each have addressed medical models of life, death and health, so unmasking the political implications of contemporary 'scientific' frameworks. Like Capra and Aries, they speak, revealingly, from the periphery, from a critical, interdisciplinary perspective, so illuminating the powerful models which represent the centre.

An initial historical approach to the management of death will therefore now be expanded, as we trace the emergence of two aspects of the management of death which have become a focus for criticism during the last twenty-five years – the felt inauthenticity of religious ritual, and the inadequacy of contemporary medical models. Ethnographic material from non-Western societies shows that death has traditionally been encountered through cultural frameworks of a religious nature. Indeed Kapferer's (1977) work on Sinhalese healing rites shows that, outside modern Western society, not only death, but also health is managed according to religious frameworks. Once we set aside our own experience of religion and medicine as distinct and separate areas of cultural and social life, we discover societies where religious thought and experience pervade, and give meaning to, every aspect of life. In the West, 'religion' has come to refer to a very distinct set of beliefs and practices. While they may retain the power to inspire emotions such as respect or even awe, as an interpretation of the nature and meaning of human experience, current religious practices often fail to allow the individual to make sense of the everyday world they inhabit. It is medical and psychological, rather than religious models of living and dying, which have increasingly been resorted to as a sufficient account of human experience. A willingness to submit to mutilating or humiliating medical treatments, and anger over the 'inadequacy' of medical practitioners, are human responses which indicate that these are models which evoke enormous expectations – ones which may be held with the unquestioning trust of a religious faith.

Illich makes a clear distinction between current and more 'traditional' approaches to suffering and death. While he is using the terms 'culture' and 'meaning' only in a very restricted sense when he assumes that they cannot be used with reference to Western society, he nonetheless raises important points when he argues that, 'Culture confronts pain, deviance and death by interpreting them; medical civilization turns them into problems which can be solved by their removal. Cultures are systems of meanings, cosmopolitan civilization a system of techniques'(1975:93).

Today, in the West, 'medical civilization' is often the context within which death is encountered, the dead are disposed of, and the bereaved seek some kind of survival. As a cultural system, it can be described as a structure of control which operates only within limited spheres. That is to say, suffering is made manageable through its removal or reduction. Suffering which cannot be effectively eradicated escapes such a model. It is, nonetheless, similarly managed in that it is distanced and avoided. Those individuals who are unable, finally, to escape suffering often find themselves isolated within their own physical and emotional conditions, deprived of any vehicle through which their experience may be made meaningful, and therefore sufferable. Geertz points out the insufficiency of commonsensical systems of thought, such as those which inform 'medical civilization'. He argues that '... the events through which we live are forever outrunning the power of our ordinary, everyday moral, emotional, and intellectual concepts to construe them, leaving us, as a Javanese image has it, like a water buffalo listening to an orchestra'(1968b:101).

As an initial premise it would seem that both medical and

religious models of ageing, dying and death have currently been
found wanting. As a cultural system, medical or scientific models are
often experiened as ultimately limited in that they make only a
narrow range of human experience manageable – and in that
distancing and control, rather than encountering and interpreting
are their primary techniques. By turn, 'religious' models are often
experienced as 'inauthentic' – that is to say, as an interpretive
framework, their symbols bear only obliquely upon the experience of
many members of Western society. Largely absent is any persuasive
fusion of the cosmic and the personal dimensions of experience,
through which each becomes re-animated by the other. Thus, for
those who stand outside or on the fringes of the established church,
or other cohesive religious groups, the legal requirement of an
institutionalised ceremony of disposal often results in the disturbing
experience of ritual which is found to both evocative, yet uncon-
vincing at one and the same time. Moore and Myerhoff point out
that '... beneath all rituals is an ultimate danger ... the possibility
that we will encounter ourselves making up our conceptions of the
world, society, our very selves. We may slip in that fatal perspective
of recognizing culture as our construct, arbitrary, conventional,
invented by mortals'(1977:18).

At the time of a bereavement, the grief of those whose religious
faith is absent or wavering can be compounded by required attend-
ance at a ritual which in principle conceals, but in practice reveals to
those individuals, the constructed, arbitrary nature of the 'given'
beliefs of the established Church – through which the self and the
surrounding world have at one time been conceived of and experienced.

To explore the nature of the 'religious' and medical frameworks
through which we currently seek to make sense of death, it is fruitful
to set them within the broader sweep of history – from the time of
early Christianity up to the present day. A theme which helps orient
discussion of this very lengthy period is the changing concept of
health. As Illich notes 'In every society the dominant image of death
determines the prevalent concept of health'(1975:122).

Capra (1982:248-257), discussing the transition from the medieval to the post sixteenth century scientific or Cartesian world view,
highlights the now unapparent etymological connection between
the words 'health' and 'whole'. Their common root, the old english
'hal', means sound, whole and healthy. 'hale', 'heal' and 'holy' are
further examples of related words whose semantic connections have
now been severed. The gradual diminishing of the concept 'health',

and the fragmentation of its semantic universe, is one aspect of a series of pervasive transformations which have been unfolding since the rise of Christianity.

Another word which has undergone changes resulting in a depleted or reduced sphere of meaning is 'hospice'. The original sense of its root, 'hospitality', was the offer of protection, refreshment and fellowship. Records of Greek centres of healing such as Epidauris in the fifth century BC, suggest a broad concept of health which encompassed diet, exercise, the emotional catharsis of theatrical performance and the interpretation of dreams. Being oriented towards an idea of wholeness which was imaged in an idealised human body, such centres excluded dying people. Within a few centuries Roman rule saw the establishment of hospitals, institutions founded on militaristic principles for the repair of members of three valued social categories – warriors, gladiators and slaves. Lacking in the power to summon a private physician, members of these three categories received a now relatively diminished form of 'hospitality'. Only with the growth of Christianity in Rome during the fourth century AD did the concept of hospitality begin to expand again, accommodating the members of all social categories and of other countries. When Fabiola, a wealthy Roman matron, became a Christian disciple of St. Jerrome she created a refuge, or hospice, for all in need of protection, refreshment and fellowship. To beggars, orphans, pilgrims, sick and dying people, Christian love was extended. No social or political boundary precluded the offer of hospitality.

It was only during the social transformations of the fifteenth century in Europe, that the concept 'health' again came to acquire a much more specific and also more limited sphere of meaning associated with control and cure. While it is a concept of health which remains with us today in a still powerful form, this century has also seen the reintroduction of the word 'hospice', used in its original sense by a small group of Irish Sisters of Mercy. In 1902, this group sought to accommodate the range of human suffering which fell outside the limits of a medical model of health – and St Joseph's Hospice for impoverished, dying people was opened in the east end of London. So successful has the original concept 'hospice' been in evoking forms of care which transcend the medical model, that by 1988 over one hundred and twenty-five in-patient hospices, and two hundred and thirty home care teams had been established in Great Britain.

With the changing concepts of 'health' and 'hospitality' as reference points, I will take up Capra's assertion that the scientific revolution of the sixteenth century was a major turning point in the way which the world was understood in Europe. Prior to this period, the hospice established by Fabiola had become the model for monastery-based hospices which functioned as way stations for pilgrims. Throughout the medieval period the legacy of Aristotle's comprehensive view of nature, combined with the Christian view of the immanence of God in all things, had given rise to what Capra describes as an organic world view. Thomas Aquinas, during the thirteenth century, brought together reason and faith in a cultural framework which asserted the inter-connectedness of every aspect of both spiritual and worldly domains. During the two centuries leading up to 1500, the role of the human being was seen to be of an interpretive, rather than predictive or controlling nature. Thus, everyday experience was made sense of through a metaphoric framework which encompassed spiritual and earthly domains within a single model.

Copernicus' discoveries in astronomy represented a profound challenge to geocentric assumptions about the physical nature of the universe. Perhaps even more significantly, in a changed physical universe, the traditional resonance of religious metaphors such as 'heaven', 'hell', or 'the trinity' was threatened. Through the work of Kepler and Galileo, Copernicus' hypothesis became established as valid scientific theory. Galileo went on to develop a philosophy which called for an empirical approach to knowledge, and the use of mathematical language in descriptions of nature. Such an approach became feasible only through the reduction of 'nature' to its quantifiable attributes – shape, number and motion. The empirical approach to knowledge was taken up and vigorously developed by Francis Bacon. Capra cites the 'Baconian spirit' as critical in the pursuit of knowlege for the purposes of control and domination rather than understanding and integration.

The more extensive system of thought developed by Descartes in the seventeenth century stemmed from an illuminating vision which he experienced at the age of twenty-three. Interpreting the experience as divine inspiration, Descartes envisaged and promoted a complete science of nature. It was grounded in a newfound belief in the possibility of absolute mathematical certainty in scientific knowledge. Being above all analytic in nature, Descartes' method stands squarely in opposition to a medieval world view which stressed the integrated quality of the universe. Thus the world view which was to dominate Western thinking, and shape Western experience, during the three suceeding centuries is rooted in the assumed authenticity of the machine as a metaphor for the material world. Graspable only through the disciplined intellect which rejects that knowledge which has not been reached by deduction, the material world came to be experienced through scientific frameworks which reduced its depth and complexity to fragmented, constituent parts.

Infused with the Baconian spirit, and effective in allowing testable mathematical laws of nature to be formulated, such metaphors lent momentum to the notion that the material world was now amenable to human control and domination. Whilst the integrated nature of the medieval world view involved the immanence of God in every part of the universe, the analytic models of the succeeding era assumed God as the (separate) creator, or source, of an unchanging, rigidly ordered natural world.

Newton's further development of Cartesian models, during the seventeenth century, ensured the extension of the machine metaphor of the natural world into the areas of human nature and human society. Rationality, as the cornerstone of a broad range of intellectual endeavours, found its full expression in Locke's theories of individualism. In a universe experienced as an assemblage of separate elements or building blocks, the human being came to be seen as a separate, inviolable entity possessing rights which were independent of larger communal concerns.

It is within the broad context of intellectual developments from the sixteenth century onwards, when contrasted with the previous medieval world view, that changes in the concepts of 'health', 'life' and 'death' become more coherent. The effectiveness of current medical practice is one aspect of a world view which must be seen as a unique deviation from the modes of thought which had prevailed and, still, persist in other societies. The model of the human body as a machine which exists independently of both the mind and of other human beings has facilitated not only knowledge of its workings, but also powerful curative techniques. Nonetheless, the effectiveness of medical models in illuminating certain aspects of the human organism has arisen to the exclusion of the broader range of dimensions encompassed by the more traditional concept 'healing'. Thus the cause-and-effect, deterministic mode of thought which had arisen by the time of Newton was readily transposed to the human body. Taxonomies of disease were constructed according to the principles embodied in Linnaean classification of living forms. Once identified in this way diseases came to be thought of as the isolable causes or sources of ill-health. With effective diagnosis they could, ultimately, be traced back to the malfunctioning of a single organ within the body.

In summary, Capra argues that medical models are, predictably, successful in the cure of an individual's disease. However, when viewed more broadly, they cannot be shown to have had any major impact upon the overall health and well-being of populations. What Capra demonstrates is the singularly innovative and influential nature of Descartes' thought and work. He also shows that many of the economic, political and social problems currently facing the world as a whole can be understood as undesirable outcomes of the far-reaching scope of the mode of thought embodied in that work. The mastery of the natural world and the resulting advances in fields such as technology, communications and curative medicine are all the product of a reductionist science which has isolated, fragmented and simplified many aspects of the natural world, ranging from the planetary system to the human body. In so doing the interdependent, integrated nature of such a world has been downplayed, thereby precipitating a whole series of problems which at source must be seen as ecological.

Capra also examines some of the responses to these problems which have arisen during the last twenty years. From the margins of established centres of power, the Women's Movement, the Green Party, and the development of holistic medicine have arisen. Stemming from a period of economic affluence in the West, their shared concerns are, implicitly, the limitations of paradigms which reflect a Cartesian world view. Not only is there a commitment to questioning current metaphors or models, such as those reflected in the marginalising of the social categories 'women' or 'the terminally ill', there is also a concern to stress currently unapparent sets of interdependencies, such as the relationship between world rainfall and world forestation, or the relationship between environmental stresses and ill health in human populations.

Alongside such movements which have arisen in the West can be placed the revolutionary or revivalist activities which are emerging continuously in non-Western societies. In many cases they represent a conscious choice to resist or reject the imposition or encroachment of a Western reductionist world view which disinvests the material world of its moral and spiritual significance. A powerful example of such a choice can be seen in the rapid and popular development of Muslim Fundamentalism in the Islamic world, of which Iran is but the most extreme example.

LIFE, DEATH AND HEALTH: THE MEDICAL MODEL

Bearing in mind the profound implications of the Cartesian world view for the way in which the human body, in growth and in decline, is thought about, I will examine in more detail the dimensions of the medical model as it is currently put into practice. It represents one of the central 'structured metaphors' through which death is still encountered in Great Britain today.

In the course of the last twenty-five years the medical model of health and death has repeatedly been questioned, modified, extended or indeed set to one side. For example, in 1967 the Hospice Movement emerged in its present form. In 1959 and 1969 two major organisations offering support to bereaved people came into being.[1] All three are expressions of rather different models of death. What I will show is how 'new' metaphoric systems such as those expressed in Hospice and bereavement organisations arise out of, and are addressed to, aspects of death which are excluded from a previous system. In the limitations of one model may be discovered the core of a successor.

Given that traditional medical models are either preventive or curative, neither therefore address themselves directly to managing the implacable and incurable processes of dying and bereavement. In hospices and bereavement support organisations, that which was marginal to a traditional medical model has been appropriated as a central area for thought and practice. I have chosen them as examples not only because they demonstrate an innovative mode of encountering death, but also because their approach has extensive implications for a far broader range of 'health' issues. These include the control of pain in chronic as well as terminal illness; the maintenance of social identity in all individuals for whom an improvement in mental or physical health is unlikely; and the negotiation of honesty and a symetrical relationship of power between doctors and all patients. Like the management of death, these are 'health' issues which have ethical and moral, political and economic dimensions.

An anthropological approach allows us to question the way meaning is attributed to the two most fundamental categories, 'life' and 'death', within the framework of a medical mode of thought. Cross cultural comparison reveals these categories to have a broad and disparate range of meanings, depending upon the social context within which people are living. Since Hertz's work on handedness (orig.1907; 1960) the notion that biological states may be variously interpreted has long been accepted within social anthropology. However, in Great Britain and the West today, technology associated with health allows for very thorough and precise descriptions or distinctions to be made with respect to bodily states. The possibility of unwavering and infallible medical interpretations has become absorbed into the way in which the body, in life and in death, is conceived of.

This is exemplified in difficulties experienced by bereaved people encountered in the course of fieldwork. Should the medical management of their relatives' death fail to conform to a very well-defined set of expectations, strong anger could be felt – for example, if a terminal illness was not diagnosed, or if they were not forewarned accurately about the time of death. Similarly, death is commonly understood in terms of a medical cause-and-effect relationship. It is the previous medical history which is often scrutinised by surviving relatives when they seek to make sense of what has happened. For example, in a large proportion of all deaths (approximately 50%) a cardio-vascular disease is given as the cause.[2] If the deceased engaged in none of the specific behaviours, worrying, smoking or drinking, commonly thought to be pre-disposing, then difficulty may be experienced by relatives in accepting the death. If however a survivor experiences no dissonance between a medical model and their relatives's death, then, as in the example in Chapter Two, death may be described primarily in terms of the medical definitions put forward by a practitioner at that time.

Thus, given the precise discriminations and distinctions of the medical model, any inconsistency or ambiguity which is encountered in practice evokes concern, if not anger. Indeed, in practice, both professional and lay people often discover that medical frameworks can raise religious, moral, and ethical dilemmas. An all-embracing, consistent and authoritative body of thought is sought after, but remains currently unavailable. As material from the popular press revealed, there is a call for clear definitions of the status of the foetus, stillborn and congenitally handicapped children, adults surviving only through organ transplant or kidney dialysis, and frail elderly people. In each case the same question underlies the debate. What is it that is being described when the words 'life' or 'alive' are used? What is their current meaning in Great Britain today ? Consider the Hindu ascetic, for whom death, as a metaphor for initiation and change, is given maximal literal expression. His initiation and funerary rites are one and the same ceremony, performed by him, and followed by a 'life'/'death' as a wandering ghost. By contrast, the 'death' of the Hindu householder only takes place mid-way through cremation when their skull is cracked open by the chief mourner (see Bloch and Parry, 1982:13). When the funeral of Indira Ghandi was broadcast live on Western television in October 1984, many viewers perceived her 'death', brought about by blows to her skull from her son, as some kind of brutal desecration of her already 'dead' corpse. Thus while the deaths of neither the Hindu ascetic nor the householder coincide with simple bodily changes such as cessation of heart-beat or breathing, reflection on the social identity of the foetus, the stillborn infant, and the chronically ill or elderly person in Britain today reveals that, similarly, there is no simple correspondance between bodily state and cultural and social category.

With the increasing refinement of medical technology, the developing foetus is now routinely observed, premature and severely handicappped infants are reared, and the adult body can be made to accept organ transplant or to survive without major organs. Indeed it can be made to continue its existence with only minimal brain function. Technological control can therefore offer bodily survival for a far broader spectrum of human beings, from the extraordinarily premature to the greatly aged, from the bodily mutilated to the profoundly mentally handicapped.

Alongside technological developments, there have been overall material improvements in areas such as sanitation, housing and conditions of work. The expectation of good health has been established, and indeed medical remedies allow the removal of bodily disfigurement, mutilation or loss of bodily control. Thus, in a material sense, the possibility of an improved quality of life has been made available. In addition life expectancy, or quantity of life, has increased at the same time.

It is the co-incidence of an overall increase in the quantity of life, and an improvement in the material quality of life, which raises questions about where the boundary between life and death lies. There is tension between the new-found possibility of survival for even the frailest human beings, and the newly acquired expectation that living should be a materially comfortable experience. Given that medical technology allows unprecedented control of the boundary between life and death, these questions are not merely abstract or theoretical. They are practical questions which have powerful emotional, economic and political implications. In today's economic climate, the expectation of a long, healthy life is shared by many, but realised only by the members of higher social classes.

Material from the popular press spotlighted areas of great ambiguity such as abortion, stillbirth, congenital handicap, organ transplant, medical care/cure of elderly people, euthanasia. In each of these areas, the possibility of making a medical intervention into a bodily condition evokes conflicting responses from different social groups or categories. For example, those espousing a moral or religious point of view may perceive such interventions through metaphoric frameworks which bear little correspondance to those metaphors which underpin an economic or political perspective.

In 1981 Dr Michael Thomas, chairman of the British Medical Association's ethical committee, was reported[3] as saying that:

> ...he regretted that the 'fantastic explosion' of medical scientific advances over the last 20 years had not been accompanied by the sort of public debate that had led to the establishment of bodies like the General Medical Council in the last century. 'I am worried about the fact that we are having a number of ethical debates which come and go without reaching any adequate conclusion. The mechanism of 140 years ago whereby the public's view became embodied in an ethical code seems to have atrophied'.

In summary a need is being expressed for widely acceptable and more refined definitions of, and distinctions between, what is meant by the cultural categories 'life' and 'death'. Whilst medical/technological skills become more precise and more powerful, their application does not fall easily within the previously well-defined doctrines of the church. Indeed these doctrines themselves are undergoing a process of change and are being interpreted more fluidly – for example, the church's teachings on pre-marital sex, homosexuality, divorce and the ordination of women.

This combination of circumstances produces a whole range of paradoxes or dilemmas. For example:

(1) The search for clarity can produce an inflexible mode of thought within which the specific circumstances of the individual cannot be accommodated, for example the introduction of a rigid legal framework within the medical management of life and death.

(2) The Christian moral imperative to 'love thy neighbour' can create insupportable pressures when thy neighbour's existence is viable only through the extra-ordinary power of medicine to keep death at bay.

(3) Through medical technology, the principle of rationality can be implemented with a rigour which excludes other aspects of

human experience such as intuition, flexibility, individuality.

Again, these paradoxes are addressed in material drawn from the popular press. Consider the death of twenty-two day old Michael Hicknott, a brain-damaged baby born prematurely after his mother's death, which drew public attention to the lack of consensus in the management of death. Bel Mooney, writing in the Sunday Times, argued that both rigid medical practice and also immutable ethical doctrines were inhumane:

> Had he lived, Michael Hicknott would have been brain-damaged - but there are countless parents who would testify to the great joy that can be brought by such a 'bleak' life. On the other hand, there are also parents who are driven mad by the exhaustion of looking after such a child, and for whom love dwindles grimly into a question of duty. Those truths run parallel ... Admittedly such agonised confusion places almost intolerable weight upon the shoulders of doctors and parents. But clarity would reduce human emotion to the level of the catechism. Naturally it would please the favoured who know God, and therefore right and wrong. It would worry the rest of us, who suspect that God only exists within the potential of each human being (a doctor, a parent, a friend) to behave rightly, with pain, dignity and love. (1983:38)

Bel Mooney writes from the premise that 'we', her readers, are not committed Christians. She asserts that the power of medical technology, through which even severely physically damaged infants can be made to survive, must be used 'pragmatically' – that is to say fluidly, with respect to the individual. What is called for is a mode of thought within which medical practice is informed by clear yet humane ethical doctrines. For the uncertainties over the boundary between life and death, arising out of its control through medical frameworks, there is felt to be no resolution which is both definitive and also humane. The rational principles through which the science of medicine is constituted often prove unwieldy in the management of individual experience. At the boundary between an individual's life and death, the precise techniques of medicine can represent a rigid system, without the flexibility necessary to accommodate all aspects of that individual's past and present experience.

For example, editorial comment in the Times Health Supplement at the time of the trial of members of the pro-euthanasia group, EXIT, drew attention to the inappropriateness of a purely rational response to individuals encountering the end of their lives.[4]

People often say they don't want to go on living. They do not want or expect a man to rush round with drugs and a plastic bag. More often it is a cry for company, reassurance, support or a symptom of depression... Reed's overzealous response, though rational, made no allowance for the irrationality of human nature.

Nonetheless within a society where a rational, analytic world view, however problematic, continues to be espoused, an intuitive or interpretive approach is not easily embraced. In 1982, Dr Garrow, a paediatrician at Whickan Hospital, spoke before a predominantly medical audience of his intuitive approach to the management of new-born handicapped infants. He had become the focus of controversy in that he had let it be known publicly that at times he allowed such babies to die. Dr Garrow alluded to the uneasy relationship between rational and intuitive approaches to medicine, saying that the clear difference between the idea of killing and the idea of not preserving life was 'ticklish in practice'. He spoke out against 'abstractions', 'principles' and 'rights', describing how he allowed a baby to 'decide its own fate' in that he followed his own intuitive responses to any 'appealing gestures' it might make. In a society where the rational, medical mode of thought predominates, Dr Garrow's public avowal of a flexible and empathic approach to the meanings encompassed within the categories 'life' and 'death' drew a powerful, negative emotional response. Nursing staff in Dr Garrow's audience clearly found the implementation of such an apparently 'arbitrary' approach very distressing.

Examples such as these reveal a persistent tension between a felt need for rigid definitions and strict procedures, and the desire for flexibility sufficient to accommodate the needs of the individual.

Nonetheless, emotional and bodily experience which otherwise remains unaccountable, does still continue to be controlled and given form through a medical mode of thought, one which is seen to embody the ideas of rationality and predictability. Comments published in the *Guardian* by K.Nichols, a clinical psychologist, drew attention to a collective myth of the infallibility of medicine.[5] He notes:

> The myth takes the form of an idealisation of the medical services, a feeling that the doctors are totally reliable in the task of diagnosing disease, repairing failing body parts and staving off death. The everyday realities of medicine, the slip-ups, errors, doubts and confusions must be denied in order to minimise anxiety. This need is in us rather than the doctors, but in its development the medical profession has elected to collude with this defence.

The implications of the 'myth of medical infallibility' are significant and merit further exploration. As the psychologist notes, it is a
myth which is embraced by both medical practitioners and 'patients'.
As shown in the examples already presented, discrepancies between
private experiences and their medical interpretation, between ethical enigmas and technological competence, all give rise to confusion
and concern. This material illustrates Geertz's discussion of the
critical role of cognitive coherence in human experience. Along with
suffering he cites 'bafflement' and 'a sense of intractable ethical
paradox' as '...radical challenges to the proposition that life is com-
prehensible and that we can, by taking thought, orient ourselves
effectively within it'(1968a:14).

Given that such paradoxes are introduced within the cultural
framing of life and death through a medical model, the myth of
medical infallibility plays a key role in allowing us to keep faith with
the practice of medicine. It is in this way that the associated 'sense of
intractable ethical paradox' or 'bafflement' is managed.

CANCER AND THE MYTH OF MEDICAL INFALLIBILITY

Illich's work on the medicalization of society (1975) and Sontag's
discussion of illness as metaphor (1983) together shed light on the
personal and political implications of the myth of medical infallibility, and the ways in which its limitations are currently becoming
apparent. As shown, strenuous attempts are being made to create a
public reconciliation between medical and ethical modes of
thought. Other attempts are being made to modify or expand upon
a traditional medical framework. Illich traces the history of today's
tenacious myth of medical infallibility. Sontag focusses specifically
on illnesses such as TB and cancer which have eluded satisfactory
medical explanations/ treatments, and have therefore remained
open to a proliferation of alternative metaphoric interpretations. As
will be shown, deaths from cancer currently represent a challenge
not only to the skills, but also the conceptual frameworks implicit
within medicine. Furthermore it is significant that cancer predominates among illnesses to which alternative approaches to medicine
have been addressed. These include the Hospice Movement and the
Bristol Cancer Help Centre.[6] As Nichols,[5] the clinical psychologist,
goes on to note in his article:

> (of the hospice) The critical difference here is that dying
> people have been told honestly of their position and the
> doctors are no longer pressured to be sources of infallible
> diagnosis and treatment. They are allowed to be honest. A real

rapport can exist between the doctor, nurse and dying person. In Illich's work on the medicalisation of society, death and its management is given particular weight (1975:122-150). He examines the contemporary Western concept of 'natural death'. Ethnographic material from non-Western societies is a reminder that death has often been thought of as an 'unnatural' occurence, an event explainable only as the outcome of deviant or malignant behaviour on the part of either the deceased or other members of their society.[7] Illich traces the historical development of Western concepts of death during the last 500 years. While Capra explores the influence of specific Western thinkers since the time of early Christianity, Illich draws on the religious imagery through which death itself has been given form and meaning.

Thus, changing religious iconography depicts the transition from the fourteenth century image of death as the indwelling, immanent condition of life, where living figures entwined with their dead counterparts in the Dance of the Dead, to the fifteenth century image of death as a controlling, natural force visited upon human beings in a once-in-a-lifetime encounter – and death was personified in the Danse Macabre. During the Middle Ages life on earth had been seen as a sacrament of God's presence, and the biological event of dying was perceived merely as a transition from a state of earthly to heavenly grace, a passage from the Church militant to the Church triumphant. Under the fifteenth century influence of the Reformation and of Lutheran thought, earthly life came to be perceived as corrupt, and redemption was only made possible through faith in God. Thus the figure of the grim skeletal Reaper embodies the idea of death as the final, definitive boundary of a corrupt earthly life. Heavenly grace or hellish punishment lay as twin possibilities on the other side of that boundary, neither of them embodying the certainty commanded by death itself.

It was this death which was anticipated by those living in the late fifteenth and the sixteenth centuries. The linear clock-time of their earthly life was bounded by an event which was encountered by the dying individual, rather than the living community. A woman or man took personal responsibility for the manner of their own death, viewing it as an occasion to which they hoped to be able to rise.

Thus 'natural death', conceived as the indwelling condition of life, came to assume the characteristics of an inevitable and important once-in-a-lifetime personal encounter. Illich cites this period as significant in the initial medicalising of death. The moment of death, to be properly managed, must be properly anticipated. Through medical folk practices, distinctions between transitory and mortal illness could be made. If a mortal illness was diagnosed the application of remedies to ease and speed the transition could be carried out under the direction of the dying person. Hoping thus to be spared overwhelming agonies, the individual sought to make a dignified exit.

Illich goes on to show the subsequent transformations of this approach and pursue their political implications. The predominant image of Death as Leveller or Grim Reaper is evoked through the words of sixteenth century liturgy,[8] pronounced whenever a corpse was lowered into the earth:

> Man that is born of a woman hath but a short time to live, and is full of misery. He cometh up, and is cut down, like a flower; he fleeth as it were a shadow, and never continueth in one stay.
>
> In the midst of life we are in death .....

In the rigidly hierarchised society of that time, the iconographic depiction of king, bishop, doctor, merchant each encountering their final deathly visitor suggests the ephemeral nature of worldly status. As Illich notes 'Precisely because macabre equality belittled worldly privilege it also made it more legitimate'(1975:134-5). Why seek to overthrow that which is shallow and transitory ?

With rise of a new, wealthy middle-class in the eighteenth century, the anticipatory comfort of equality in death gave way to the concept of 'natural death' as that which money could ensure, or reserve, for certain social classes. Medical remedies, once an aid in the transition from life to death, now assumed the new role of a valuable commodity, disparately accessible to rich and poor. Similarly, medical skills and knowledge were firmly appropriated as the exclusive property of the doctor. By the nineteenth century the unprecedented power to step between the individual and their death was attributed to members of the medical profession.

In the twentieth century the idea of equality in 'natural' death assumes new political implications. With dying perceived as the predation of multiple killer diseases, 'health', and indeed 'life', come to be seen as that which medical technology underpins. As shown previously, distinctions between 'life' and 'death' become matters arising out of, and discussed in terms of, a medical mode of thought.

From another culture Bourdieu offers a parallel example – of a Kabyle woman making a conscious distinction between a former social role, 'dying', and a current, medically defined condition, 'dying'.

> In the old days, folk didn't know what illness was. They went to bed and they died. It's only nowadays that we're learning words like liver, lung ... intestines, stomach... and I don't know what! People only used to know (pain in) the belly... that's what everyone who died died of, unless it was fever ... (1977:166)

As a set of metaphors the hegemony of a medical model is such that major inequalities in the distribution of wealth, and in the quality of living and working environments, can be subsumed, and thereby masked, within claims for equal access to medical care and therefore to a 'natural death'.

In summary Illich, by exploring the concept of 'natural death' as one particular, developing metaphoric interpretation of death, shows its key role within the hegemony of a medical model. Through this imaging of death two myths are promoted – one is the myth of medical infallibility; the other is the myth of a deterministic, unilinear relationship between equal access to medical services and 'social progress'. Illich asserts that 'The myth of progress of all people towards the same kind of death diminishes the feeling of guilt on the part of the 'haves' by transforming the ugly deaths of which 'have nots' die into the result of present underdevelopment, which ought to be remedied by further expansion of medical institutions'(1975:146).

Illich's work gives very useful insights into the ways in which current medical frameworks have evolved. His appraisal brings out the political implications which secure the continuity of such an approach.

In a very different fashion Berger's portrait of an isolated country doctor, John Sassal, shows how the practice of medicine can expose the practitioner to the limitations of his model (1976). Sassall, the Fortunate Man of the book's title, finds himself in the privileged position of 'gentleman' within a small economically depressed rural community. More than any sense of medical inadequacy in the face of incurable illness, Sassall is dogged with an awareness of the more pernicious inadequacy of medicine as a remedy for cultural and economic deprivation. Berger writes:

> I do not want to exaggerate Sassall's dilemma. It is one that many doctors and psycho-therapists have to face: how far should one help a patient to accept conditions which are at least as unjust and wrong as the patient is sick ? What makes it more acute for Sassall is his isolation, his closeness to his patients and a bitter paradox which we have not yet defined.
> I believe that Sassall's disquiet is provoked... by the contrast between the general expectations of his patients and his own. (1976:141)

Berger's exploration of the experience of a single medical 'insider' lends support to Illich's argument which stems from a more generalised, historical perspective. Together their work indicates important dimensions of the historical background and current cultural and social context of contemporary initiatives such as the Hospice Movement. Whilst a medical framing of 'life', 'death' and 'health' produces apparently insoluble paradoxes, the myth of medical infallibility remains as the prevailing orientation towards the practice of medicine.

Illich's argument that medical frameworks carry powerful political implications is borne out in the fact that class-based differences within mortality statistics were already being made evident in the early part of this century by Dr T. H. C. Stevenson, superintendent of statistics at the General Register Office (1928). Townsend notes that '...his special interest was the influence of wealth and culture on mortality and morbidity'(1979:369).

Whilst awareness of this 'influence' has therefore been long established, the 1980 Black Report on the persistence of class-based inequalities in life-expectancy, despite the introduction of the Welfare State, was semi-suppressed. Patrick Jenkins released just 260 xerox copies of the original report, and it was only after two years that Townsend and Davidson made it widely available in a shortened form (1982).

Though the relationship between social class and health has to some extent been acknowledged within the medical profession, its political implications remain submerged within the more dominant emphasis on changes in dietary and exercise habits to be made by the individual. Death, as framed within the mortality statistics, nonetheless remains as a powerful challenge to a victim-blaming approach. Geographical areas identified within the Black Report as having a particularly high early mortality rate have been the focus of research into the environmental/ cultural conditions of social groups and categories where death comes earlier (See Townsend, Fillemore and Beattie, 1987). Using anthropological and oral history techniques, this research reconstructs what might otherwise remain as the purely 'medical' histories of such populations.

Turning to the ideology of the Hospice Movement, and the individuals who represent the majority of hospice patients, it becomes apparent that cancer deaths have contributed to the modification of a medical mode of thought. A close look at the nature of cancer reveals its relationship with the emergence of the Hospice Movement.

Cancer is an unpredictable, invasive illness, not as yet satisfactorily encompassed within current medical frameworks. In 1986 it was the stated cause of more than a quarter of all non-violent deaths.[2] Illich has stressed medicine's central defensive/aggressive role at the boundary between life and death. Public debate and the attitudes of bereaved people confirm the presence of a widespread emotional investment in this state of affairs. As Illich suggests, the myth of medical infallibility defines 'bad death' as that which takes place without past or present medical treatment. It is disordered, unpredictable, uncontrolled. Nonetheless, despite access to medical treatment, almost a quarter of us will die after a protracted period of uncomfortable or painful illness for which, it is commonly thought, there are no adequate medical remedies.

Cancer, with its invasive yet elusive qualities, is therefore 'bad death' of another kind. It is the death which reveals the inauthenticity of the myth of 'natural death' as that which is experienced by the consumer of medical services. Lying outside simple, conventional medical frameworks or interpretations (being thought of as incurable, inexplicable), cancer attracts a proliferation of alternative metaphoric associations.

Sontag writes from the proposition that 'the fantasies inspired by TB in the last century, by cancer now, are responses to a disease thought to be intractable and capricious – that is, a disease not understood – in an era in which medicine's central premise is that all diseases can be cured'(1983:9)

What Sontag suggests is that an illness thought of as incurable, and therefore fatal, attracts a fluid range of metaphors which expand into areas of life lying beyond the more limited scope of medical frameworks.

An additional example is AIDS, an incurable disease acquired, like TB, through contagion and experienced, like cancer, as a stealthy, invasive killer. Lying beyond the curative frameworks of a medical model, its associations with 'uncontrolled' and 'unnatural' sexual mores have been elaborated extensively.

Like Illich, Sontag effectively includes a historical perspective in her argument. Perceptions of TB in the nineteenth century provide a further example of the possibilities for metaphoric elaboration offered by an illness without a simple, medically identifiable cause or cure. Only with Koch's discovery of the tubercle bacillus in 1882 did the disease's associations with romanticized poverty and aesthetic enfeeblement give way to the more prosaic processes of innoculation and sanitary inspection.

Lacking a simple biological cause, and indeed failing to manifest itself in a single, isolable form, the causes of cancer are variously interpreted, whilst its source is variously located. As Sontag shows, the nature of the self, that is to say the personality, is often seen as a major predisposing factor in cancer sufferers. Thus a self-pitying, emotionally repressed individual is thought to be particularly prone to the illness. Similarly, a personal failure which produces a sense of hopelessness or resignation is thought of as a predisposing circumstance. Sontag argues that to attribute causation to the personality, rather than to a simple biological source is to associate blame of some kind with the occurence of cancer – and that that blame is subtly attached to the ill person themselves. As a result, a disease thought to stem from a repressed emotional style and a sense of personal hopelessness comes to attract stigma of a particularly humiliating kind. In an almost punitive sense, the malignancy which arises from within individuals perceived to be somehow lacking, is then seen to take over that individual in a parasitic fashion. It diminishes them further as mutant, alien cells replace 'you' with 'non you'.

Again responses to AIDS sufferers can be seen as a parallel example. Assumed to be members of a separate and disordered social category, their sickness is not only seen to reveal their deviance, but also acts as a stigmatising barrier which marginalises and distances both their social category and their disease.

In tandem with the shaming of the individual in this manner, there are connections being made between cancer and the perceived ills of the environment. Blame attaches to a whole range of factors, from food additives through to airborne radiation. Whether from within or without, cancer is thus understood to result from the perceived ills of our time. Indeed Sontag traces a changing perception of conducive conditions or personality traits. The Victorians thought of grief and rage, poverty and overwork as its causes. This contrasts with the emotional isolation and material excess currently identified as predisposing conditions. In the absence of simple medical explanations, cancer is seen to embody the broad dimensions of experience defined as deviant or troubling. Processes of this kind – such as an 'unnatural', overcontrolled emotionality which gives rise to growing inner corruption – are then used metaphorically to identify other non-bodily processes such as moral corruption.

Sontag writes during the mid 1970s, a period which saw much speculation about the causes of cancer. Subsequent research[9] has substantiated many of the 'fantasies' which she discusses, thereby underscoring the limitations of medical models which fail to encompass the social and environmental circumstances of cancer patients.

The prevalence and complexity of cancer not only allows for the generation of metaphors or theories which transcend the limits of the medical model, it also brings home the unpredictability of human mortality. Cancer is imaged as a stealthy, insidious invasion of the body, a 'malignant growth', the source and extent of which are hidden and capricious. Whilst mortality statistics show class-based inequalities in the incidence of cancer,[10] there still remain few simple, cause-and-effect medical links between human behaviour and cancer. The exception is the relationship between cigarette smoking and lung cancer.

Given that cancer cannot be distanced as a disease which only results from quite specific forms of behaviour, the sense of vulnerability experienced by each and every individual is managed through a 'conspiracy of silence', the fostering of cancer's invisibility. As Sontag notes, an individual suffering from heart disease, whose death is, statistically, relatively imminent, may be freely informed of their condition. To inform the individual of a cancer diagnosis is not only to condemn but also to stigmatise the patient.[11]

The ideology of the Hospice Movement, which has arisen largely in response to the needs of cancer patients, can be seen to be linked with cancer's metaphoric associations with the perceived ills of our time. The Movement gained its most powerful recent momentum in 1967, through the setting up of St. Christopher's Hospice in London. Hospices have proliferated throughout the country since then. So effectively does the concept of Hospice care attract money that government policy[12] has been instituted in order to curb the charitable establishment of hospices which the NHS is then pressured to maintain.

Given that repressed emotionality, social isolation, material excess and environmental pollution are currently seen as the predominant social ills of Western society, the values brought together within the ideology of the Hospice Movement represent a readily acceptable alternative. For example, helping patients to express, and come to terms with their feelings is regarded as an important aspect of their care, pastoral suport and counselling being provided for this purpose. Indeed it is the range of emotional rather than bodily experience at the time of dying which has been the focus of Kubler-Ross's widely read work (1970;1975). Her writing/ counselling oriented towards 'the dying' is complemented by workshops for 'the living', where the expression of powerful negative emotion is a major focus. In addition to emotional openness, the Hospice offers devoted care to each and every individual. The Hospice maxim, 'You matter because you are you',[13] resonates within a society where cancer is understood as the fate of a traumatically diminished self, finally

ousted by alien disease cells. Similarly the management of a stigmatising disease by making it visible and evident is one of the Hospice
Movement's particularly powerful gestures.

In summary, illnesses such as cancer, which resist simple medical
interpretations, are currently imaged and conceptualised in terms of
the perceived social, psychological and bodily ills of our time.
Whenever cancer is diagnosed, medicine is revealed as limited and
fallible, and the myth of medical infallibility stands unmasked. What
is thereby revealed or underscored is:

(1) the inevitability and unpredictability of each individual's
death.

(2) the cultural and environmental, rather than purely medical
causes of death.

(3) class-based inequalities in wealth and in working and domestic conditions.

In remaining resistant to medical intervention, cancer not only
reveals its limitations but also, consistently, brings home an awareness of the universality of human mortality.

MALIGNANT GROWTHS AND METAPHORIC EXPANSION

Having traced the implications of the scientific or Cartesian world
view, I will introduce an example of a present-day form of Hospice
care. As noted, since its inception at the time of early Christianity,
hospice care represented an offer of protection, refreshment and
fellowship to anyone in need. Inclusive and broadly based, it is a
form of care grounded in an organic, holistic, interpretative world
view. Its currrent resurgence comes at a time of increasing dissatisfaction with what formerly appeared as the limitless possibilities of a
scientific model of the human being and the planet. It has emerged,
nonetheless, in a social context where scientific, medical models
continue to predominate.

In 1981, in the south east of Scotland, Strathcarron Hospice
offered terminal care to 131 patients, 128 of whom were suffering
from cancer. In caring for these patients, the hospice addresses the
limitations of traditional medical models, as they are revealed
through the metaphoric associations of cancer.

Support is offered to dying people in the form of pain and symptom control, and extensive nursing and pastoral care. In comparison with traditional approaches, the breadth of this care reflects
the richer and more expansive metaphoric framework of this Movement. Rather than a simple alternative, this framework can be seen
as both an expansion and a transformation of traditional models.

Three aspects of cancer make it particularly difficult to incorporate the treatment of patients within a traditional medical model.

(1) Cancer patients are relatively young, large in number and suffering from an illness which is likely to be terminal at some stage. Of a total of 141,618 people who died from cancer in England and Wales in 1985, approaching a half, 61,379, were less than seventy years old.[14]

(2) A patient's condition can often be diagnosed some months or even years before it slowly culminates in death.

(3) Their illness can take one of a considerable number of forms, the course of which is never entirely predictable. Symptoms vary and can be distressing.

In the face of this particular combination of attributes, the limitations of medical models become apparent. For example the customary attempt to halt or slow down the progress of a tumour can reveal medicine's most aggressive dimensions. Sontag notes the metaphors drawn from a military domain which are used in descriptions of treatment. On behalf of cancer 'victims', a 'fight', 'crusade' or 'war' is waged against the disease. 'Invasive', 'alien' or 'atavistic' cancer cells 'colonize' a body once 'defences' are lowered. 'Malignant' tumours can be 'bombarded' with radiotherapy or chemotherapy; 'radical' surgery is another possibility. Mutilations or amputations may be the only way in which the disease can be 'conquered'.

While such valiant attacks contribute to perceptions of cancer as a physical elaboration of political or military threats, the disease itself remains, and is the cause of almost a quarter of all non-violent deaths. It is only by systematically obscuring the nature and incidence of cancer – that is, by withholding information and by removing patients from home to hospital – that the myth of medical infallibility can be upheld.

In turn this strategy of maintaining an uneasy silence itself reveals a marked discrepancy between refined diagnostic technology, and confused moral or religious codes which offer few guidelines concerning the management of such knowledge and skill.

Finally, the suffering which cancer can entail is not easily managed through a system which interprets pain as a symptomatic byproduct of diseases which can be cured. Chronic pain associated with cancer has been defined as a situation rather than an event and is described as unending, liable to increase, apparently meaningless and totally pre-occupying for the sufferer (Twycross, 1975:13). Using the term 'culture' to refer only to traditional, non-Western societies, Illich again argues that 'Culture makes pain tolerable by integrating it into a meaningful system, cosmopolitan civilization detaches pain from any subjective or inter-subjective context in order to annihilate it'(1975:93).

The chronic pain associated with an incurable illness is a double challenge to 'cosmopolitan civilization'. Not only is it associated with a terminal illness and therefore medical failure but also, customary pain 'killers' may no longer annihilate pain in the way an individual has come to expect.

In Strathcarron Hospice three individuals skilled in the full range of traditional medical techniques are relieved of the doctor's implicit commitment to preventive or curative work. Their skills are used only to alleviate suffering which is acknowledged to lead to death. Once heroic, 'curative' techniques are foresworn, the removal of the patient from their social/domestic context is less necessary. The temporal boundary between initial diagnosis and biological death is freed from both the constraints of interventionist treatment, and also the isolation of the 'terminal' ward where those 'on their way out', 'for whom there's no hope' are lied to by emotionally withdrawn relatives during rigid visiting hours. Being no longer set apart, or exposed to surgery, individuals dying of cancer gain the opportunity to live as before. Their difficulties and their suffering, whether domestic, bodily, emotional or spiritual, can be managed with the help of an extensive body of hospice staff and volunteers. Movement into and out of the hospice is continuous.

For example, patients living at home may visit the hospice two or three times a week for daycare, or may be admitted briefly for pain and symptom control; relatives visit freely and may spend nights in the hospice; patients dying in the hospice may make short excursions, or longer visits, both to their homes and to other places (shops, the countryside) which have been integral to their lives. No boundary lies between living space and dying space. The process of biological deterioration takes place alongside all the other processes which together constitute 'life'.

In this way traditional medical models are both expanded and transformed. Though established skills and techniques are retained, their aims and objectives are transformed. Being firmly directed towards improving the quality, rather than increasing the quantity of life, a 'medical' approach assumes the character of a collaborative rather than a combative strategy. This strategy is exemplified in the control of pain. Extraordinarily complex and refined technological procedures such as nerve blocking are consciously and deliberately complemented by counselling, cuddling, and 'diversionary' approaches such as craftwork, gardening, music and travel. Pain is therefore one example of the kind of bodily experience which, in the hospice, is approached from a holistic rather than traditional medical perspective.

This chapter presents the broad historical context of current dilemmas associated with the management of health, life and death through a medical model. The power to maintain and to prolong very frail human lives, within a social context where an improved material quality of life is at least evident if not fully realised, raises questions concerning the quality of each individual life. Decisions about how such newfound power is to be used must take into account the need for a clear ethical framework which accommodates the varied circumstances of the individual.

Light is shed upon such dilemmas by the work of Illich, Berger and Sontag which sets the issues within a political context, thereby showing the value of a broader perspective in the search for resolution of some kind. Though the power embodied in medical techniques produces a variety of conflicts, it has nonetheless taken predominance over, and indeed masked, many of the broader cultural and social dimensions of human life.

While Illich (and Berger) argue that the narrow focus of a medical perspective effectively downplays inequalities in the distribution of wealth and the resulting quality of life, Sontag shows that prevalent, incurable illnesses such as cacncer reveal the limitations of this perspective and readily evoke the wider political implications of ill-health and its distribution.

Throughout this chapter a historical perspective has made it possible to focus on the way in which differing approaches to the management of death have both gained ground and then given ground to a successor. The example of a hospice allowed us to explore responses to the limitations of a medical model. In later chapters, field material from this context is contrasted with material from a residential home for elderly people. The resulting insights show the framing of universal experiences – pain, physical and mental deterioration, and loss – within institutions which co-exist in a society where both traditional and more innovative approaches to death are simultaneously pursued.

Chapter Four

Setting the Stage for Death

Two institutions to be found within contemporary British society, a residential home for elderly people and a hospice, are spaces within which death regularly takes place. However, while a hospice is seen to offer a more open encounter with death, a residential home for elderly people is recognised only implicitly as the place of death for individuals admitted to its care. Through ethnographic material, I will show how these institutions embody the sets of ideas which were discussed from a historical perspective in the previous chapter. Furthermore, in that they are rooted in two contrasting cultural traditions, these institutions provide frames, or stages, which can create radically different kinds of experience among those who live and die within them. Thus the focus of chapter, and indeed those to follow, is the cultural and social framing of human experience. Through the extensive body of anthropological work addressed to ritual, symbol and metaphor we can gain insights into how this 'framing' operates.

As noted, an anthropological perspective allows the Western perception of 'religion', and therefore religious ritual at the time of death, as a discrete category of experience to be contrasted with the more overt coherence between death ritual and other aspects of life within more traditional societies. Thus Du Boulay's work (1982) shows that in rural Greece the relationship between the categories 'life' and 'death' is structured through the same principles or patterns expressed in marriage rules and dance. Similarly, Okely's work among gypsies (1983) shows the boundary between the living and the dead being used symbolically to affirm the gypsy/gorgio boundary. An anthropological approach thus allows coherent circularities to be discerned within the relationship between life and death in other societies. The issues of life can be seen to be put to use metaphorically to give form to death, whilst the event of death is similarly elaborated in such a way as to affirm the validity and permanence of the issues of life. In the creation and re-creation of this circular process, some aspects of death as a biological event are being highlighted while others are downplayed.

It is to the question of how the performance of cultural metaphors frames and shapes the quality of human experience that we now turn. La Rochefoucauld has suggested that 'Neither the sun nor death can be looked at with a steady eye (orig. 1678; 1967:13).

His statement is about the role of metaphor in the human encounter with death. The eye, wavering in its glance towards the sun, is an apt analogy for the human encounter with death and indeed for the metaphoric process itself. La Rochefoucauld's statement is quoted on the title page of Hinton's 'popular' book, *Dying* (1967). Hinton's choice of this statement indicates both the resonance of La Rochefoucauld's use of common experience, sun-gazing, to evoke the quality of a more opaque experience, the contemplation of death, and indeed the felt need for such analogies in areas of experience such as death.

The nature of metaphoric thought and expression has been the subject of extensive work. In addition to their salient contributions to debates about research methods, Lakoff and Johnson (1980) also draw upon the ideas of Ricoeur[1] to show how human experience comes to take on particular qualities. Like Ricoeur, they question the perception of metaphor as a peripheral, poetic/decorative linguistic flourish. Rather, the notion increasingly assumed within social anthropology is that most thought is of a metaphoric nature. As noted in earlier methodological discussion, Lakoff and Johnson argue that human beings do not experience and understand the world in which they live in a direct fashion, but rather through an inherited system of culturally-specific constructs or metaphors. As an alternative to what they term the 'objectivist' and 'subjectivist' myths, prevalent within Western society, they offer the 'experientialist' myth. This term refers to society's metaphors or hypotheses about the nature of the world, tested through experience in the world, and discarded or developed depending on their usefulness or richness. Metaphors of this kind operate by revealing some aspects of human experience, for example love, work, death, spotlighting some of their dimensions, and masking others. Death is an area of experience which more than most evades comprehensive metaphoric interpretation.

For example, it can evoke intense emotion; it can raise profound questions about the nature or meaning of life; and, furthermore, the nature of what it represents, beyond physical extinction, will remain mysterious. Given all this, the contemplation of death, like the sun, is an unsteady process, made possible only through elaborately conceived and persuasive metaphoric systems. This book describes acts and utterances which constitute a cultural and social response to death. They are the sets of lived metaphors through which death is being encountered. According to the view presented by Lakoff and Johnson, I will look at them as interpretations, as ways of seeing, which not only highlight but also downplay one area or another of the events and experiences associated with death.

Lakoff and Johnson's work implies the made-up quality of metaphoric systems. If there are 'truths' they must be seen as specific to their cultural and social context, rather than as an aspect of some enduring, universal 'truth'. Creativity is the hallmark of the metaphoric process, in that it develops continuously through the flow of social discourse – and in that it never reaches completion. This brings discussion to the question of persuasiveness and how one set of metaphors rather than another is experienced as a convincing description or re-description of reality.

La Rochefoucauld's analogy of sun-gazing has been cited as a popularly quoted and therefore illuminating evocation of the encounter with death. Lakoff and Johnson use the term 'experientialist' in arguing that 'reality' is the experience which human beings create for themselves through their use of metaphor. I have described a system of metaphors as hypotheses or ideas about the world which are validated only through direct experience. However the term 'experientialist' also describes the origins as well as the continuing means of validating such a metaphoric system. Lakoff and Johnson show how very simple bodily experience often provides a grounding for conceptual thinking. Thus in statements such as 'I get a lift when I see you', or 'I may fall into a depression', intangible emotional experience is given form through metaphoric use of the basic 'up'/'down' orientations of the body. Gazing at the sun is, of course, another example of a common physical experience which has been used metaphorically to evoke the experience of encountering death.

Thus, in asserting that metaphoric concepts have an experiential grounding, Lakoff and Johnson are describing a circular process in which simple bodily experience in the world provides an experiential basis for metaphoric thought. That thought is then used to structure experience in the world, thereby finding confirmation or contradiction of its authenticity. One metaphoric system, validated in this way, may then be used to structure another, for example in the Western cultural concepts 'time is money' and 'argument is war'.

Metaphoric thought can be described most simply as seeing one thing in terms of another. Lakoff and Johnson stress experience in the world as both a common source and a validation for this process. Returning to death ritual and the way in which it works, this approach is invaluable in that it enables us to look in much more detail at the themes of authenticity and cultural consistency.

For example, Du Boulay and Okely's work (1982 and 1983) both show death ritual structured in terms of other aspects of a particular society – that is, one thing, death, being seen in terms of another, a marriage pattern or an ethnic boundary. As I suggested earlier, the process does not operate in one direction only. Okely points out '...the boundary between life and death is used to make symbolic statements about another boundary'(1983:230).

In these examples it is therefore bodily or in-the-world experience which can be seen as the basis of metaphors through which death is encountered – for example the flowing quality of blood; the body's visible and invisible surfaces; and the historical and geographical circumstances of a community. Used metaphorically these very immediate experiences allow other less tangible phenomena to be grasped and indeed to be manipulated. Such systems may then be used to make other, possibly more abstract phenomena accessible to understanding.

Realised in thought, language and action, systems of this kind 'take place' within the time and space of everyday. In this way abstract schema, grounded in basic physical experience, resonate back, and give meaning to that world from which their substance has been drawn. As Bourdieu says '...the mind is a metaphor of the world of objects which is itself but an endless circle of mutually reflecting metaphors'(1977:91).

The work discussed so far goes a long way towards showing how metaphor operates and, therefore, how it becomes persuasive. The metaphoric process has nonetheless been shown to be creative and inevitably incomplete. Ricoeur describes it as the bringing together of two previously unconnected ideas, a calculated error which re-describes the world in which it takes place (1978:21-24). For example, in the statement 'He wolfed down his supper', the idea of 'man' and the idea of 'wolf' come together in such a way as to re-describe the eating behaviour of the man. Following this argument, words themselves must not be seen simply as labels corresponding unequivocally to objects out there in the 'real' world, but rather as vehicles through which that 'reality' may be experienced. Indeed words can be seen as institutionalised metaphors, metaphors which have ceased to surprise or create new experience. Ricoeur describes them as 'metaphor(s) on the road to extinction' (1978:143). In this dynamic process all metaphoric systems are therefore susceptible to change. In the highlighting of some aspects of a phenomenon, scope inevitably remains for the re-inventing of that which is downplayed.

How then, in ritual, can a society's fluid and possibly inconsistent metaphoric system come to be experienced as an unquestionable representation of wholeness or order? Ritual takes place, by definition, in times and spaces set apart from the everyday world. Nonetheless, it is potentially a profound influence within that world. Again a circular relationship is in operation. As I will show, ritual draws power through the appropriation of the material of everyday life – for example, bodily functions such as birth, breast-feeding, menstruation. That everyday life, or rather the metaphoric system through which it is experienced, may then find both validation and completion through the power and influence of ritual forms.

This relationship between carefully bounded non-ordinary ritual space and the everyday world within which it is embedded is illuminated in Ricoeur's work on textual analysis (1978, 1981). Extending his use of the term 'text' to refer to speech, action or performance, he argues that discourse, written down as text, has both an internal or sense meaning, and also a referential meaning which transcends the limits of the text itself. The sense meaning can be thought of as an internal self-referential, semiotic system. It makes sense or has meaning purely within its own terms. Referential meaning stems from the relationship between 'text' and the world. It concerns what the text discloses of the world through its being in the world. In addition reference concerns the meanings accruing to the internal relations of the text by virtue of their location within the time and space of the world. Thus language, when used in the construction of texts, is transformed from a purely self referential system into one which transcends itself, finding meaning through its referential meaning in the world. Within the relationship between internal sense meaning and self-transcendent referential meaning lies considerable scope for creating particular sets of meanings, for highlighting certain aspects of reality and for downplaying others. Here the important issue of power is raised.

Geertz's discussion of the question of religious belief (1968a:25-26) is of particular relevance in this connection. He argues for a relationship between belief and the acceptance of an authority which can transform experience. Believers are those who willingly become susceptible to the power embodied in a particular system. Through imagery, trance or charismatic personality, power of this kind may be expressed. A familiarity with recognisable ritual forms, by definition distinguishable from the secular, common-sensical world of everyday, and a willingness to submit to their power, would seem to be essential dispositions in the believer. An analogous context is the theatre. The fictional reality produced through stage sets, actors and musical or other effects is accepted and 'believed' by the theatre-goer. The quality of a performance is often judged largely by its power to uphold such an illusion. It should maintain the audience's unawareness of the re-hearsed and carefully contrived nature of the fictive world in which they have elected to 'believe'.

In his published diary Frisch describes a chance experience of observing the unintentional framing of people and events within the stage's proscenium arch during the hour before a rehearsal (1950:63-65). He notes the transformation of trivial actions and objects when captured, fleetingly, in this space. Suddenly they acquire a 'non-ordinary' weight and significance. This leads him to reflect how eras and continents can be evoked at will within the finite, fictive time and space of the stage play. As each object, gesture or utterance is pre-sented, it takes on expansive referential meanings which transcend the immediate physical world of actors and props. Offstage, for example, chairs are understood largely in relation to other household objects of the category 'furniture'. This could be described as the internal or sense meaning of a chair. Onstage, a chair can assume a vast breadth and subtlety of significance depending, for example, on who uses it and how.

This example takes us a long way towards the heart of the ritual process. Both theatre and ritual are extra-ordinary contexts in which the material of everyday life can be made to demonstrate what Esslin describes as '...the inherent symbolism of reality itself'(1982:10). One actor or one object can stand for a whole class of men or chairs, and can represent the essence of that class through its presence on the stage.

As already shown, many of the conceptual systems through which we perceive and experience the world are grounded in our bodily experience of that world. In a ritual context that relationship between abstract thought and physical experience is often inverted. Metaphoric allusions to primary biological experience, usually the implicit ground-ing of more abstract schema, are made demonstrably explicit. As Fernandez says '...metaphors provide organizing images which ritual action puts into effect'(1977:101). He draws on the example of the native Americans of the North Pacific coast. He quotes Boas's com-ments on '...the use of metaphorical terms in poetry, which in rituals are taken literally'(Boas:1911). Thus potlatch, the native American ritual consumption/destruction of material wealth, is described by Boas as 'closely related' to the metaphor 'devouring of wealth'.

In summary, it can be said that the everyday or experiential grounding of conceptual systems is an important aspect of their persuasiveness. As a rule the sources of common metaphors remain implicit, resonating back into the tangible, surrounding environment in a way which is largely inaccessible to the conscious mind. Indeed the work of Ricoeur and Lakoff and Johnson has been profoundly innovative in that it has made explicit the experiential grounding of metaphoric forms. The role of metaphor in the creation of meaning is anything but apparent. Thus, for example, Bishop Jenkins' explicit references to the metaphoric rather than literal role of the 'worldly' events which constitute the Christian gospels[2] have been seen as potentially disruptive to the religious experience of many believers.

When framed within ritual time and space, the revealing of the normally veiled, literal grounding of conceptual systems potentially reanimates or revitalises those systems in their capacity to describe or interpret the world. As noted, Moore and Myerhoff have drawn attention to the dangers inherent in this process (1977:18). In presenting the implicit grounding of metaphoric thought for view in an open and deliberate fashion the risk of revealing the made-up, arbitrary quality of that thought is of course incurred. It is nonetheless the concrete representation of organizing images which lends a sense of integrated wholeness to the believer's experience of the world and of themselves.

The framing of ritual time and space has already been noted as one crucial element in this process. In addition a willingness to believe, to submit to the power embodied within ritual forms, is also critical. Moore and Myerhoff describe how knowledge is imparted through ritual in the form of postulates which '...render it unverifiable, separate from standards of truth and falsity'(1977:18). In his work on the nature of symbolic forms, Turner (1967:19-17) addresses the question of how this process is achieved. He shows how literal representations of metaphoric images in a ritual context – a candle, a black ribbon, bread, wine – have a multivocal power. In this respect they are like the stage chair, flower or king, which transcends its own immediate self and is transformed into a representation of the essence of all chairs, flowers or kings. Central to Turner's approach is the idea that such objects, and indeed gestures, smells, music and the structuring of time and space, can all have an expansive set of referents ranging from the physiological to the most abstract areas of life. In other words conceptual schema and their experiential origins are brought together and fused. In this way abstract thought is reanimated by primary experience, whilst simultaneously giving form and meaning to fundamental experiences such as birth, copulation and death.

Death itself is a good example of this process. It is commonly made use of metaphorically. As noted earlier, in British society its figurative use imputes an ultimate or extreme quality to the emotions or events of life. This is exemplified in expressions such as 'dead centre'; 'dead right'; 'I'm dying to meet you'; 'You'll die when you hear this'; 'I'm tickled to death'.

By contrast, in societies where death is understood as change or transition, metaphoric 'deaths' are often enacted in order to bring about ritual movement or passage, as in initiation. It is in this process that Bourdieu's description of mind and world as 'an endless circle of mutually reflecting metaphors' (1977:91) is borne out. In British society, metaphoric language emphasises the biological finality of death, for example 'terminally ill', 'on her way out', 'lost'. This in turn is reflected in our metaphoric use of death to lend an ultimate or extreme quality to everyday happenings. In societies where images of transcendence and continuity are stressed at the time of death, we find a corresponding metaphoric use of death to suggest transition.

In describing how metaphors and their more concrete sources come to be fused within ritual, Turner talks in terms of the bi-polar or dualistic aspects of all dominant religious symbols. Encompassing both the physiological/emotional and the abstract/conceptual domains, such symbols can be so manipulated within the ritual context as to evoke any one level or area within the symbol's sphere of reference. Whilst the participant's attention is thus focussed, the broader sphere of the symbol's reference nevertheless continues to make itself felt. With the imagination, intellect and bodily experience simultaneously engaged, the participant's experience shifts continuously from partial to total awareness and understanding. In this way the possibly inauthentic and undoubtedly limited 'reality' of everyday life is not only re-presented as valid and unquestionable; it is also experienced as but a part of what Geertz describes as a 'correcting and completing' totality (1968a:39).

It is this experience of wholeness, made possible only through submission to the constraints of ritual time and space, which may be carried out into the less predictable world of everyday life. There the experiential sources of conceptual thought again become veiled. Having been revealed in the ritual context however, their power to impute authentic meanings to experience-in-the-world is restored.

In ritual processes associated with death, at a time of potential chaos and incompleteness, the symbolic manipulation of objects, space and indeed the corpse itself, can serve to transform that present experience of confusion and loss by placing it within the context of a set of meanings which resonate throughout the entire cultural system.

Levi-Strauss offers the example of death ritual among the Bororo (1973:298-320). The death of a member of Bororo society is seen as the violation of culture by nature. This idea is given tangible form in the reciprocal killing of a large animal by man. Once avenged in this way, the spirit of the deceased is thought to be received into a society of souls. Such a society is re-created through dances performed by men from whichever half (or moiety) of the tribe the deceased was not a member. Levi-Strauss describes Bororo death ritual as 'a dazzling metaphysical dance'. He shows that it can be seen to 'correct and complete' the experience of an everyday world where separation and inequality predominate between moieties, clans and gender and where 'men die and do not come back'. As Levi-Strauss points out '... the image a society evolves of the relationship between the living and the dead is, in the final analysis, an attempt, on the level of religious thought, to conceal, embellish or justify the actual relationships which prevail among the living'(1973:246).

In summary, ritual can be seen as the literal presentation and manipulation of the set of metaphors through which death is encountered in a particular society. Within the framing of ritual time and space, everyday objects and familiar spatial and temporal arrangements are re-ordered, thereby evoking participants' most fundamental physical and emotional experience, and bringing it into line with the most abstract cosmological theorising. It is through these processes of framing and re-ordering that the expressive symbolising power of objects/events is maximised. Spanning both a biological and an intellectual plane, symbols create within the participant an experience which is not only authentic, but also exclusive. As noted, Moore and Myerhoff use the word 'postulates' to describe the form of knowledge apprehended through ritual (1977:18). That is to say, the power of ritual is very much bound up with its capacity to exclude alternatives. Selectively highlighted aspects of experience in the world are transformed into a representation in which life as lived and life as imagined are fused. In such a context the inner turmoil of individual survivors' grief is given selective expression in images or outward forms which have referents within the more expansive, and more ordered world view shared by the entire society. In this way death ritual provides both an inspiration for, and an interpretation of, the quality of individual experience.

DYING AND THE CONSTRUCTION OF
NON-ORDINARY TIMES AND SPACES

Informed by the preceding discussion of how ritual comes to act persuasively upon its participants, I will turn to the question of how experiences associated with death come to take on particular qualities within the special, 'non ordinary' contexts which our society sets aside for dying.

A residential home for elderly people and a hospice are two such contexts, non-ordinary places within which the dying of residents or patients is an inevitable occurrence. As already noted, the culture of each one is different and gives particular forms and qualities to experiences associated with death. In both contexts the same issues emerge continuously – for example, patients' experience of themselves as changing rapidly; staff's ambiguous caring/controlling role; the entrenched nature of the boundary between life and death. However these issues can emerge in radically different forms. Even very similar comments made with respect to those approaching death take on very different meanings when uttered in one or the other context. For example:

(1) 'You know they're pampered here, they're really pampered.'
(2) 'They're really spoiled here, they deserve it.'

These two sentences are statements made by staff about people who are likely to die in the near future. Statement (1) was uttered in a residential home for elderly people and invokes the fictive notion that very elderly people are not approaching death – and therefore do not have special needs. Statement (2) is an inversion of (1) and was uttered in a hospice. It acknowledges the literal reality that patients in the hospice are dying and that they do have special needs.

The following sentences are remarks addressed by staff to the same categories of people.

(1) 'I'll carry you both out on my back.'
(2) 'I'll carry you home on my back, you're so tiny.'

Sentence (1) was uttered in a residential home for elderly people. It is a teasing remark which obliquely alludes to the physical condition of two elderly women and the limitations of the care which staff offer. The speaker was a small, slight porter/handyman and the women he addressed were large and immobile. Sentence (2) is another teasing remark in that this speaker too will not do what she promises. It was uttered in a hospice, however, and does refer directly to the physical condition of the patient and, implicitly, to the idea that the nurse can support the woman through her frailty.

Though each of these two pairs of sentences might appear to say the same thing, their utterance in one or the other of two very different social contexts in fact lends a very different meaning to them. Comparing similar statements in this way provides a clear illustration of the points already discussed concerning the way in which otherwise trivial remarks or gestures begin to take on new and quite specific sets of meanings when framed within ritual, or non-ordinary times and spaces. Both the residential home and the hospice, by virtue of their non-ordinary functions, have parallels with the stage in that the meaning and the quality of everything which is framed within these institutions begins to resonate in quite specific ways. This chapter offers an account of life, and death, within a residential home for elderly people. It will demonstrate both the special resonance of everyday utterances and acts, and also the ways in which their meanings may be manipulated within. this context.

HIGHFIELD HOUSE

In Highfield House the Local Authority houses forty-five elderly people who cause concern or experience difficulty in living alone or with younger family in the outside world. Most of them have applied for admission and the majority are accommodated in their own single bed-sitting rooms. Carpet-tiled, with teak bedside furniture, wardrobe and built in wash-hand basin and mirror, the rooms overlook lawns, trees and flowerbeds at the periphery of the city. Most of the home's elderly residents bring favourite ornaments, photographs and religious pictures or objects in with them. Some bring their own armchair, rug or small table and, together with pot plants, these valued possessions fill the light sunny bed-sitting rooms. Small lounges and alcoves are also available for the elderly people to sit together and there are three televisions for them to watch. Meals are waitress-served at small tables in a dining-room where floor to ceiling windows open onto the gardens.

There are other services offered. Rooms are cleaned regularly and thoroughly, and bed-linen and personal clothing is laundered and returned to rooms. If anyone becomes ill or unable to get about, care assistants give nursing care or assist with bathing or walking. When elderly people come to live in the home they give up their own private accommodation, knowing that they will be able to stay on in the home for the rest of their lives.

The forty-five elderly people living in the home during my nine month period of fieldwork often needed help from a care assistant. Many of them were very old, more than half over eighty-five years old, and most over seventy-five. While sixteen of them needed little special help, ten could walk only with a zimmer frame and therefore had to be bathed by care assistants. Seven people could not communicate easily, either through deafness, stroke or confusion, and a further twelve could neither communicate nor walk with ease. Some residents had multiple forms of dependency – for example, among those already referred to, three were totally immobile, and five were troubled with incontinence. Within ten months of my initial entry into the home approximately a quarter of the elderly people I met had died, usually within the home itself.

The home's material circumstances, as described above, lend themselves to the maintenance of an attractive image of the homeliness, security and independence of 'adulthood'. However the mental and physical losses experienced or observed by the elderly people living together at close quarters are an unequivocal representation of biological processes which lie outside the curative frameworks of medicine. Indeed they are peripheral to the prevailing cultural categories of both 'life' and 'death', in that 'life' is constituted largely through images which exclude dependencies of the kind described here.

The residential home is therefore a dying space concerned primarily with the slow process of deterioration. Not only are the illnesses of old age often chronic rather than acute, they are also accompanied in many cases by other gradual losses such as blindness, baldness and immobility. Death itself tends to arrive slowly, from a multiplicity of ailments rather than a single and specific disease. McDonald expands upon this point when she describes the quality of her experience of being seventy years old:

> One doesn't just die all of a sudden. It is a process and one we may be conscious of for the last ten or twenty years of our life, which if you think about it, may be a quarter or more of your lifetime. I find myself wondering why this is not more talked about and why it has not become the common knowledge of our lives. I am self conscious in writing this. For after all, no one speaks of dying until they have only a few months or weeks or hours to live. This is society's definition of dying. It asks that I deceive myself and others about my daily awareness that my body is using itself up; it prevents me from calling this process by name for myself and others. (1984:108-109)

McDonald is acknowledging her entry into a social category to

which many negatively perceived aspects of bodily existence are now
implicitly distanced in the West. They range from a (sexually) un-
attractive appearance, an inactive body and an unreliable memory,
through to incontinence, dementia and death. The occurrence of
any one of these conditions prior to old age is recognised as at best
a misfortune, at worst a tragedy. Indeed the wholeness of the adult
is made questionable through the presence of one or more of these
conditions. Distanced to old age, such conditions are kept firmly in
place through the silence required of older people.

Within the residential home the process of ageing is submerged.
The role of the Matron is critical to its submersion. Spatially,
temporally and hierarchically she is so located as to be able to
promote a figurative representation of a homely enviroment which
may then be used to transform the experiences identified by
McDonald as 'dying'. Those elements of the home and its inhabitants which approximate to the cultural categories 'life' and 'adulthood' are selectively highlighted through metaphoric strategies
which simultaneously downplay evidence of the slow collapse,
'dying'. Only when the 'deadness' of an elderly person is finally given
open acknowledgement through coffin, hearse, undertaker and
flowers, do some of the elderly inhabitants and care staff of the home
watch and possibly follow the body to the funeral.

The role of the Matron stands in opposition to the role of her care
staff. The authority vested in this role is expressed in her social and
spatial distance from staff – and from residents. For example, while she
and her two deputies have exclusive use of a matching dinner and tea
service, staff bring in their own mugs kept in a separate cupboard in the
kitchen. Eating and relaxing similarly take place in separate rooms –
Matron's office and the Staff Room – and indeed during sequences of
duty the Matron lives in a flat within the home. Similarly, her white
uniform dress contrasts with care staff's blue-checked overalls – and
her personal clothing is laundered within the home where a machine
will be put on solely for a few items of her clothing, rather than
including them in a larger load of residents' laundry.

Set apart in this way she is distanced from the literal evidence of
residents' increasing physical frailty, conditions which she possesses
the medical and administrative capacity to exercise some control over.
She can be compared with her staff whose daily tasks of washing,
dressing, bedmaking and managing meal times involve constant
exposure to human frailty and decay. Unlike the Matron, staff lack
nursing qualifications and are given no medical information concerning the condition of those in their care. In addition they lack her

authority to draw directly upon the expertise of outside agencies
such as doctors and the hospital. While the Matron may re-create
the conditions necessary for the imposition of the categories 'life'
and 'death' upon an ageing population, staff's work involves them
continuously in the tension between the figurative and the literal
reality prevailing within the home.

THE MATRON AS SENTINEL

The Matron spends much of her working life at a desk facing the
ever-open door of her office. From this position she looks out into a
carpeted foyer where a coffee table with flowers and magazines
stands surrounded by armchairs and pictures. She faces the home's
locked glass entrance door and, beyond it, the three-sided entry
courtyard. From the courtyard a curving drive leads away towards
the main road and two neighbouring institutions, County Hall and
the local hospital, both of them closely related to life within the
home. Beyond lies the city.

The courtyard is fairly well-hidden from the main road. It allows
for access of all kinds. New residents, visiting family and friends,
staff, doctors, health care officials, food, rubbish and the dead all
pass into and out of the home through this space. The Matron has
visual control over it.

Away to the right of the Matron's office the foyer leads off towards
a complex of rooms comprising the staff room, kitchens, washing
and ironing rooms, the medical room and the dining-room. Once
past this space the carpeted foyer gives way to the long lino-tiled
corridors along which are lined the thirty single and seven double
bed-sitting rooms where the elderly people live.

To the left of the Matron the foyer gives access to a small visitor's
room, a lounge (used irregularly by a small group of elderly women
and by day-care visitors), and the two sets of double doors leading to
the morgue. Beyond and also above the morgue lie two flats, the
upstairs one belonging to the Matron and the other used by her two
deputies.

Thus the rooms overlooking and bounding the courtyard on
three sides are the Matron's flat, the foyer, the staff room and just
two of the thirty-seven bed-sitting rooms where the elderly people
live. The remaining thirty-five of their rooms face away outwards
towards the gardens and the countryside to the northwest of the city.
This form of spatial organisation is illustrated in the accompanying
diagram.

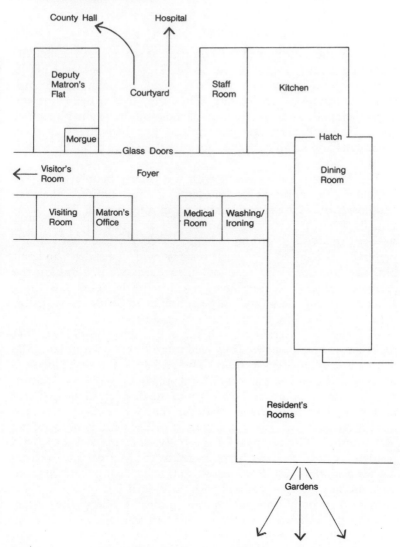

Figure 1: The Structuring of Space at the Periphery of Highfield House.

The diagram illustrates the spatial relationship between Highfield House and the outside world as it is mediated by the Matron. While some residents's rooms occupy similar space on the floor directly above the foyer, only two have visual access to the courtyard.

CONTROLLING THE CARE

Located at the periphery of the home the Matron is responsible for admitting elderly people to the home. This process leaves her in possession of a great deal of medical, social and financial information concerning the individual. While they live in the home she holds their pension book, their medicines and their valuables in her office. She will also have determined just how many clothes, ornaments and small items of furniture they have brought in with them.

The Matron's involvement with the elderly people who have 'settled' in the home as its 'residents' is more limited. She may administer medicine in the dining-room after a meal. Very occasionally she will serve the main course at lunch time, carefully selecting the food according to her knowledge of each individual's preferences. She will sit over breakfast with a resident on their birthday and open and read out their cards while admiring the carnation button-hole they have been given by the home. Last thing at night she will sometimes say goodnight to residents in bed in their rooms, blowing them a kiss where appropriate.

It is when an elderly person living in the home becomes ill that the Matron again becomes involved more directly with them. She will go in to visit them in their room and summon their doctor if necessary. If they become very ill and are about to die, the Matron may sit with them through the night in the downstairs sickbay and deal with their immediate relatives. When a resident dies, she usually lays out their body, packing its orifices and bandaging the feet together. The removal of the body from the sick bay (or a resident's room) may also be managed by the Matron, she overseeing the maintenance of secrecy as staff usher living residents into their rooms. Her final contact with the elderly person is when she releases their body from the morgue under her flat to the undertaker in the courtyard. Relatives deemed inattentive during the resident's lifetime may also find that the Matron seeks to retain some control over the elderly person even after death.

For example, when a resident's two neices and a nephew appeared for the first time at her funeral, their behaviour was interpreted by staff as cold and ungrateful. 'Its their guilt' they said. The Matron declared herself all the more determined that the resident should have a headstone and that she was going to have Masses said for her – that would use up a bit more of her remaining money (and keep it from her undeserving family).

METAPHORIC SCENE-SHIFTING: 'THE HOMELY HERE-AND-NOW'

As forty-five elderly people edge their individual ways forwards to death in the homely here-and-now of Highfield House, the Matron effects critical shifts of meaning within their immediate environment. As indicated, she operates at a fixed distance from the processes they are undergoing. This suggests that the home's boundary, the Matron's stable position, is the point from which power emanates. A figurative set of meanings created at the periphery provide an interpretive framework for all that goes on within.

The literal meaning of daily life within the home is that forty-five people have lived so long as to have outgrown their places within the outside world. Much of what is said and done within the home readily takes on a set of referential meanings to do with deterioration and death. Residents are now separated from a past life, and from the roles and relationships through which it was constituted. In addition their bodies have begun to change, in some cases fairly rapidly, in ways which can only lead to their death. For the first time in their lives they are without the prospect of future change – that is change other than the gradual physical deterioration which, in most cases, will take place within the home up to the time of their deaths. The domestic and nursing services which elderly people are offered in the home are a way of managing the practicalities of this process of deterioration which takes place without the constant support or intervention of family or friends belonging to the past. It is the Matron, however, who transforms the home's literal referential meaning, supplying in its place a figurative set of meanings associated with homeliness, security and independence. Located at the periphery she is well placed to make interventions in the way in which the events framed by the institution are interpreted, in the self-transcendent process whereby a set of purely semiotic sense meanings acquire a particular set of referential meanings.

Thus, for example, not only does the residential home lie within a boundary which separates it from the surrounding world; it also encompasses a whole range of institutional boundaries, of a kind which inhibit the making of connections. In this condensed world of ageing and dying, there is an essential introduction of distance between people and things, ideas and knowledge, and, ultimately, life and death. The complex bounding of time and space within the institution is a necessary condition for the continuous mis-reading of the literal referential meaning of what goes on within it.

In summary, the residential home is a space visibly set apart, which has a quite specific role or purpose. Unlike almost any other single-purpose building or institution, it is a true cul-de-sace where future alternatives are lacking. In this respect it stands in an iconic relationship to human biological existence which, regardless of a society's processual twists and turns, leads inevitably to a single event, death. In the bounded, condensed space of Highfield House, an awareness of the transitory, mortal nature of life, customarily diffused through a cultural stressing of development and accumulation, is brought home. Like acts or utterances staged within a proscenium arch, the details of life in residential care readily assume non-ordinary meanings – that is, they become 'matters of life and death'. And bearing the extra-ordinarily loaded capacity of any ritual or indeed stage production, the meaning of life in residential care is susceptible to the power of director, shaman or Matron. Like the writer's critical choice of one word rather than another within the dozen or so lines of a poem, so the Matron's manipulation of one event or one individual has an extensive resonance within the condensed semantic space of the residential home.

The example of the residential home demonstrates the role of a boundary or frame in the creation of a time and a space within which events or acts acquire expressive power, the meaning of which is open to manipulation. An environment peopled within by heavily wrinkled, immobile or confused individuals is a powerful evocation of death. When carefully controlled, the literal referential meaning of such conditions can be transformed – and a figurative state of homely independence fostered. In such a context 'pampering' comes to be seen as a form of care which is both unwarranted and inappropriate.

PASSAGE THROUGH RESIDENTIAL CARE

The following ethnographic material traces the movement of individual elderly people into and through residential care, highlighting the metaphoric strategies through which their passage is managed. Fieldwork reveals this passage to be contained within an otherwise hidden social, spatial and temporal loop which links the twin processes of admission and exit. While an elderly person may seek admission in order to make a life for themself in residential care, the institution, through the person of the Matron, is oriented towards managing their transition from life to death. As noted, a resident's initial entry is directed by the Matron within the carpeted public space in and around her office. Its flowers, coffee table, magazines and pictures are an effective representation of the figurative reality of homely independence which, it will be shown, is used extensively to mask the looped passageway through Highfield House.

Having been brought in through the public space of the courtyard, the new resident can expect to be allocated a room on the first floor of the building, oriented away from this point of contact with the outside world. Literally 'put out to grass', their remaining 'private' space overlooks lawns, hedgerows and countryside. As noted, the peripheral homeliness of the institution does not extend into the unvarying furnishings of the residential corridors. Thus, any transformation of the living accommodation into a personal space must be wrought by the resident themself, using the few possessions they have brought in with them. The bedrooms have no electric power points and the home has no payphone.

The passage of deteriorating individuals through Highfield House is submerged in this unchanging, depersonalised environment. Only the small bedside rugs, the trinket boxes, the remnants of former dinner services or table linen, and the mantlepiece clocks serve as personal reminders – or iconic representations – of entire, lost domestic contexts. Remaining figuratively alive in the memories and the reminiscences of individual residents, the past is embodied in such small inanimate objects. They stand as sad reminders that, just as they have survived the homely spaces where once they were framed, so too they will survive the dwindling physical presence of their individual owners. Past, present and future are thus evoked and brought together in a continuum. These are the symbolic gestures of individuals and not of the institution. The institution manages the temporal continuum which links past life with future death by submerging it, rather than giving it overt acknowledgement.

Having been moved from the periphery to the centre, upwards and away from their point of entry, the individual resident is required to conform to an institutional division of time and space. Care staff gently direct the new resident from early morning tea in bed, to breakfast, to a seat in one of the lounges, to lunch, and so on. Care staff make their bed, wash and iron their now-labelled clothes and determine where and when they will sit to receive their food. Every aspect of the resident's environment is shaped by care staff.

For as long as an elderly person is capable of meeting the requirements of the category 'resident', they will remain at the centre of the institution. Framed within institutional time and space their individuality, as embodiments of human deterioration and decline, is submerged within this depersonalising social category. Any physical or mental deterioration, however, may lead to the beginning of a movement back towards the periphery, and out of this category.

Those who become incontinent, unable to walk without support, or perceptibly 'confused in their minds' will find themselves moved downstairs to what staff refer to as the 'frail' corridor. In their use of the term 'frail', staff hint more openly at the loop or passageway which is threaded through the intractably rigid time and space of the home. Thus residents' everyday comings and goings, back and forth between bedroom, bathroom, lounge and dining-room, are in reality a one way movement through the non-ordinary space of the 'frail' corridor, its name referring directly to their own death-evoking physical and mental conditions. Should staff fail to attend to the home's implicit task – of channelling deteriorating elderly people towards their deaths – then the carefully submerged disorder of ageing bodies might rapidly emerge to make visible and explicit the true nature of the institution.

Residents from the 'frail' corridor may also find they are no longer accepted in the lounges where fitter residents pass their days. Care staff will seat them in the alcove nearest the dining-room and it is here that once again they become prominent, visible and singled out for attention as an individual rather than as a member of a category. Becoming more nearly the corpses which are the home's unspoken product, they are recognised swiftly as the staff's primary focus. Not only staff, but also the more healthy and mobile residents recognise an emergence of the literal movement towards death. It is rare to see one of the fitter residents sitting in the very accessible and convenient alcove area.

Similarly in the dining-room 'frail' residents are moved forwards, closer to the hatchway into the kitchen. Referred to as 'the little people' – who receive smaller meals – it is this group who will be addresssed by Christian name only and will tend to be given nicknames. As confusion and an increasing lack of bodily control erode all but the last vestiges of an elderly person's individuality, a fictive persona is often predicated upon them. Roleless and physically incapable, their attributes are inverted in nicknames such as 'King Arthur', 'Queen Gertrude', 'the Ballerina' (a squat, totally immobile woman), and 'the Two Musketeers' (two women, one very unsteady, one very poor-sighted, who arm-in-arm steered each other slowly through the home). Through such nicknaming a grim literal reality is both acknowledged and humourously diffused. It is the names, or nicknames, of these residents which will be listed and underscored in the report book where care staff record the events of one shift for the benefit of those taking over. The phrase 'Remaining residents no change at the time of report' is written beneath the list of individual names and encompasses all those whose slow ageing still remains submerged within the institutional category, 'resident'. A fictive sense of stability or permanence is thus imposed upon a gradually fading population.

The 'little people' however are beginning to move away from the centre, a movement which in time will lead them back to the periphery. From their prominent position in the alcove it is this group who are most exposed to the passage of a corpse from sickbay along to the morgue. Similarly it is to these individuals that the clothes of the dead will be given, sometimes within a day or two of the funeral.

As their physical deterioration increases and illness sets in, these individuals will be cared for in one of the two sick bays on the 'frail' corridor. As they move visibly closer to the literal reality of dying their previously ambiguous status, betwixt and between the categories 'life' and 'death', is finally left behind. No longer subject to the required uses of time and space, the very poorly individual will receive frequent attention from the Matron, the only member of staff with medical experience – and in addition from outside doctors. As noted, the Matron sits with them as they are dying, and lays out their body before it is wheeled along to the morgue beneath her flat, once again at the periphery of the home. The body passes back into the outside world through the morgue doors into the courtyard, the Matron guiding the coffin into the hands of the undertaker.

As shown, it is the Matron's position at this peripheral point which empowers her in a central transforming role. Whilst the continuum of life and death is charted in the visible passage of individuals through this building, she nonetheless promotes an illusion of 'life' as a stable and enduring state, to which the would-be resident may aspire.

To follow are four figurative representations of the 'homely here-and-now' of Highfield House which the Matron helps to promote. Each one reveals the strategy of metaphoric transformation which masks institutional processes pragmatically addressed to the management of bodily deterioration. They are:

(1) a Guide Book given to prospective residents and any family they may have.[3]

(2) the Name of the Home.

(3) a Valentine's Card sent to residents by volunteer helpers, the Friends of Highfield House.

(4) an Open Day, or summer fete, to which all associated with the home are invited.

Whether written down or performed, these four representations of the homely-here-and-now are oriented towards the resident or relative and re-assures them that entry to Highfield House is entry to a favourable life in 'care'. As will be shown, each representation has a set of additional, largely implicit meanings. Once set within the cultural context of the wider society and of residents' lost past lives, present dependencies, and pending future death, those otherwise implicit meanings can be read out.

(1) Guide for Prospective Residents

Local social services offer a guide to elderly people contemplating admission to Highfield House. On the first page, in 'A message to you from the Director of Social Services', there is an acknowledgement that:

> ... many people are apprehensive about applying for a place in a home.

Though the language of the guide is gentle and circumspect in style, its content advises the would-be resident that tenancy or ownership of their home must be given up; that their furniture cannot be accommodated; that the officer-in-charge will take possession of their money, valuables, pension book and medicines; that the times and places for receiving visitors are circumscribed; that the use of alcohol and tobacco must be moderated. In the context of a residential home for very elderly people this shedding of possessions, responsibilities and personal space readily takes on one particular set of meanings – that death is the impending reality. Indeed those who continue to live alone in extreme old age often fear the spectre of outsiders intruding upon personal space such as cupboards and drawers after their death.

Offered prior to admission, the guide book can be seen as an attempt to transform the otherwise frightening meaning of a residential system of domestic and nursing services.

Thus the guide book acknowledges the possible apprehension of its readers, being offered in the hope that:

> ... it will serve to allay some of the worries you may have.

In accordance with this hope, it seeks to soften its stipulations in subtly persuasive language such as:

> ... you will be encouraged to...
> ... you are expected to...
> ... it is common practice for...
> ... in the interests of your safety...
> ... you are strongly advised...
> ... you are asked to remember that...

It represents the home as:

> ... well furnished, everything possible having been done to make it as homely and comfortable as possible...varied and interesting menus are provided... a range of activities are arranged within the home which may include concerts, socials, table games and a library service.

In resonant language such as this the outsider's perception of the institution as some kind of last resort where the waiting game begins, is metaphorically transformed in a figurative representation which stresses material comfort and enjoyable sociality.

(2) The Name of the Home

In the naming of the residential home a similar metaphoric transformation is introduced in order to mask its less welcome implications. Despite the fact that the word 'home' implies something more than just a house, the prefacing of the word 'home' with the name of a category, 'old folks' or 'dogs', rather than an individual, 'Mr Wilkinson', immediately inverts the more positive meaning of the word. Notions of hearth and home sweet home, of the private and the domestic, then give way to images of a public, rule-bound space into which the individual is 'put away'. Thus, although Highfield House is described as being 'as homely and comfortable as possible', the stigmatised word 'home' is not used to name it. Instead a name becomes a title in the substitution of the word 'house' for 'home'. For example, where institutions have been established in rather grand properties, formerly owned by wealthy families, the legacy of titles such as 'Metcalfe House' or 'Grosvenor House' is pressed into service, thereby masking the institutional with something of the dignified and the stately. This practice is extended in the naming of modern, purpose-built homes such as Highfield House and indeed staff refer to an overcrowded institution as a 'heavy house'. The word 'home' is used to name only one of the forty-one institutions for elderly people in this region of the North East. Preferred are titles such as 'Palatine House', 'Gladstone Hall', 'Greenfields House', 'Bydale Lodge', 'Grove Park', 'The Lawns' and 'Moorcroft'. Overall it is the title 'house' which predominates, being used to name twenty-nine of the forty-one homes in the region.

In the rigorous exclusion and inversion of the word 'home' and its associations with category rather than individuality, the cultural manipulation of awareness is exemplified. Rather than being 'put away into an old folks' home' or 'admitted to care', the elderly person 'becomes a resident in Metcalfe House'. Through the use of this particular cultural linguistic device, dependency and impending

death are metaphorically transformed and rendered less perceptible
to those confronted with admission to an institution.

The describing and the naming of the residential home are two
areas amenable to transformative interventions. In addition a figurative representation of the home is also given literal form in events or
performances which take place at the periphery of the home. These
events arise from the efforts of the Matron in conjunction with
outside helpers or volunteers. The two I will describe are the sending
of a Valentine's card to the residents, and the Open Day. A group of
people known as the Friends of Highfield House are responsible for
both.

(3) The Valentine's Card

The Friends of Highfield House are a group of about eight or ten
middle-aged women and men whose regular involvement with
residents is largely confined to the organisation of a weekly bingo
session. Their role in creating a figurative representation of residents
is however more far reaching. Using the occasion of St Valentine's
Day and its associations with the offering of romantic love between
individuals, the Friends addressed a poem to all those encompassed
by the institutional category 'resident'. After some initial difficulty a
Valentine's card which contained no implicit or explicit sexual
reference was bought. A verse was typed on the back of the card
which was then pinned on a notice-board outside the dining-room in
such a way that the card's printed message for the individual was
obscured. It read as follows:

> We love to be among you
> To share in all you do
> The residents of this home are dear to us, 'tis true.
> So upon this special day
> We are pleased to write these lines
> To the friends of Highfield House – you all are Valentines

In these lines the literal meanings associated with an institutional
category, 'resident', are entirely supplanted by figurative meanings
associated with Valentine's Day. Those to whom it is addressed are
very old people who have little option but to live among others who
are similarly categorised by their age and their degree of dependency. To 'love', to 'share in', to be 'dear to', to experience a 'special
day' and, indeed, to be 'a Valentine' are the experiences of individuals involved in or open to the possibility of romantic love. The
senders of the card have appropriated an expressive form from this

area of life in order to address those socially categorised as unavailable for romantic love, and who live with and are cared for by those with whom they have no longstanding ties of blood or affection. Only dependency and age have brought them together.

Thus the senders of the card are addressing a category, 'you all are Valentines', in such a way as to transform its implications through an evocation of the 'special' individualizing experience of romantic love. So flimsy is the illusion, that cards with any sexual content were dismissed by the Friends, lest reference to a more literal expression of romantic love should draw attention to the literal reality of ageing bodies, culturally perceived to be unsuitable for lovemaking. In such a context, helpers' sensitivity to language or images of this kind is clearly heightened.

(4) The Open Day

This is an annual occasion when outsiders come into the home and its grounds to buy products such as the plants which residents have propagated. When I attended I found that the residents themselves were largely conspicuous by their absence from this event. A few fitter individuals ran stalls and a selection of the infirm were lined up, blanketed in wheelchairs, with one care assistant per chair to attend to them. However the majority of residents could only be glimpsed as they watched the event from upstairs windows. The jazz band, the fortune teller, the rummage stalls and the teas served by staff and Friends successfully predominated. The ostensive purpose of the event is fundraising, money being used to buy a third television set for the home. However the vitality and sociality of the tea shop and the fairground, in briefly supplanting an everyday atmosphere of boredom, isolation and weariness, offered an effective literal representation of the guide book's figurative description – that is, of a homely, comfortable environment where varied and interesting menus, concerts, socials and table games are provided.

As a summer-time occasion, the Open Day is staged almost entirely outside or on the periphery of the home. While teas were served in the dining-hall, the majority of space within the home, the bed-sitting rooms, sickbays and corridors, is effectively not 'open' to outsiders. Diverted from any confrontation with the literal reality of ageing in residential care, outsiders encounter only glimpses of the life of a resident. Both are figurative. One is the small group of elderly people who, briefly, are given control over a stall; the other is the row of frail residents who, briefly, are taken outside the building and are seen each to receive the undivided attention of one care assistant.

Lakoff and Johnson argue that '... people in power get to impose their metaphors'(1980:157). In the hierarchical ordering of residential care, metaphors such as names and descriptions, projected by powerful members of Social Services Departments are taken up and given literal form by the heads of institutions under their authority. Scripts assembled by the middle-aged, at a distance from the literal reality of ageing are given material form in performances promoted by the Matron at the periphery of the home. Outsiders may thus be reassured. Of more central importance is the exposure of care staff and residents to periodic special events which tangibly reveal the metaphors through which care is continuously being made acceptable to them.

Indeed, when the Matron herself serves the main meat course at lunch-time, slowly and carefully choosing the slice of ham appropriate for each individual resident, she is providing an additional figurative re-description of the home. Her 'performance' of care is in marked contrast with the normally rapid spooning out of food by the kitchen staff. Similarly, when the Matron seats herself at a resident's birthday breakfast table, sharing in the opening of their cards and chatting in an extended and leisurely fashion, she is again giving literal form to an otherwise figurative notion of 'care'. And again, this contrasts strongly with staff's swift expressions of humour or affection as they sweep the dining-room floor around her. Figurative 'care' is being performed before residents and staff, both of whom are involved more literally in the management of dependency.

In summary the example of the residential home shows the biological processes of ageing and dying being managed in culturally contrived, socially maintained isolation from any overt social or emotional experience of transition. The confined, condensed nature of such an institution provides an example which richly illustrates the strategies of distancing and separation, less obvious but nonetheless powerfully pervasive, within the wider society. In drawing upon anthropological perspectives, developed through the study of ritual within more traditional societies, insights can be gained into the way in which the manipulation of society's metaphors can profoundly alter both the meaning, and also the experience of ageing and death. We move on now to look more closely at that experience, from the perspective of the care staff, and from the perspective of the residents themselves.

Chapter Five

Keeping Them Going: The Work of the Care Staff[1]

While the Matron of Highfield House exercises powerful control over both the literal and the figurative reality of life and death within the home, her care staff occupy a distinctly deferential position in relation to her authority. The exercise of authority in the home is unlike that to be found in institutions such as those devoted to accumulating profit. In the latter the aim of the institution is one which brings most reward to its more powerful members. As a result their purpose and authority is sometimes subverted by less powerful members, particularly if they lack the incentive of profit or promotion. By contrast the underlying purpose of the residential home is the management of physical deterioration and dying. Thus, for care staff, the authority vested in the Matron is a crucial reference point in the management of these processes.

When the Matron expressed her authority in a very direct fashion, she would be described by staff as 'on the warpath' or 'having a purge'. Even when care staff perceived her behaviour to be unjust, they offered little resistance to it. As a care assistant in her fifties said:

'You feel like school girls, being told off. You feel like arguing your case – but I think its better to just say nothing'

Thus staff colluded in assuming the status of schoolgirls. By attributing ultimate responsibility for what went on to the Matron, they created for themselves an outside source of authority in their management of residents. When the Matron chose to scold a young domestic worker publicly in the kitchen, staff comforted the sobbing girl by telling her to try and accept what had happened. Thus Norman, the porter/handyman, drinking tea and eating sandwiches, said:

'Calm yourself, Lorraine – it'll blow over man – don't think about it – put it out of your mind'

Susan, the cook, similarly said:

'I've had it – from the Matron and the residents. Don't let it get to you. You can't do nothing about it'

Unlike many areas within the public world, Highfield House is therefore a setting where all those in authority are female, and indeed where power is highly centralised within the hands of a female officer-in-charge. Norman, the sole male employee, was in many ways an ambiguous and a marginal figure. While occasional staff shortages saw Norman donning a white coat and assuming, rather uncertainly, the role of care assistant, his customary position as porter/handyman involved continuous movement across the boundary between the home and the surrounding world. Charged with fetching prescriptions and small items of residents' personal shopping, Norman was not only peripheral to the home's all female hierarchy, but was also one of the few members of the institution, staff or resident, to move freely between the inside and outside world. Within the home itself his handyman tasks corresponded largely to those forms of labour traditionally seen as men's required contribution to the family home. Female staff had a corresponding role in maintaining a figuratively homely environment, a role which has parallels with women's naturalised care work within the family. The absence of senior male staff is in keeping with the low status 'homely' rather than high status 'medical' nature of the institution, one where suffering which falls outside the limits of the medical model is managed. Indeed geriatric medicine itself is seen as one of the less prestigious specialisms within a medical sphere. For the women employed as care staff, their paid care work was tailored to the demands of their unpaid domestic work. Not only did they willingly allow the Matron to retain ultimate responsibility for the intractable nature of residents' deterioration, but they also indicated no desire that their daily work should result in promotion and the possibility of one day stepping into her shoes. For many the domestic work required to meet their husbands' needs was a more immediate priority, and the ultimate outcome of their paid work was either marriage, motherhood or retirement, rather than promotion.

Unchallenged in her position, the Matron often remained physically within her office for a large part of the day. However her name was in constant use throughout the home in persuading residents to comply with staff's wishes. Indeed, residents themselves, when in conflict with one another, would threaten to report misdeeds to the Matron. Such was the power ascribed to her presence within the home that Mary, the assistant Matron, would insist that the residents all developed problems as soon as the Matron was seen to disappear out of the main door. Jokingly Mary told the Matron to put a sack over her head when she went out, so retaining the powerful illusion of her presence within the home.

Care staff's willing subservience to the Matron's authority was compounded by their very marked lack of information concerning events other than their own immediate tasks. This, together with a lack of any medical knowledge concerning individual residents, effectively absolved staff from ultimate responsibility for what went on. When I declared my concern over causing pain to a resident in sickbay while helping her to sit up and take food, the care assistant working with me replied:

'Well you can only do your best for them you know'

Willingly debarred from ultimate authority, care staff create for themselves a circumscribed scope for power within which they can only do their best.

Thus in the particular circumstances of the residential home, the authority vested in the Matron by her employers, the Local Authority, is rarely challenged by staff. By chance, the shoes I wore at the outset of fieldwork gave my footsteps the same sound as the Matron's. Care staff's faces, turned towards me as I entered the staff room, revealed the awe in which she was held. I quickly abandoned these unsuitable thin-soled shoes as, unlike the Matron, fixed and at a distance in her office, my assumed role as care aid involved the endless and exhausting movement through the building which brings exposure to the physical evidence of deterioration and decay.

A willing acceptance of the sometimes harsh exercise of authority by the Matron is one indication of the demanding nature of care staff's role. By looking more closely at who the residents are, and how the institution seeks to manage the final stages of their lives, further insights into the quality of the care staff's working experience can be gained.

One of the first jolts experienced by the (non-elderly) fieldworker entering a residential home for elderly people is that their notions of the scale and the stages of the human life cycle no longer fit. Those who live in the home are very, very old. Many of them were born some years before the outbreak of the Boer War, one or two being already in their mid-teens at the time of Queen Victoria's death. Seemingly, the residents belong in a history book rather than a home. While individuals who die before the age of seventy may well leave gaps – empty social roles, ruptured relationships, unfinished business – those who survive the age of eighty may find they have toppled over the edge of the social 'map'. Within Highfield House, elderly people often made comments such as:

'I've outlived my generation.'

'Most of my friends are ... (dead and gone)'

'My generation has gone. I'm 85 that's old enough.'

'All my generation has gone now; only the dregs are left.'

With the loss of one's generation comes the loss of all the networks of professional, social and kinship roles within which one was formerly imbedded. In their seventies, eighties and nineties, elderly people may become prominent as individuals, marginal to the rest of society. Their homes, or their membership within the households of the next generation, may be withdrawn from them and, perhaps for the first time, they are singled out by the 'Authorities', the medical and social services.

By pressuring elderly individuals into accepting residential care, their marginality is recognised, and contained within a space which is physically, socially and structurally marginal to the rest of society. It is transformed into an institutionalised marginality. Admission to residential care is therefore the experience of individuals no longer able, or perhaps willing, to live out the requirements of their former social roles. Their awkwardly prominent individuality is managed through the imposition of the social categories of an institution such as Highfield House.

The following ethnographic material shows that attempts to submerge individuality within institutional categories are an intrinsic but problematic aspect of the culture of institutional care. Within the home, membership of one category or the other – staff or resident; Matron or Care Staff; 'fit' resident or 'frail' resident – is given marked, material expression at all times. Thus, residents eat and drink from sterilised plastic crockery, care staff use chipped, unsterilised mugs and plates, and the Matron and her deputies have exclusive use of a matching dinner and tea service. The style of dress and the use of space for washing, eating and relaxing is also different and separate for the members of each institutional category. So rigidly and visibly is social category expressed that the passage of any one individual through the institution has little impact. While the Matron and her deputies work in daily rotation, care staff change shift at eight hourly intervals, and residents pass through the home in a matter of weeks or years. The absence or permanent loss of the individual is thus made irrelevent to the daily unfolding of this hierarchical pattern of social categories. At the death of a resident their room, clothes and dining room place are soon assumed by another member of the category. No visible record of their presence within the home remains. This overdetermined expression and separation of social category is mirrored in the rigid structuring of institutional time and space.

Paradoxically, the imposition of institutional categories can, of itself, serve to heighten a painful sense of one's own individuality. For residents, the rigid timetabling through which 'normal' rules of eating, sleeping, hygiene and dress are maintained, can intensify their awareness of the bodily changes they are experiencing. For example, a frail stroke victim may spend fifteen minutes walking the fifty yards from their bedroom to the dining room, in order that a meal shall be eaten at the time which is appointed for those categorised as 'resident'. During this period the elderly person is inevitably made uncomfortably aware of their immobility, finding it difficult to use speech to deflect their consciousness from the interminable nature of the journey. A painful sense of individuality arises out of an attempt to conform to the timetable set up for all the members of one social category. As the journey is repeated at every successive mealtime, the increasingly extended period of time required serves as a reminder of the process of deterioration which is taking place.

Between those categorised as 'care staff' and 'resident' a physical closeness not customarily found outside sexual or familial relationships is permissable. This too can bring about a problematic awareness of individuality. In the roles of resident and care assistant, individuals continuously share intimate contact in bathrooms, bedrooms and toilets. It is through personal care of this kind that staff control and distance the literal reality of the ageing process, thereby making the promotion of a figurative reality possible. Nonetheless, it is often at the end of these spatially confined interactions that a resident will insert a joking/threatening reference to their (individual) closeness to death. Similarly care staff, whether in seeking to care for, or to control a resident, are repeatedly exposed to situations which evoke a personal, individual response.

Thus, for example, the care assistant who assists the frail stroke victim to walk the corridor to her meal is herself constrained and made very physically aware of the unconscious ease with which she, as a younger individual, can make the otherwise very brief journey. A range of personal feelings may arise. For example, she may feel compassion and question the value of imposing movement upon someone who is very elderly and handicapped; she may feel frustrated, fatigued and bored by the physical constraint being imposed upon her; or she may feel a sense of tongue-tied inadequacy if she attempts to alleviate the unpleasantness of the resident's experience. In addition she has to manage an extended period of physical confrontation with the conditions of old age. All these feelings must somehow be subsumed within the working role of care assistant.

In summary, while residents are continuously made aware of the ageing process as they move here and there according to the requirements of a rigidly repetitive institutional system, so care work, similarly, involves staff in the literal confronting, and then figurative distancing, of elderly individuals who are moving through a difficult and often lonely stage in life.

A very young and inexperienced care aid gently pinched the wrinkled skin on a resident's arm, commenting reflectively:

'That's how your skin goes'.

A resident's photo of himself among former police colleagues, taken in the 1930's, led her to wonder aloud how many of them were dead, to comment on the swift passage of time and to wonder what she'd be like when she was old. Such thoughts must have been common among new staff, yet this form of overt expression was very rare.

The uneasy awareness of individuality, produced through the imposition of institutional categories, is managed by staff in a variety of ways. These include (1) a stressing of group style among themselves, and (2) a vigilant control of the expressions of individuality offered by residents.

(1) Nice-natured Women

Among those categorised as care staff, conformity to a very well-defined style prevails and these individuals can be said to constitute a distinct social group. Membership of this group is very positively perceived, and relationships within it are characterised by deference and a desire to please rather than offend. To appear 'canny' or 'nice-natured' is to qualify for acceptance. Any requests for help from one staff member to another are delicately prefaced by phrases such as 'if you don't mind', 'if you've got a minute' or 'could you do me a favour'. Care assistants compete with one another to answer the summons of a bleep which interrupts a coffee-break. Similarly, the exchange of cigarettes or small food items between staff invariably follows a complex pattern of offering and refusing, offering and refusing, until finally the gift is placed firmly in front of the would-be recipient. Frequently care staff can be found with several un-smoked cigarettes lying before them on the staff room table.

Those who fail to conform to the style adherred to within the group are silently but strenuously excluded. An over-effusive or noisy manner in dealing with residents, a tendency to work at the wrong pace, or an unwillingness to work hard, can all lead to a staff member finding themselves permanently seated at the less sought-after staff room table, the one exposed to the gaze of the Matron across the courtyard. Yet even this process is subtly accomplished, accepted members of the group being unwilling to risk censure through the overt expression of critical personal opinion of another member, whether present or not.

This striking solicitousness of each other by the staff, the carefulness with which they continuously interact with one another has the effect, even purpose, of creating and maintaining a cultural solidarity which serves to define and express their identities in the home as caring staff, rather than as individuals. The ethos of care, customarily employed in the management of residents, is also used in such a way as to seal off staff from residents. It provides the staff with a corporate means of protecting their individual vulnerability during the stressful contact with ageing/dying residents. In a context of care the cultural elaboration of this caring style helps distance the care givers from the care receivers by providing a conformist and well controlled model for caring behaviour. In this way individuality is subordinated to a concept which defines and separates that caring category for whom a future remains.

Only once was the shared fate of both staff and residents made explicit. It took place in the staff room when one of the older care assistants reported the discovery of her post menopausal bleeding and bluntly declared her fear of cancer. Profound silence greeted this confession, and minutes elapsed before the jokes and the rationalisations could be mustered in response. An explicit intimation of mortality had crossed the barrier from residents to sit among the staff, thereby posing a particularly overt challenge in the exposure of the vulnerability of one staff member to the care givers as a whole. The unwelcome challenge was met with the only appropriate response – silence.

(2) Making History: a Record of Dying

The submerging of their own individuality by staff is complemented by other institutional processes which provide a means of controlling or interpreting the inevitable manifestations of individuality among residents.

Perhaps the most succint and concrete example of this form of control is the Report Book. Lying open on one of the staff room tables, it is permanently accessible and frequently read by staff – for interest as well as information. Every eight hours, at the change of shift, they list the dozen or so names of residents who have become prominent as individuals, whether through illness or through some particular form of behaviour. Beneath this list the additional sentence 'Remaining residents no change at the time of report' encompasses the anonymous majority who have adherred to the behaviour required of those categorised as residents. Prominence is thus achieved by those who have failed to conform. Reputations are built from the noteworthy events of each eight hour shift.

For example, when Mabel Edgar, an eighty-nine year old resident, was finally moved from a double to a single bed-sitting room, she declared herself 'as happy as a pig in shit'. In an environment purged of bad language the humourous vulgarity of Mabels's remark resonated throughout the building. Its entry into the Report Book brought it to order, the utterance of the word 'shit' sanitized through the use of the letter 'S' followed by a blank line.

Similarly, when Granny Foster assertively offered night staff 10p to turn off the corridor light outside her room, her name too appeared in the Report Book:

Granny Foster is now into bribery and corruption.

The morning after Gertie Swinburn, ever wakeful, had slept until 5 a.m. a care assistant made the following entry:

Gertie Swinburn made history – slept until 5 a.m. The little darling.

As the common property of the staff group, the Report Book is a vehicle by means of which the individual responses of its members are transformed to become the jokes, the comments and the castigations of the group. In this way staff culturally manipulate the behaviour of those categorised as residents by singling out those who fail to conform. When a resident apologised for speaking harshly to a care assistant the reply came back:

'That's alright but we get annoyed too you know – and we're not allowed to say anything.'

By making explicit the constraints on individuality among staff, the care assistant both accepts the apology and attempts to put the elderly lady in her place, back among the residents where her individuality may become less perceptibly troublesome. The exchange was later reported to another care assistant who commented:

'Well, that's something, an apology from Mrs King. That's going down in the Report Book.'

In this way the force of a confrontation between two strong personalities was dissipated, brought to its conclusion in the pages of the Report Book.

The vigour of these, and many other of the entries within this record, testifies both to the distinctiveness of particular experiences of old age, and also to the singular acuteness of staff's responses to those who undergo them. Written just prior to leaving the home at the end of a shift, the Report Book offers care staff a means of reflecting on, and giving order to, the fragmented and often overlapping experiences of the eight hour shift. In her chosen use of language, the staff member invariably leaves behind her a record, not only of particular events, but also of the style in which they were managed.

The Report Book can therefore be seen as a cultural interpretation of a struggle to retain fading individuality on the part of residents, and a struggle to restrain such intrusive individuality on the part of staff. This restraining control of resident individuality is transformed in the record, by humour, into a guide for the successful and caring manipulation of awkward events which otherwise might disrupt the rhythm of life in the 'homely environment'. Edited and summarised in the pages of the report book stand the lives of those who have outgrown the social categories of their own society. As argued in earlier chapters, 'life' is, currently, a limited and excluding category of experience. Separated off from 'death', 'life' refers to a concept and an experience which precludes any association with decline or loss – and social death, in some form, is the fate which threatens those unable or unwilling to conform to its limited models.

KEEPING THEM GOING

Gathered in the staff room, care assistants grumbled about Mary Crawford, a resident who persistently argued that she felt too unwell to come down for breakfast. The Assistant Matron joined the group, pondering on what the real cause of Mary's problems might be. She wondered if Mary was depressed, adding hastily that of course she was not to be 'pandered to' or she would 'just give up'. Angela, a care assistant, replied:

'Yes, we've got to keep them going'.

The irony in her voice was clearly perceptible.

Angela's succinct, ironic statement carries a powerful resonance within the context of the home. It hints at some of its carefully hidden issues or questions. For example, to what end are staff keeping these elderly people going? And where is it that the residents are going to? To openly address these issues would be to acknowledge, explicitly, that all the residents are going to die soon. Irony therefore emerges as one of the few ways open to staff of alluding to the true nature of their work, and of the current and future conditions of those who they look after. The duties required of care staff do, however, provide unequivocal evidence of the home's implicit purpose.

'Keeping them going' involves care staff in a two-fold set of duties. It is the care assistants' responsibility to ensure that the bodies, the beds and the clothing of all residents are clean; that a rigid regime of meal-times and bed-times is maintained; and that a minimum of emotional and physical distress is manifested among their charges. In thirty-seven identical single and double bed-sitting rooms, in lounges, bathrooms and dining-room, continuous adherence to this task is the overt pre-occupation of all care staff. Two sickbays and an unobtrusive mortuary are the only spaces which attest to their more covert task of supervising the process of dying and the event of death. It is required that both tasks will be pursued simultaneously, that the slow deterioration of elderly people will be managed within the virtually undifferentiated spaces of an institution set apart amidst lawned gardens at the periphery of the city. In such a context, the conceptual categories 'life' and 'death' intrude upon one another continuously. If the figurative 'homely here-and-now' is to be maintained, a constant vigilance is necessary to the maintenance of distinctions and separations.

One strategy through which the boundary between life and death is continuously maintained is the cultural transformation of institutional space. Admission to institutional space is not made available to individuals whose death is apparently imminent. Bedfast, incontinent or dementing people are excluded. Thus the greater part of the home, the upstairs bedrooms, the lounges and the small scattered tables of the dining-room, is maintained ostensibly as accommodation for the 'living', for mobile, continent residents still able to wash and feed themselves.

Nonetheless doubts and ambiguities as to the nature of their social status have already been introduced through the losses inherent within the admissions procedure. The new resident has therefore not only experienced an implied social death, but will also, at some point, begin to display some of the conditions which preclude entry, and portend imminent death. In such a situation care staff are continuously involved in making a subtle and gradual spatial separation between those fitted to remain with the areas which can be described as 'living' accommodation, and those whose membership of even this ambiguous category is increasingly open to doubt.

One by one, failing residents are moved downstairs to bedrooms on the 'frail' corridor, within a few yards of the two sick bays where dying people are cared for. As noted already, such residents find their armchair in one of the lounges supplanted by a seat in the open alcove at the beginning of the 'frail' corridor. Increasing immobility and the need for regular 'toileting' rapidly curtail their movement outside those areas of the home associated with illness and with death. It is in this way that care staff are able to create a somewhat precarious distance or spatial boundary between 'fit' and 'frail' residents.

The time and place of death itself nonetheless remains unpredictable, and at any moment this boundary can become particularly fragile. Within the confines of the institution, its random occurrence is always an implicit possibility. Throughout each night care staff check the breathing of all sleeping residents at hourly intervals. Taking day-time naps on her bed, a female resident whose breathing was very shallow shocked more than one care assistant by her resemblance to a corpse.

Should one of the 'fitter' residents show a sudden deterioration, care will be taken to move them downstairs to one of the sick bays. Failure to note the signs of imminent death can involve staff in the unorthodox removal of a corpse from upstairs 'living' accommodation in a wheelchair. The small lift is intended for the living only and cannot accommodate a stretcher-borne body. Nonetheless sudden deaths can and do occur among the category of 'fit' resident and staff express strong dislike of what they describe as the 'degrading' removal of a seated corpse, the improper fusion of the two categories of the living and the dead.

Though properly managed deaths take place in the sickbay, ambiguities are still encountered in that the corpse must then pass through the space of the living on its journey to the mortuary. An impromptu transformation of this space is effected through the deliberate closure of lounge and bedroom doors en route, and the strategic positioning of staff members between the 'frail' who doze in the open alcove and the passing corpse.

In the mortuary, at the periphery of the home, the distinction between the living and the dead remains at issue. The Deputy Matron, when asked if a recently deceased resident had been coffined, misheard the word 'coffined' and interpreted the question as:

'Has Mrs Atkinson been coughing ?'

Only later was she able to laugh about the horror which this mistake had aroused in her. Similarly, a member of the domestic staff suggested that a particular corpse was not in the mortuary when she cleaned it and jokes were made about the deceased popping out to the toilet. Night staff were horrified to discover the morgue doors flapping open in the wind at dawn one day. Mistakenly thinking a corpse was in the morgue at the time, they feared that both corpse and trolley had rolled out into the courtyard and away down the drive.

Thus the allocation or transformation of limited institutional space can be seen as a cultural strategy through which the conceptual categories of the wider society may be given expression. The dilemmas introduced by setting elderly individuals apart in the 'living'/'dying' space of the institution may in part be managed through physical manoeuvring of this kind.

Another important strategy in the creation of separations and distances is the use of linguistic transformations. Thus the manipulation of space is complemented by forms of verbal manoeuvring, or metaphoric strategies, through which the more intractable ambiguities of the system are distanced or transformed. For example, the search for a refined medical framing of the biological process of dying which pervades the wider society finds parallels in the institutional setting. Though a precise medical understanding of residents' physical condition is lacking, care staff nevertheless make implicit distinctions between the categories of 'fit' and 'frail' residents through a subtle and often humourous use of language. Two examples illustrate the process through which membership of one category or the other is imposed upon residents:

(1) Alice Dixon was made to come down from her upstairs bedroom for breakfast when she was feeling unwell. Her subsequent attack of faintness was viewed with angry scepticism by staff. They interpreted it as 'dramatic', an 'Oscar-winning performance', mimicking her 'ohhs' and 'ahhs' and the way she had clasped her hands over her heart. In words and in actions they metaphorically transformed Alice's physical distress into a theatrical performance, thereby refuting evidence of her possible transition to the category 'frail' resident and affirming her membership of the category 'fit' resident. The fragile, arbitrary nature of such a distinction was later affirmed when staff not only allowed Alice to return to bed but also requested Matron look in on her, saying,

'We don't want a dead body on our hands'

(2) Mabel Carstairs, a resident in her mid nineties, refused outright to come downstairs for breakfast one morning. Huddled deep beneath her bedclothes, she spoke bitterly to me of her sleepless night, her desire for death and her unmet need for sympathy and understanding from staff. Coming out of her room, I was asked by a care assistant:

'Oh, is she still playing the dying duck!'

As in the previous example, a resident's distress is interpreted by staff as play-acting and her status as a 'fit' resident is affirmed. In her choice of metaphor,'dying duck', the care assistant both reiterates the notion of a theatrical performance and also denigrates its quality. That Alice might aspire to death in the role of a 'dying swan' is both suggested and mocked in the choice of 'dying duck'.

Distinctions between an inability, as opposed to an unwillingness, on the part of the resident to 'keep going' are not easily made or maintained by care staff. Earlier examples showed that in a context such as the residential home a living horizontal body can be powerfully suggestive of a corpse. Doctors visiting sick residents often imply that one state can quickly lead to the next when they assert the medical dangers to the lungs of a horizontal position. For example, after a fall a resident was prescribed a week's bed rest by medical staff at the local hospital. Contrary advice from the resident's GP (that bedrest would endanger her lungs) lead to a compromise on the part of care staff. The resident was isolated in sick bay for a week – but propped up uncomfortably on pillows in a wheelchair.

The suggestive sight of a horizontal body is more than matched by the ominous presence and smell of a resident's urine and faeces. Asking for advice about the handling of 'accidents' when I began fieldwork, I was always told, 'You avoid them'. Incontinence must nonetheless be managed and staff deflect its threatening power by inverting the name of that which they are required to handle. By taking one of the more potent and offensive names by which faeces are known – 'shit' – and reversing the order of the letters to create the word 'tish', the full force of the event is both acknowledged and subverted. 'Tish' is used, either as a noun or a suitably regular verb, by the staff as a group and requires no ammendment when entered into the Report Book in the staff room. Official acknowledgement of its force is given in the form of an additional 30p pay for every day on which a staff member has handled it. In order to receive this money, staff are required to enter the letter 'F' for foul linen in the appropriate box on a time sheet. Within the home, staff's use of the word 'tish' represents both an acknowledgement and an inversion of the power of incontinence, a verbal form which corresponds appropriately to the physical act of first handling faeces in order then to remove them. Outside the home, the wage clerks receiving time sheets in County Hall are not required to confront the evidence of incontinence and, for their eyes, the prescribed euphemism 'foul linen', aptly makes reference only to that which can be measured in financial terms, the supply and laundering of linen.

If those who have what are referred to as 'accidents' do not display
signs which presage imminent death, staff are able to deflect the
impact of their occasional double incontinence by creating metaphoric shifts in the social status of incontinent people. By figuratively attributing a lazy disposition or a child-like status to the
residents, the literal implications of lost bowel control are veiled. For
example, when a care assistant discovered the draw sheet of one of
the fitter residents was badly streaked with the stain of faeces, she
turned it over rather than changing it. In doing so she said:

> 'If he can't be bothered to wipe his arse then he'll just have to
> put up with it. It's just laziness. It's not as if he's incontinent.'

To soften the harshness with which she had refuted the evidence of
deterioration she added:

> 'I get nasty after I've been on for eight days'

And indeed she had worked an eight hour shift on eight successive
days.

The interpretation of incontinence as a social misdemeanour,
rather than as an aspect of physical deterioration, allows those who
are required to confront it in order to remove it, to figuratively
diffuse the power of an act which signals an approaching death.
Another resident, Ethel Brandon, who had retained the ability to
walk, to converse and to feed herself, suffered from fairly regular
bouts of double incontinence. Being cleaned after an 'accident' she
was told by the care assistant concerned:

> 'You've dirtied your knickers, you naughty girl. You said you
> hadn't. You should get up in time. You must know when you
> want to go to the toilet. We all do.'

By interpreting Ethel's incontinence as a childish accident, care staff
are able to distance themselves from the disturbing literal evidence
of physical deterioration which they are required to handle. Whilst
the incontinence of young children may be frustrating, its implications are far less threatening than the incontinence of elderly people.
Like the verbal inversion and transformation of the potent 'shit' into
the essentially meaningless and amusing 'tish', old age incontinence
is reinterpreted as childish wilfulness.

Examples of field material drawn from among the residents of the
'frail' corridor show that in this contrasting location staff are ready to
affirm evidence of a deathly status. In opposition to the 'dying ducks'
up above, these residents are described as:

> 'just like a little corpse'
> 'just a little skeleton'

While staff interpret the waning mobility or incontinence of 'fitter' residents as playacting or childish wilfulness, they perceive aspects of the physical condition of the 'frail' as signs of imminent death. Two examples illustrate this:

(1) In March 1981 a 'frail' resident, Mrs Watson, was said to have had a 'collapse'. Lacking in medical knowledge, staff nonetheless made grim note of the 'signs' of imminent death, sunken eyes, rattling breath and a bluish tinge to her nose. Feeling her forehead they exchanged knowing looks, saying:

'Poor little soul. Two o'clock will test her'

In fact Mrs Watson remained wearily alive for another three months, despite staff's repeated assertions that she was:

'on her way out'

'likely to pop off soon'

(2) In February 1981 a care assistant announced that there was little hope for Molly West, a 'frail' resident who had spent several months in sick bay.

'Well its a blessing really. She's just a vegetable. Poor little soul'

Three weeks passed, the care assistant maintaining that 'it could be any time now'. In June 1981 Molly was reinstalled at her table by the dining-room service hatch. She lived on in the home for almost another two years.

These examples illustrate an implicit social process of categorisation through which distinctions are introduced within the slow and uneven deterioration of the members of an ambiguous social category. It is this complex, unpredictable process of decline which predominates within the home, among the 'fit' who ail and the 'frail' who linger. In asserting the liveliness of members of one category, and anticipating the demise of members of the other, staff maintain meanings and distinctions associated with the conceptual categories 'life' and 'death' which prevail within the wider society. One last example, a brief case study, shows how uneven the processes of physical deterioration can be among very elderly people. It describes staff's attempts to overcome some of the ambiguities raised in the case of one of the elderly women living in the home. Repeatedly they manoeuvred her back and forth between the two categories, 'fit' and 'frail' resident.

Alice Hepple, a small, thin and rather confused resident, was admitted to care when her dependency proved too overwhelming for her daughter to manage. Alice was nonetheless communicative, mobile and well able to feed and wash herself. Repeatedly staff led Alice into the lounges implicitly reserved for 'fit' residents. They offered her a walking frame rather than their supporting arms, saying:

'Go on Alice. Walk with the ladies !'

Alice, however, failed to take up a place among 'the ladies'. Conspicuous as she tottered aimlessly in the corridors, Alice rendered herself a highly ambiguous individual to the eyes of staff. Though she continued to walk, eat and speak, it was with increasing difficulty and reluctance. Always in the wrong place at the wrong time, Alice was confused and slow-moving. Staff's ineffectual attempts to impose membership of the category 'fit' resident were eventually abandoned and within six weeks of her admission staff led Alice to a seat in the 'frail' alcove and a new dining-place beside the service hatch. No longer urged by staff to conform to the behaviour required of 'the ladies', Alice was described at this point as looking 'just like a little corpse' when she slept. Like Mrs Watson and Molly West, Alice nonetheless failed to deteriorate or 'pop off' as anticipated. Living on for another four months, she regained speech, appetite and mobility, this time unaided. The former 'little corpse' was re-categorised a second time when staff described her as 'coming out of her shell'. Her re-entry into the category 'fit' resident was confirmed when a voluntary helper offered her a dance one afternoon.

Alice Hepple lived and died in Highfield House in the course of one six month period. Her gradual deterioration proceeded unevenly and was managed by staff through a series of physical and verbal manoeuvres which served implicitly to set Alice firmly to one side or another of a conceptual boundary between 'life' and 'death'.

In summary the position of staff can be seen as essentially paradoxical. As subordinates of the Matron and as members of a society in which death is distanced and disguised, they readily conform to the figurative transformation of the home's purpose which the Matron offers. Yet continuous exposure to the literal evidence of ageing and dying repeatedly subverts their attempts to adhere firmly to this cultural strategy. The following examples reveal the ambiguity of their perceptions:

> (1) Two care assistants, Maureen and Janet, were discussing a conversation between Monica and her husband, Billy, the previous night. In response to Billy's enquiry as to what kind of day she had had, Maureen told him:
>
> 'Hectic. Lifts off and on'
>
> Billy replied:
>
> 'By, what a good job you're doing. You must get a lot of satisfaction doing so much good for all those elderly people'
>
> 'He was being serious ?' Janet asked.

Maureen nodded and the two women exchanged small,silent smiles. The quietly humourous conspiracy of this wordless exchange reveals their awareness of the figurative nature of a representation of their job which Billy, naively, had interpreted in a literal sense. Nonetheless their awareness remained tacit. (2) The day after a resident, Charlie Lumsden, had died, another resident, Ethel Robson, asked a care assistant, Kathy, if there was a morgue in the home. Kathy replied:
'Yes there is. Its a sort of Chapel of Rest. Its very nice'
Turning away from Ethel, Kathy gave me the same conspiratorial look, saying nothing.

Just as Kathy transforms the bare room with its slab and small table bearing a cross, candles and flowers, into a Chapel of Rest, so staff, like the Matron, transform the bleak literal meaning of the home. Whilst their faces may betray an awareness of this deception, their perception of ageing/dying as a disordering and potentially uncontrollable process firmly inhibits any explicit acknowledgement of the literal meaning of their role within the home.

The material discussed in this chapter describes the care staffs' continuous involvement with ageing and dying. Their labour constitutes not only the physical management of dependency, but also its metaphoric ordering and distancing. In this way, their work underpins the Matron's promotion of a figurative reality within which 'life' and 'death' are preserved as rigidly opposed categories, and ageing itself is effectively submerged.

Chapter Six

One-way Journeys: Residents' Experience[1]

Care staff, as we have seen, are committed to defining and maintaining the two institutional categories of 'fit' and 'frail' residents in permanent opposition to one another. Residents, by contrast, are involved in somehow making a transition between these two categories, from the independent adulthood of the past, to death which lies ahead. Not only are residents seeking to manage their own bodily experience of ageing, but also the process of ageing as it is made orderly through the controlling care of the staff.

The confining of dying and death to certain spaces within the home is complemented by the confining of the idea and the expectation of death to those residents perceived by staff to be 'frail'. Yet in the following examples, 'fit' as well as 'frail' residents are making clear assertions that their death may be imminent:

'I'm old – I'm eighty seven'

'What can you expect ... I won't live much longer'

'You can be struck down in a moment'

'You can't turn the clock back'

This is in contrast to the staff's strategy of distancing such a possibility. Residents' oblique, sometimes humourous, statements therefore represent a powerful challenge, either to care staff themselves, or to the institution as a whole. They reveal residents' awareness that life within Highfield House is transitory, that the timeless, repetitive routine of institutional care imposed upon them can create only an illusory sense of permanence.

For example, when a care aid takes early morning tea to a resident, his arms are deliberately folded, corpse-fashion on his chest, and he grins at her.

Whilst a 'fit' resident, Nellie, was naked after her bath, she recounted to staff her dream in which she saw her body laid out in its coffin. In preparation she had already removed her wedding ring, not wishing it to fall into the hands of undertakers. Shocked, eyes-to-heaven glances were exchanged among staff. They were lost for words through which to deflect the residents's dangerous revelation of the incipient fate of her body.

Seeing staff empty rubbish into plastic bags or sweep remnants of food from the floor onto a shovel, residents joke, saying:

'You can put me in there too'

or

'Sweep me up too. You might as well'

Staff struggle weakly for another joke which can effectively counter, and diffuse the power of this embarrassing honesty. Indeed residents' use of rubbish as a metaphor for themselves, though made oblique through humour, nonetheless constitutes a succint and powerful statement about their marginalised social status, as well as their fragile physical state. Through the style and the timing of explicit statements about their own mortality these elderly people, like other marginal social categories or groups, are able to make powerful gestures by bringing to the surface that which is muted within the dominant group. Structurally weak they gain stature by reducing the figurative to the literal, thereby drawing attention to the one incontrovertibly human event which remains to them.

Thus while staff are made aware of the literal reality of ageing through repeated physical contact with the bodies of residents, the remarks of residents are additional, unequivocal and, as I have suggested, unanswerable reminders of the imminence of death within the home. Nonetheless institutional time or space is not made available for open discussion of the experiences of aging and dying. McDonald discovers this in this wider society:

> I ... feel shame in talking about my bodily discomfort, aware of the stigma 'old people are always complaining'. But the fact is we spend our lives conveying to others how we feel in our bodies ... suddenly in my sixties, when my body is doing all kinds of things, sending me all kinds of messages, I am not supposed to talk about it. (1984:109)

So too, in Highfield House, residents are discouraged in their attempts to open discussion or make enquires. Two examples illustrate this point:

(1) When former cancer sufferer, Maggie Carstairs, was ill in bed, her arm swollen and mottled with red patches, she was visited first by the Matron and then by a care assistant. The Matron set the tone with forceful, joking sympathy:

'What are we going to do with you Maggie!'

'Throw me in the river !' replied Maggie, laughing.

A care assistant came in soon after, she more subdued and

down-to-earth in her manner.

'Do you think this is the end ?' asked Maggie, not laughing this time. Again denials and jokes were offered by the care assistant in reply – she hoped there would be a really good funeral tea – Albert, Maggie's husband, also a resident, would have to see to it all. She wanted lots of squashy cream cakes.

(2) Ninety-seven year old Hannah Cartwright was one of a small group of elderly people who were transferred precipitately to Highfield House when wiring in another residential home was found to be dangerous. These people were given black plastic bags for their belongings the night before moving and were told of their various destinations only as they were bundled into cars. In Highfield House Hannah ailed and, after a painful, sleepless night, she asked a care assistant:

'Haven't you got something for me ?'

'Why no Nellie. We wouldn't do that. We wouldn't do that!' came the firm and conclusive reply. After her sudden admission to Highfield House Hannah had been moved from one room to another.

'You've moved again Nellie!' was the remark of many staff that morning.

'I think this will be the last time' was Hannah's reply to each one. It drew no further comment.

In these descriptions of two brief interactions between residents and staff, four separate and very direct references were made by a resident to their own death:

'Throw me in the river!'

'Do you think this is the end ?'

'Haven't you got something for me'

'I think this will be the last time'

Not one of these attempts brought forth any honest or extended discussion of the literal reality which was being being referred to.

In such a setting token remarks and gestures of an aggressive or joking kind seem to represent the only viable means remaining to residents of raising this most personal and significant issue. Hence the examples of barbed humour quoted.

The assertion of the imminence of their own death is one, particularly salient example of the impromptu strategies through which residents seek to negotiate their passage through Highfield House. It provides a starting point for looking more broadly at the question of how residents seek to maintain a viable sense of personal and social identity, one which can encompass both the losses sustained at admission to care, and the future prospect of the loss of their own life.

Insights into this question can be gained by exploring the meaning and the role of the memories, possessions and personal style remaining to residents. The record of their past lives is, in most cases, available only in their own verbal accounts, but it is also embodied, implicitly, in their possessions and their gestures. Personal identities, therefore, consist in the selective oral accounts of what has gone before; in those remaining personal belongings through which memories are evoked; in the scars or bodily weaknesses which mark some of a lifetime's formative incidents; and in the gestures and speech patterns through which the institutional present is negotiated. Assigning meaning to these materials requires an awareness of the part they play within a death-imbued context.

Those individuals who take on membership of the institutional category, 'resident', become one of a far from homogenous population. Whilst sharing membership of an age-based social category, 'the elderly', residents differ in age across the thirty or more years from the early sixties to the late nineties. Some residents first met seventy years previously on the long benches of a local village school. Some recognise one another from their former, prominent professional positions within local small town society. For some, Highfield House is the last in a long series of institutions which have accommodated them throughout their lives. And, as already described, the range of dependencies to be found among residents is large.

Thus, in terms of age, former place of residence, social class, and degree of dependency, those individuals who find themselves encompassed within the monolithic institutional category, 'resident', bring with them a disparate range of past lives. What they all have in common, however, is the experience of living in the same institutional space, and of having no additional domestic context of their own. Similarly the requirement that all but the bedbound should eat together in the dining room brings constant exposure to deteriorating strangers and therefore a reminder of the imminence of their own deaths. As a result each resident's sense of personal identity is under threat. They share a severed connection with their past, a present life among individuals whose age, degree of dependency and social class varies enormously, and an exposure to the idea of death and the process of dying.

To find out how residents manage this threatening set of circumstances three questions can be posed. First, what is the significance for residents of their former way of life ? Second, how do they make

sense of the transition to institutional life ? And third, through what
strategies do they maintain their social identity within the home ?

TWO LIVES

Material drawn from two tape recorded life-histories, one of an
eighty-four year old former 'shopgirl', Ethel Carr, one of an eighty-
two year old former schoolmaster, Arthur Grant, gives an initial
insight into residents' perceptions of a former self and its subsequent
transitions.

Ethel Carr had been born in the local town in 1896. Having
served an apprenticeship in the confectionery trade, she was set up
by her mother in a small business near the town centre. Like about
a quarter of the female residents, Ethel had no children and,
unmarried, she worked on in her shop for more than forty years,
supporting her parents in their old age. Ethel and I had lived a few
streets from one another, albeit not simultaneously, and her recorded life-history took off from points of shared knowledge – local
people, shops, doctors' surgeries – into an assemblage of snapshot
incidents spanning the previous sixty years.

The following extract from the record exemplifies the mix of broad
appraisal and highly specific incident which characterised the form of
Ethel's reminiscence. It sheds light on the first question, concerning
residents' perceptions of a former way of life. She told me:

> 'Ah, but you know, people were different in them days to what
> they are now. It was true friendship and true neighbourhood,
> you know. They were very friendly, helped a lot. Oh, I never
> need want a thing. I just need ask, you know. Used to open the
> shop door and shout. One woman said to me, 'Do you want
> anything down the street ?' I says, 'Well, bring me two kippers'.
> I like kippers for me tea. They used to be very cheap in them
> days. Anytime she passed, doesn't matter if the shop was full,
> she used to shout, 'Do you want any kippers, Miss Carr ?' I
> used to say, 'Do you think I live on kippers !' By, its a different
> life now, isn't it, not the same. Because I was young then, you
> know, and energetic. See, the College boys all used to come.
> They couldn't get anything at College in them days. And they
> used to come 'bout ten o'clock and I used to make little buns
> and fill them with cream, and sell them for a penny. And I used
> to make, perhaps, four, you know, trays of those. They called
> my shop 'the Bun Shop' at the College. Its mixed now, isn't it,
> girls and boys. Eh, yes'.

Ethel's clear sense of herself within the context of 'them days' can be set alongside the powerfully recalled account which Arthur Grant, former schoolmaster, gives of himself during adolescence. Born in 1898, one of the five children of a mining family in a local village, Arthur grew up within the rigid framework of the United Methodist Chapel. 'That was our life – chapel', he told me,

> 'But at weekends, Saturdays, we were real toffs – when we grew up to about sixteen, seventeen. Real toffs. If you weren't playing football for the football team, get our best suit, walking cane, walking stick, white gloves and kid gloves. Posh. Down to town. Marketplace. Spend all afternoon and part of the night there. 'Course the marketplace was full then, of stalls, you know. Big band show, like. Randolph Williams' big organ used to take up the whole part of the place and play marches. There were quack doctors there and all sorts of things, pulling teeth out and selling patent medicines and all sorts of things. The place was packed besides the closed-in market where you could go at any time. The whole square was filled up. So we had to go down there every Saturday, or down onto the racecourse for a cricket match or something like that. We were always poshed up. All went together. Real lads. Cane, straw benchers. One and sixpence for a straw hat with a green band on, two and sixpence for a bigger one, very hard, a cord round the back to fasten onto your lapel here with a button so the wind wouldn't blow it away. We thought we were the bees' knees then. Striding away down to town there, walking of course. Walking sticks, some had chamois gloves, you know, some patent leather ones. All had walking sticks. One or two had spats. We thought we were something.'

In the case of both Ethel and Arthur, a former self survives in vivid snapshots of energy, youth and self-importance – 'real toffs', 'young then, you know, and energetic', 'the bees' knees'.

With regard to the second question, concerning the transition to institutional life, both these residents had found it to be a period of demanding change and loss. How they each understood and made sense of their losses was, however, rather different. In both cases, critical events which had taken place in late adolescence, in the years around 1915, were seen to be influential with respect to their circumstances in 1981. References to these events were offered readily. Rather than the outcome of any prompting on my part, speculation and appraisal were some of Ethel and Arthur's primary pre-occupations, as well as those of many other residents.

Ethel Carr identified a personal relationship, with her mother, as crucial to the lifecourse she was to follow. 'Mothers shape their daughters' destinies', she said, going on to describe her mother's 'narrowness', her refusal to admit potential marriage partners, friends even, to the family home. After a harsh apprenticeship in a town some twenty miles away – where she was woken with a thrown apple at five a.m. and worked until breakfast at eight a.m. – Ethel began business life at the age of twenty.

'Oh, I was too young. My mother put me in and I had to bake and manage all the business. I had no youth, I had no youth. Because, I mean, I had to work practically night and day.'
Ethel said:
'It's hard, a life on your own. You take a lot of knocks. People think there's a lot of things you don't know about, not having been married'.

It was during this same period that Arthur Grant finished his very successful education at a prestigious local school. Rather than a personal relationship, it was a world event, the Great War, which Arthur saw as crucial to all that followed. He told me:

'I was called up straight away. After that – fini. No more fiddling (violin playing). Two and a half years in Italy. Made a wreck of me. Came back with nothing, not a halfpenny, no money. I applied for college of course and credentials were alright. I managed to get in, on the understanding that I passed the doctor, coming straight from the war. If he had failed me I don't know what I would have done. So I persuaded him to let me, I pleaded with him. I'd been wounded slightly, but it was malaria and poison gas. I knew what was wrong. I said, 'Give me a chance, man'. I said, 'I can last two years of this, after two and a half years of that'. He says, 'Alright, Mr Grant. Ten and six, please.'

Of his present health and circumstances, Arthur said:

'I'm getting weaker every day. I mean, this gas comes back every now and again and malaria – warm days – hits me now and again. So I just come in here (his bed-sitting room), and wait 'til it oozes out. Say nothing. I don't even bother telling the Matron. I get through. I know what to do. You know yourself. You know what to do. But its very noticeable now that the three of us in here that were in the First War – there's George, big Jimmy and meself – all our legs, they're going. Sometimes we can't walk. They're afflicted in the same way.'

'Nobody would believe it, nobody would believe it. We're suffering for it now, but there we are. It comes back now and again. I don't wake up screaming or anything like that, you know, it doesn't affect me in that way at all. But I know when the malaria comes back and I know when the gas comes back. Feel rotten. Just have to square up to it, that's all. Frostbite. All for sixpence a day.'

In Ethel's case, admission to residential care came after a period of thirteen years spent living in local sheltered accommodation for elderly people. She understood her admission to be on account of 'bad arthritis' in her hands which, temporarily, left her unable to lift a cup. Of the transition to institutional care, she said:

'Dr Unstone put me in here. I rue the day I came in here.'
She told me that she'd only intended to stay in the home for one month and had cried for a week when she first arrived. Time had dragged on and on and now she was resigned:

'I won't live much longer. I'm eighty-four. All my friends are dead.'

– but resistant:

'You lose your independence when you come to these places. I've never had a mistress, you see, I've never had a boss. I'll never be happy here, but I'll have to stick it, 'cos I won't live that long, much longer.'

'And the money they take off you – hundreds of pounds just for a few weeks. Of course they'll bury me and everything. I'm all on my own, so I have no worries on that score. You never think about old age, do you, you never think. You ought to prepare for it.'

In common with a number of other residents, Arthur had been admitted to care after a major operation which, it was decided, left him unfit to continue living alone. Widowed for forty years, he'd been living with a brother, the two of them looked after by a housekeeper. He said:

'Oh yes, we had a real good time. Then of course, both of us having the operations and his mind went. That was it. He died nearly two years ago. Couldn't carry on meself, not in the house by meself. Housekeeper was a bit older than we were and she retired. There was just the pair of us left, except for me little sister. I did all the housework, painting, decorating, all the lot. Too much. However, I'm not grumbling.'

'So me son brought me to live with him. 'Course being daft, I had to take ill as well. I had an operation meself and they had me into here. Stirred me up a little bit, she (the Matron) did, she cured me. That's the way it goes. I'm not grumbling.'

Arthur's repeated verbal commitment to 'not grumbling' reveals a more resigned stoicism than is evident in Ethel's account. Though hindsight had lead Arthur to the opinion that his chapel upbringing had been 'strict, very strict, too strict', he retained faith in the value of discipline in schools, 'the kids thrived on it'. Acceptance and stoicism were evident when he offered the view that:

> 'You never know how things change in the world. Where you get to. How things link up, or break up. That's life, you take it as it comes. Sometimes its good, sometimes bad.'

Material from Ethel and Arthur's life-histories spotlights some shared aspects of the lives of many residents – for example, the transformative role of the First World War for male residents; women's unquestioning commitment to caring for elderly parents; the management of hardship through both stoicism and determined independence; pride in former roles and statuses; bitterness over losses by now forever irredeemable.

These two life-histories also indicate that, depending on gender, residents perceive and experience the past, and its relationship to the present, somewhat differently, and this is confirmed by information from other residents of Highfield House. Gender is also of significance in issues raised by the third question, concerning strategies through which social identity is maintained or negotiated within the residential home.

GENDER AND THE EXPERIENCE OF ADMISSION TO RESIDENTIAL CARE

While the home accommodates forty-six residents, almost three quarters of them were women. Of the twelve men living in Highfield House during my stay, three allowed me to tape their conversation with me. While many of the women spoke freely about their past lives, only two, when asked, were willing to speak in what they saw as the formal setting of a taped conversation. The discrepancy between women's and men's willingness to give a single, extensive account of their past life is echoed in the style and content of what was said – both on tapes and in more informal conversation. In particular, men's chronologically ordered accounts of former roles and the positions they held contrasts with women's vivid and more fragmented asides which describe dramatic events from the past or humourous personal interchanges. Humm (1987) discovers a corresponding contrast in written autobiographies submitted by young women and men seeking admission to North East London Polytechnic. She describes how 'Women students created an "episodic" memory of affective words triggering physical or emotional moments'(1987:20).

.It is revealing to look, briefly, at all twelve of the home's male residents. Two of them had spent long periods in institutional care of some kind and remained very much on the fringes of life in Highfield House. Three were frail and/or confused, speaking very rarely and with little coherence. One shared a double bed-sitting room in the home with his more outgoing wife, and spoke only rarely himself. Of the other six, five were prominent within the home, among them the three willing for their life-histories to be taped. Together, that minority of five male residents who were free from extensive handicap or disability represented a strong, articulate presence within the home.

Arthur Grant offered his life-history in a lucid, linear form which began by tracing the passage from schooldays shared with three of the home's other residents; included reference to the predominance of chapel and music practice in his early life; and went on to his wartime experience, his teaching career, his retirement, and his children and grandchildren's careers – 'They're all B.A.s except me. All comfortably well off there, now. No worries. And that's the story'. Details of Arthur's social life, his courting days and his marriage were given only in response to my further questioning.

Like Arthur Grant, George Smith too had been born in 1898, into a large mining family in a local village. As in Arthur's case, Methodism had provided the framework for George's early life, one within which he had remained throughout his life.

> 'During the whole of my married life I was in the Methodist Church. Now everything that took place, I was always active in it. Nearly every event or position, I was in it.'

This sentence, 'every position I was in it', provided the starting point for the whole of George's life history as he chose to present it – a detailed list of a lifetime's significant roles and achievements. George's oral record is complemented by three Local History books he has written, and an album of his certificates and photos made by a nephew. In his 'secret drawer' (a locked drawer built into every residents' wardrobe), George kept a little cardboard box containing a British Legion medal and a Christian Endeavour badge. They were to be passed down to his nephew when he died.

Albert Lyons was another of the five prominent male residents, older than George and Arthur, approaching his ninetieth birthday. He entered Highfield House with his wife, living on there alone after her death. Albert Lyons spoke freely at all times, his conversation consisting almost entirely of the stories which go to make up his life-history. Like George, Albert complemented his tales with scrap-books of photos and press clippings. On tape, it was his career as plumber, joiner and concert party entertainer; his father's career at the colliery; and his grandfather's career as agricultural engineer and night-watchman, which provided a framework for the story. In addition to scrapbooks, still noticeable consequences of industrial injuries to Albert's eyes and feet provided prompts for the re-telling of dramatic incidents from his working life. He also used my tape-recorder to re-create his former role as concert party entertainer, painstakingly retrieving half-forgotten monologues and music hall songs.

The ease with which men offered accounts of public roles and positions as life-history contrasted with the richness and diversity of women's references to the past. Evers (1981:108-130) discussion of the different meanings of institutional care for women and men sheds light on this contrast. She argues that while the identity of retired men rests on the honourable performance of their past employment, women's identity continues throughout life to arise out of the quality of care which they provide within the home – 'a woman's work is never done'.

The shift into institutional care therefore had different implica-tions depending on the resident's gender. Most of the women found themselves bereft of their identity as domestic carer. The men not only experienced continuity in receiving care from women; they also discovered new scope for public 'role-playing' once they moved out of a more private form of domestic life. Thus for Arthur Grant, George Smith, Jack McIntyre, and Albert Lyons, the public sphere of a residential 'home' represented a context where an acceptable male dependence on female care could quite appropriately go hand in hand with public reference to, and re-creation of, their former professional, or quasi-professional roles. Jack McIntyre, prominent as the residents' male representative on the Friends of Highfield House committee, was aware of the fusion of domestic and public worlds within the home. 'In your own home', he told me, 'you arrange your social life outside, but here you do it all in the same place, on the job'.

What then were the important reference points for these elderly men engaged in managing the transition to residential care ? Albert Lyons' wife had died after they both had moved into the home. He often told told me how she'd been taken away from Highfield House for hospital treatment, how he'd seen her funeral cortege pass by the home, but was too unwell to attend. In referring frequently to his bereavement Albert was an exception, in that the other men had been admitted after a long period of widowerhood. For them, dependence on female carers, unrelated to them, was acceptable, while the loss of an active role within the outside world was still felt. Within the home, it was therefore through reference to, and re-creation of, the public roles of that outside world that they sought to maintain their social identity.

How did the implications of admission to care and the way in which they responded to it differ for women ? Like Arthur Grant, Ethel Carr's personal history is an account of a working life outside the home. However, as in the extract presented earlier, it was told through a mosaic of interchanges with neighbours, shopgirls, customers and family – and not as a linear progression from schooldays through to retirement. On admission to residential care, Ethel had burnt most of her photos taken in and around the shop. Prominent among the remaining few was one which marked a lost personal relationship. Kept on her bedside locker, the photo showed one of her sisters, a former hospital matron. Ethel told me:

'She was at Edinburgh Royal. She went when she was eighteen and she died at sixty-two, and she was at that Edinburgh Royal all those years. She was a real sport, she was short and very fat. I think an awful lot of her. I don't think so much of the other one. But I was upset when she died. She died at sixty-two, and she'd been in hospital life all that time. And when she died they found her dead in bed. She had heart, well she was so fat, you know, little and fat, and liked her food – big, fat rosy face, you know, jolly. They found her dead in bed, in the hospital. And the secretary wrote and said that she had spent her life looking after other people but at the last she needed no-one. Wasn't it lovely put ? She died suddenly. Yes, I was sorry about her. I often think about her, poor girl.'

Small personal possessions, photos, table napkins, jewellery, were the prompts which repeatedly brought such memories to the surface of the women's minds. By contrast, the men's rooms were often strikingly bare, containing little from which details of their tenant's identity might be detected. While men were willing, at a single sitting, to offer a lengthy account of themselves, women, involved in the continuous handling and re-arranging of remnants of a lost domestic context, gave evidence of their pasts in vivid, fleeting asides, which were repeated on many occasions.

For example, one of the institution's daily routines evoked a

highly specific personal memory for ninety-two year old Grace
Heslop. Highfield House took responsibility for all residents' personal washing, and staff frequently returned small piles of ironed
laundry to their rooms. When I handed Grace her clean napkin and
handkerchief she was prompted to give me an account of her early
married life. The damask napkin, labelled with the former couple's
initials, was a remnant of the table linen she received at her wedding
in 1916. She had been engaged for only a month in 1914 when her
fiance, later husband, left to fight in France. He survived World War
One, only to be killed in World War Two, leaving her with a teenage
daughter and a seven year old son. Two figures which were repeated
often, and usually together, by Grace were her age, ninety-two years,
and the length of her widowhood, forty-four years. Her account of
an incident in her long distant married life was prompted by an
emotive co-incidence of the time of year and the handling of the
napkin. November 9th, the previous Sunday, had been Armistice
Day. 'You get over it', she said, 'its just these times that bring it
back'. For Arthur Grant, war had meant a threat to his career and,
now, a physical vulnerability. For Grace Heslop, war meant a lost
relationship, one which otherwise might have sustained her
throughout old age.

Whichever article of personal memorabilia evoked emotion and
reminiscence, for women it was often a bereavement or an illness
which came readily to mind. Very often these experiences bore a
particular relevance to the institutional present and to the quality of
the resident's old age. Recurrent themes were the deaths of their
elderly, sixty or seventy year old children; the loss of younger
children who might otherwise have cared for a resident in old age; or,
very commonly, the death of a male partner who had provided a
lifetime's social, emotional and financial support. Now, as a resident's body became demandingly weaker, that source of comfort
was no longer available to them.

For example, Mabel Carey's mention of her husband's recent
death, precipitated by my comment on her snake ring (worn by him
through two world wars) was rapidly followed by a description of her
son's much earlier but most horrific death by drowning in a cess pit
in India.

Mabel's friend, Hannah Archer, also a resident, had had eight
children by her now dead husband. Her story of a lively family life
led her back repeatedly to Vera, her quiet and clinging daughter who
had died in her forties from heart trouble. Hannah had overridden
Vera's pleas not to be admitted to hospital, and it was there that she

died within a few hours.

In these examples it is the dead rather than the surviving child or sibling who absorbs the attention, or whose photo is framed on the locker. In the opening remarks they made to me, the women often referred to an earlier bereavement of this kind. Framed within a present of accumulating losses, these deaths were sources of emotional pain which lay very close to the surface.

The changed significance of earlier bereavements was made explicit by a resident, Annie Crosby. She told me:

> 'I had a stillborn boy, you see, and I had a terrible do … a complete hysterectomy. And of course when I was younger I didn't feel it so much but now I've no-one to care for me'.

Similarly, a reference to the death of a male partner was often the starting point for an appraisal of the circumstances which led to a female residents' admission. For example, when I went into ninety-one year old Mrs Porter's room, she showed me her husband's photo on the dressing table and said, 'he was the best husband in the world'. She began to cry and told me there had been an accident four years previously; he had been sent to a nearby hospital and she had come to Highfield House. He had died in hospital and she had stayed on in the home 'to sort myself out', 'get myself pulled together'. At admission, she had 'vowed' she wouldn't stay long but, finding everyone so kind that she remained, to see how things went. She knew her house in the centre of town was too big for her. Having decided to stay, she said it was important to accept the rules and regulations of the home. There had to be someone at the top and what they said had to go. She had been in charge of a local sweet factory and knew that this was how it had to be. She said a lot of residents grumbled and complained when they had no cause to. She talked a little about the local town, what a close-knit, friendly town it was. She said she had never been back since her admission four years previously – she was 'too much of a coward'.

Many other female residents echoed Mrs Porter's slow acceptance of the inevitability of residential care and, like her, attempted to make the best of it. After Alice Johnson's husband had died she had little alternative but to accept admission to the home, since her daughter was already pre-occupied with care of Alice's son-in-law who had suffered a heart attack. She had 'broken her heart' coming into the home, but had got used to it and settled down. She had been there for two years. Most of her family lived just around the corner in the local village.

Janey Firth had had two strokes and eventually became bed-

ridden at one of her daughters' homes. The GP had tried repeatedly
to persuade her to go into a home. She had refused, but after the
second stroke she 'studied and studied' and decided she would be
better off in a home. She was totally dependent on her daughter and
would never get back to her own place. She said:

> 'You're well fed here, very comfortable. But its not like your
> own home'.

Childlessness, the death of children and the death of a partner
were not the only recurrent themes voiced by the home's elderly
women as explanations for their present situation. Breakdown in
health was another. Janey's perception of her second stroke as
having a determining role in her subsequent admission to care was
echoed by other women who identified one specific breakdown of
health as crucial to the move into care.

For example, Lily Armstrong seldom allowed a day to pass
without mention of the doctor who 'tried out' a powerful drug on
her, causing a black-out in the street. At ninety-two, Lily had lived
alone and, though she continued to play bowls for her city up to this
point, the injuries resulting from her collapse led rapidly to her
permanent admission to Highfield House.

Similarly Nellie Baldwin told me:

> 'I fell off a bus was the thing – I never claimed for it. It was a
> foggy day, foggy night, on the bus – somebody got off and I
> started to follow them ... I could have complained because the
> conductor wasn't on the lower deck. A fall brings anything on.'

SELF-SUSTAINING STRATEGIES

The material presented thus far indicates those areas of past life to
which the residents refer most frequently and most readily. Much of
it was offered in fleeting conversations as I cleaned residents' sinks,
returned their clean laundry or helped them into the bath. It was not
the outcome of structured interviewing, but of a spontaneity which
suggests that it reflects issues which constitute a private undercurrent to residents' daily lives.

An institutional present can thus be conceptualised as a framework or grid through which the past is viewed, some of its aspects
taking on new, pressing meanings, others fading into insignificance.
On the evidence, men's former careers or positions assumed a new
significance for them in the diminished 'public' space of Highfield
House. For women, specific illnesses and the loss of significant supportive relationships provided a way of making sense of their transition from care-giving to dependence on the care of other women.

These points can be explored more fully by examining the details of daily interactions between residents within the home. Social identity was not only achieved and maintained by re-creation from salient fragments of the past; it was also tested out and if necessary modified continuously in day-to-day experience.

The context for the continuous endeavour was, as noted, the confined space of the home, shared with a far from homogenous population, where living and dying went on at close quarters. The assertion of personal identity and the creation of space between the self and undesirable others were implicit, interrelated objectives which underpinned much that took place. Framed in a fairly imme-diate sense by the frequent occurence of death, these objectives reflected not just a sustained commitment to the past, but also an urgent shielding of the self from the prospect of deterioration of which the presence of other, 'frailer' residents constituted a constant reminder.

Sissy Crowther, a childless widow, in her eighties, had come to Highfield House after an unsuccessful attempt to live with a nephew and his wife. She referred to her admission as a personal decision to try to be 'independent' and 'make my home' in the institution. Eight months later she found herself both physically and socially very vulnerable. She shared her bed-sitting room with Ada Brown, a sixty-two year old mentally handicapped woman. Things went badly between them. Sissy told me:

'Do you know I pay £86 per week to stay here. And I have to share a room with her !'

She found Ada a great nuisance, as the latter would come in during the afternoon, when she was asleep on the bed, and put her radio on loudly. She also put it on loudly at 6.30a.m.. Staff told her off but Ada insisted she had the Matron's permission. Mrs Crowther went on to say that Ada had once walked into the room saying:

'Have you got that bloody heater on again !'

Mrs Crowther said:

'Well, I'm not used to that sort of thing. Language like that. I don't know what my nephews and nieces would say if they knew. Well, I wouldn't tell them. Of course I tend to give in to her which doesn't help. She is a bit simple, you know.'

In the dining-room, residents were given, and retained, the same seat for every meal. Sissy Crowther asked to be moved into an alcove seat at the far end of the room. She said she preferred it. 'I can be away from ... people, here'. She felt she had come into the home too soon. She should have waited another two years. It was not only the social class, but also the bodily implications of contact with other residents which Sissy began to find oppressive.

As I re-arranged the blanket box and commode she had brought into Highfield House from her home, Sissy told me how helpless she felt. Every day it got worse. She had been in the home for eight months and she felt she had deteriorated enormously in that time. Although she knew she was old, she had never expected this kind of deterioration. Some people had been in seven, eight or even eleven years, she said, and it did not give her much to look forward to. She was not happy there, she would just have to make herself happy.

Sissy managed the oppressiveness of her environment by withdrawing into the dining-room alcove and by refusing to speak to her room-mate, Ada. She also drew on her former identity, as a middle class voluntary worker, decorated for organising canteen services during the last war. Despite increasing mobility problems, she took on the role of visitor to the more genteel, but sick residents, with whom she shared a similar class background. After asserting that she would make herself happy, she appeared minutes later in the bed-sitting room of another resident, former opera singer, Elsie Hall, where I was cleaning the sink. In fieldnotes I made the following observation:

> Elsie was in bed, curtains drawn, looking and feeling very unwell. Sissy came in to 'visit' and played the sensitive, caring, middle-class sick visitor to perfection. It was an impressive effort on Sissy's part. Elsie Hall was very pleased to be visited and rose to the occasion with a great show of emotion and pained feebleness.

My initial sense that Sissy's visit to Elsie was far from a casual 'dropping-in' was borne out in the frequency with which other female residents took opportunities to move into a caring role. Bereft of most domestic tasks, they were nonetheless surrounded by 'frail' residents who provided scope for expressing the identity of informal carer. So great was the choice of potential recipients that telling discriminations were often made.

Ethel Carr told me that a very confused resident, Alice Hepple, had begun to call for her all the time. Drawing on the metaphor of parental obligation, Ethel avoided the commitment, saying:

> 'Alice's not one of mine ! Gran Robson is a different case. I could adopt her. She's such a character.'

And indeed Gran Robson was strong-minded and alert, if a little unsteady on her feet. In discriminating between the two, Ethel knowingly withdrew from contact with the very confused resident.

She was aware that she would not only have little success as her carer, but in failing would risk acquiring a similarly undesirable identity. Hence the double meaning of 'Alice's not one of mine'. Ethel disclaimed not only responsibility but also the possible imputation of some shared origin. By contrast, through leading Gran Robson from lounge to dining-room, or on walks in the grounds, Ethel was able to identify herself publicly as an able, kindly carer.

Her visibility in this informal role can be set alongside the public positions which male residents took up within the home. Rather than the outcome of personal negotiation, Arthur Grant, Jack McIntyre, Albert Lyons, and George Smith all accepted roles prescribed by the institution itself. For example, Arthur sold newspapers in the dining-room each morning, and directed the residents' rehearsal of a song he had set to music. George Smith propagated cuttings from his plants and sold them to raise funds for the home at Open Days. Though this project had been shared with a female resident, Grace Heslop, she told me that her contribution had not been acknowledged when the final sum was publicly announced. Albert Lyons kept a pile of cards and a list of all residents' birthdays in his room. Dutifully he sent them out on behalf of the other residents, a formal rather than a personal gesture. His choice of card was often inappropriate as he now had difficulty linking names and faces. When an elderly person died in the home, Jack McIntyre would attend their funeral as the residents' official representative. He also made the public announcements in the dining-room whenever a rehearsal of Arthur's song was due to take place.

In summary, those aspects of their past and present lives which elderly people choose to talk about in the context of the home provides an important starting point in understanding how they experience the transition to care. Life histories show positive images of a former self being vividly recalled as lively reference points within a less glowing present. It is also evident that the question of how such a present had occurred is pressing. Residents trace links between the events of a long distant past, more recent bereavements and breakdowns in health, and their current life in residential care. Personal qualities, such as stoicism or determined independence, developed throughout a long lifetime, are invoked as still dependable strategies for survival.

Though women and men enter the same institutional context, its implications differ, depending on gender. For women, their lifelong commitment to providing domestic care and emotional support within key personal relationships is robbed of a focus. Memory draws them back to those individuals who have once been the recipients of their care; fellow residents are perceived as a possible source of substitutes whose presence might provide a way of re-creating an earlier role. By contrast the men, who made up just one quarter of the home's population, draw on an identity arising out of their public working life. This is apparent in their recorded life histories, and exemplified in their willingness to take on public roles within the home.

This chapter concludes with a discussion of one event which took place within the home, the creation and rehearsal of a song by the residents. It represents one of the public acts initiated by two of the most prominent men living in Highfield House.

JUST A SONG AT TWILIGHT

In the spring, prior to my period of fieldwork, an Easter card bearing 'inspirational' verses had been sent to Jack McIntyre, one of the group of men whose friendship stemmed from shared childhood residence in the local village.

> 'We liked the words so much', Henry told me 'that we asked Arthur to set them to music'.

Using the verses, Jack and Arthur Grant intended to prepare a song for performance at the Christmas concert held every year in the home. Previous concerts had attracted the attention of local television, thereby making it very much a public performance.

The verses can be seen as a fragment selected by a particular group of residents from their external environment and appropriated for a specific purpose within the home. They are meaningful to the extent that they can absorb and embrace that which is critical within the bounded social context of their peformance. Indeed they become filled with meaning through their deliberate adoption into the lives of those who sang them.

Thus the creation and preparation of the song for performance within a public setting represents a series of conscious, independent choices and decisions on the part of certain of the fitter residents, men and one or two of the two women. As representatives of a common memory of significant events, experiences, roles and status within the former village and the city of which it is now a suburb, Jack, Arthur and others of this group offer a reference point of some kind to those residents whose present withdrawal into deterioration belies their former awareness and involvement with the affairs of the locality.

Staff too are not unfamiliar with the biographies of those associated with this group. Their relationship with these individuals arises less from the close physical contact used in care of very dependent residents, and more from the complex verbal interaction needed to ensure co-operation from those more accustomed to independence and respect. In her discussion of the relative ease with which male geriatric patients could accept the care of female nurses, Evers also notes that it is only upper class women who learn to find it appropriate to receive domestic care from other women (1981:110). Interestingly, either an independent role in business, or a sheltered world of wealth and high status, characterises several of the female members of the social group associated with the creation of the song.

Having identified the source of the song and discussed the common attributes of those who constitute its source, it remains to explore the social and cultural meaning of the statement which it represents. It is a statement which serves both to articulate, and to reinforce the more disparate attempts made by the socially isolated to interpret their relationship to their present situation.

During the late autumn of 1980, many of the residents of the home met together in the dining-room once or twice a week to rehearse the singing of the verses, 'Hope', now set to music composed by Arthur Grant.

HOPE

1 There's always a <u>hope</u> – though it may be quite small
2 There's always a <u>star</u> – tho' the darkness may fall
3 There's always a <u>gleaming of gold</u> in the grey,
4 There's always a <u>flower</u> growing wild by the way.
5 There's always a <u>song</u> floating out on the air,
6 There's always a <u>dawn</u> to the night of despair –
7 There's always a <u>path</u> for the faithful to tread,
8 There's always a <u>bend</u> in the <u>roadway ahead.</u>
9 There's <u>always</u> a <u>hope</u> – but we've got to <u>believe,</u>
10 We've got to be ready to <u>see</u> and <u>receive</u>
11 The hints and the signs
12 Although faint they appear
13 To <u>wait</u> and to <u>trust</u> till the meaning grows clear.
14 And when through the murk of the shadows we grope
15 <u>We've got to remember</u>
16 <u>We've got to remember</u>
17 <u>There's always a hope</u> !

(Arthur Grant's underlining)

From their imprecise, inspirational sentiments the verses are readily identifiable as an example a particular genre of quasi-religious texts and poems, often to be found on calendars and greetings cards, and perhaps best exemplified in the work of 'Patience Strong'. Like magazine horoscopes, it is the vagueness of this form of writing which is particularly important in that it allows the reader to impute their own specific meaning to its imagery.

The verses were originally printed on an Easter card. Their theme is 'Hope', that which was given to the world through the resurrection of Jesus Christ, and is central to the Christian concept of Easter. Written in the characteristically imprecise style of their genre, the verses were found to be appropriate to a quite different point in the Christian calendar when detached from an original context of chicks, rabbits and budding flowers. Sung by very elderly people in the dark November afternoons leading up to Christmas, the words which had previously lent vague Christian undertones to Easter's association with spring, fine weather and fresh hopes now took on a more profound and urgent 'religious' reference.

It is that more profound and urgent set of meanings which is revealed if the images used in the verses are seen in relation to the comments and conversations which pattern the daily round within the home. Familiarity with the texture and the quality of residents' daily lives is enlightening in suggesting why these particular verses spoke to them with such clarity. Such was the energy generated in the appropriation, transformation and rehearsal of these verses that it may be inferred that the residents concerned recognised certain very crucial themes traced in the simple images of these lines. I will now discuss the resonance of these simple images – of old age (1), of the natural world (2), and of afterlife (3) – and so describe the three themes which are of particular significance for those who age in residential care.

(1) Images of Old Age

'There's always a dawn to the night of despair' (line 6)
This line is perhaps the most immediate point of identification with the verses for residents encountering the bodily conditions of old age. It readily articulates the experiences of those condemned by too many daylight hours of dozing to suffer the persistent aches and pains of an ageing body through long wakeful nights.

'And when through the murk of the shadows we grope' (line 14) is similarly resonant for those whose failing limbs and eyesight are tried by the unceasing requirement to edge their way back and forth along the corridors which lie between bedrooms and dining hall. Such experiences are also alluded to in the phrases:

'though the darkness may fall' (line 2)

and

'the bend in the roadway ahead' (line 8)

a bend which may appear at times unattainable when a zimmer frame compensates so poorly for the limbs' lost vigour. The word 'grey' in line 3 has multiple reference points in a bland physical environment where extreme old age and lack of fresh air are everywhere reflected in greying hair and flesh, and all movement is made across monochrome lino and carpet tiles. Any gleaming of gold to be found in these grey surroundings arises from such chance events as a joke, a visitor or a burst of spring weather.

Through the imagery of bodily discomfort the concept of a journey is implicitly traced – for example:

'there's always a path for the faithful to tread' (line 7)

and

'when through the murk of the shadows we grope' (line 7)

Suggested through the imagery of physical suffering, the motif of a journey is implicitly lent additional associations with the Christian ideology of life as pilgrimage. As they grope through the murk of the shadows, it is the faithful, the believers, who find a path and a bend in the roadway ahead. It is a journey of suffering, a night of despair, which not only has an ending or a dawn, but also leads towards meaning.

Remembering that, in one form or another, many residents have experienced a dramatic change in their domestic and social circumstances brought about by deterioration in their physical state, the significance of a journey motif within the chosen song becomes apparent. In many cases changes in personal circumstances have occured at a time in life when the uncertainties and upheavals of youth have long since given way to the stability and predictability of a long-established marriage within a familiar and well-ordered domestic environment. Bereft of reference points previously taken for granted the resident confronts a solitary one-way journey into an indeterminate future. This period of up to thiry years following retirement is singular in its lack of classificatory markers comparable with the various rites of transition whereby the individual has negotiated their passage through the earlier years of life. As Hazan asserts in *The Limbo People*, a study of a Jewish day-centre for elderly people '... the elderly are confronted with two conflicting dimensions of time. Their position in society consists of static elements

whereas the unavoidable process of disintegration changes conditions and abilities'(1980:47).

The conflict between two very different dimensions of time is
particularly marked for people who age in residential care. While the
rigidly repetitive routine of the institution creates a sense of timeless-
ness, the individual's subjective experience is of a personal time
dimension characterised by progressive physical decline.

Remarks from residents such as:
'You never know what to expect when you're getting old. You
never know what's coming next'
'I never thought I'd come to this'
or, as Ethel Carr put it:
'You never think about old age, do you, you never think. You
ought to prepare for it.'
attest to the fact that the unprecedented bodily experiences of ageing
in the unfamiliar environment of residential care may bring with
them an acute sense of disorientation or discontinuity between past
and present. As in Sissy Crowther's case, when changes in the body
multiply, the experience of an unanticipated rupture in one's path
through life can breed a growing sense of uncertainty and insecurity
with respect to the future.

Thus, when Mrs Porter received an unprecedented number of
cards and presents during the week leading up to her ninety-first
birthday, she confided her appreciation of these gifts to a staff
member – and added a query as to why people had been so kind to
her this year. Was it to be the last ?

Thus to those whose passage through physical deterioration is
contained and constrained within the static and repetitive routine of
the institution, the motif of a journey which is traced in the imagery
of physical suffering has a very personal significance. The song
acknowledges the fact that, though staff may manage a repetitive
cycle of admissions and exits to and from the institution, the resident
encounters a solitary one-way journey into unknown and uncertain
personal territory. The acknowledgement is couched in a form
which not only offers comfort by asserting an end to suffering, but
also lends purpose, meaning and therefore dignity to that suffering
by implicit reference to the Christian concept of life as pilgrimage.
Though a present of discomfort and constraint continues to repli-
cate itself day after day, as the resident moves back and forth
between the same bed, armchair and meal table, their sense of
uncertainty about the nature of their fate as individuals is both
acknowledged and transcended through the image of a painful

journey which leads towards a meaningful destination.

(2) *Images of the Natural World*

In common with many poems and texts of this kind, images of the natural world are used extensively in these verses – for example:

a star, a wild flower, a dawn, a gleaming of gold in the grey, a song floating out on the air, and a bend in the roadway ahead.

In the In Memoriam columns of provincial newspapers similar examples are to be found.[2] These images are used to fulfil two different purposes in the verses, 'Hope'.

First, the external world of nature is used to give metaphoric form to the hopes and fears associated with human hardship and struggle. For example:

'There's always a star – though the darkness may fall' (line 2)

and

'There's always a flower growing wild by the way' (line 4)

In this way the uncertainties of human life are placed within the broader context of the cycle of nature and the message to the reader is that present hardships or discomforts can be accepted as part of a larger pattern. Comforts and relief will come in their own good time, just as spring follows winter and sunshine follows rain. In other words, it is not for the individual to strive for, or seek to possess, happiness. It will come like the flower growing wild by the way and the song floating out on the air.

Second, the images are used to endorse and validate the Christian message by drawing on that separate body of folk wisdom, the Lore of Nature. For example, line 1 expresses the rash and contestable assertion that, however small, there is always a hope. The form of this line is echoed in the following seven, all of them variations on the adage, 'Every Cloud has a Silver Lining', all of them referring to that which, by the Lore of Nature, is firmly held to be 'true'. By the eighth line the validity of the first line is well established and the reader/singer is open to the injunctions of the third verse.

Thus images of the natural world are used:

(1) to suggest that both suffering and its relief are inevitable, each to be accepted in its turn, that 'into every life a little rain must fall'.

(2) to invoke a body of folk wisdom which lends further weight to the message of Christianity.

These roles are essentially overlapping, or mutually reinforcing. The presentation of suffering as something to be accepted as part of nature's cycle underscores the song's Christian injunctions that the individual should be humble, patient and trusting.

What can be inferred from residents' choice of verses bearing messages of this kind for their public performance? Examples of residents' private comments, presented earlier, suggest that the uses to which images of the natural world are being put in these verses correspond to many of the strategies through which residents seek to come to terms with their present situation.

It must be remembered that residential care is made available only to those:

... in need of care and attention not otherwise available.[3]

No matter what form of response residents offer, their continued and inevitable presence within the home ultimately represents passive acceptance of care. The active seeking of alternatives is no longer an option for them. And indeed, when new residents are asked how they are settling in, they offer replies such as:

'I'm beginning to but it will take time. It takes a while to get used to it, but I'll just have to'

'I accept things the way they are here. I have to, there's nothing else for it'

'You never know what's coming next. You just have to accept it'

To express acceptance in words such as these is to betray the helplessness and desperation from it stems. It is the one strategy open to all who encounter hardship and loss of power yet it inevitably implies personal failure and loss of integrity.

Hence the significance of the use to which natural images are put in the verses. As noted, they describe a present condition of darkness, despair and greyness. All that remains to the faithful is hope. Only by 'waiting' and 'trusting' can they hope to stumble upon the 'wild flower', the 'song' and the 'bend in the roadway ahead'. Couched in religious terms which are validated by references to the natural world, the acceptance of hardship assumes a dignity and stature which distinguishes it quite clearly from resignation, apathy or passivity. In their singing, residents are implicitly invoking the authority of two traditional sources of truth, Christianity and the Lore of Nature. Thus they validate their one remaining option, acceptance, and allay any notion that it may be little more than a giving up.

As the comments of new residents testify, they keenly feel the loss of alternatives and accept residential care because they have no choice. Earlier we saw that, for more settled residents such as Arthur Grant, their acceptance was elaborated, through reference to cultural values rooted in their past lives, into a system through which dignity and status may be acquired. Proverbs, aphorisms, systems of authority rooted in former professional lives and religious texts are all cited in support of residents' acceptance of present circumstances.

Thus, Albert Lyons, complaining that care staff had hurt his back by dropping him hard onto a chair after his bath, curtailed his resentment with the opening line of a hymn:

'Well...we but little children, frail and helpless all ...'

He expresses acceptance of his present helplessness, and interprets it in terms of the Christian metaphor of human beings as children and God as father.

Ethel Halliwell also ended a series of complaints with the biblical text:

'We must learn not to kick against the pricks'

Like a religious ideology or system of order stemming from a previous professional life, other sources of folk wisdom are made use of in the same way. As we saw, Ethel Carr drew on the adage, 'Mothers shape their daughters' destinies', when seeking to make sense of her current lack of family to support her in old age. Similarly, Sissy Crowther, struggling to make herself happy, drew courage from the aphorism:

'Nothing ventured, nothing gained'

The value which is attributed to some form of stoic acceptance is also revealed in the transformation, through language, of unhappiness or the unneccesary display of helplessness into a form of illness and therefore pathological. Thus Albert Lyons described his homesickness as 'get-out-itis', and Bill Headley's willingness to allow staff to shave him was described as 'lazyitis'.

In these and many other examples, as in the chosen verses, traditional sources of authority are invoked to validate a patient, trustful and accepting response to hardship. By drawing on such traditional values as discipline, hierarchy, and Christian humility and trust, residents are able to impute meaning and therefore grace and dignity to an otherwise demeaning acceptance of failing health and lost independence.

(3) Images of an Afterlife

Though I have dwelt so far on the relevance of the song's images for the present circumstances of residents' lives, the original significance of its metaphors must not be overlooked. Thus the 'dawn to the night of despair', the 'flower' and the 'song' are all faint hints or foretastes of that much happier life which lies beyond death. I suggested that the appropriation of the verses by the residents lent them a more profound and urgent religious significance than was originally intended on the greetings card. Sung by those for whom death is an everpresent possibility, the Easter message of the gift of hope for the resurrection to eternal life has a very immediate personal relevance. The resurrection ceases to be an intangible precept of the Christian religion and instead assumes the pressing reality of an imminent event. Closing a 'choir practice' Arthur Grant, in his role of choir master, sought to encourage the more faint-hearted by promising a growing repertoire by that time next year. Awareness of what the future held led him to add the proviso:

'...if we're all still alive by then'

Thus underlying the significance of the verses for a here-and-now which is centred around the constraints of ageing in residential care is a more fundamental layer of meaning associated with the immediacy of dying.

Set to music, the image of a pretty landscape with wild flower, song and star constitutes a vehicle whereby residents may implicitly affirm that their bodies are failing, that they stand very close to personal annihilation or transformation to an unknown state. The preparation of this statement for expression in a public setting is an acknowledgement of all the private statements which, as we have seen already, are being made in bedrooms and bathrooms throughout the home. Talking with Grace Heslop, resting in her room after a period of ill-health, the subject of her daughter's family, living in the north of Scotland arose. Stressing their remoteness she told me that in the past she had had to fly up there:

'I'll fly there again', she added, 'either here or here'

Her hand, raised from one level to the next revealed the meaning of her words. Little distinction remained between plane flights and heavenly flights. My suggestion that a few day's rest would help restore her strength brought the reply:

'If not in this life, then in the next. I'll be ninety-three next month, you know'

Comments such as these suggest that the Christian concept of the resurrection to eternal life, alluded to throughout the verses, constitutes a public acknowledgement of residents' private preoccupations with the nature of their own death. It is upon this preoccupation that the overall sense of the verses bears most directly. The slender hopes and the faint hints and signs, apparent only to the trusting as they grope for a path through the murk of the shadows, all refer to that most critical but elusive of goals, the discovery of meaning. Pre-occupation with the approach of death inevitably presages repeated reflection upon the long life that has gone before.

Those who care for the residents are aware of, and skillfully avoid, the rambling repetitiveness which periodically comes to the fore in conversation with elderly people. The young are locked within the linear flow of a time dimension directed towards the next days off and the forthcoming summer holiday. They lack the telescopic vision of elderly people for whom meaning lies not in the foreseeable achievements of the future but rather in the collapsing, condensing and integration of the decades which separate past from present experience.

This aspect of growing old, the search for meaning through repetition and reminiscence, has been discussed by many writers on the subject of ageing. Myerhoff, describing the elderly members of a Los Angeles Jewish Day Centre, says 'Their histories were not devoted to marking their successes or unusual merits. Rather they were efforts at ordering, sorting, explaining, rendering coherent their long life, finding integrating ideas and characteristics that helped them know themselves as the same person over time, despite great ruptures and shifts'(1978:33-34).

The search for coherence, the creation of life history which transcends the changes and losses of the recent past, represents a major if unacknowleged pre-occupation of the residents of Highfield House. Faced with the certainty that one's past life is one's whole life, that admission to care has brought with it social death in one form or another, the achievements and the regrets of the past assume their ultimate dimensions. Nothing further promises to dwarf, diminish or erase them and it is to these events and experiences that the memory returns during the vacant hours which remain. As the verses repetitively assert:

'We've got to remember
We've got to remember' (lines 15,16)

As shown, women living in the home feel the need to repair gaps and to come to terms with losses, often by focussing on the meaning of relationships now curtailed by death. And many men seek to sustain or find new forms for the roles through which integrity has previously been established.

As already noted a sense of uncertainty can arise through admission to care and the loss of the assumed reference points through which the self was formerly defined. For many residents this sense of dislocation remains and conversation returns endlessly to the events which conspired to produce the present situation.

This point is illustrated by the example of a now aged child's desire to account for and place a parent who was lost to them many years previously. The postcard pinned beneath a religious text above Elsie Crawford's bed showed a Lancashire churchyard with graves prominently framed in the foreground. After many years of family life in the North East, Elsie had travelled back to Lancashire in her old age to find her mother's grave. Her purpose satisfied, Elsie told me she felt 'easier'. Moreover, in the same churchyard she said she had 'found' some of her old schoolfriends by picking out their names on headstones. Her journey had served to give form and order to a long distant past and her black and white postcard recorded its permanence.

Returning to the choir practices, the 'public' context within which the song was first manifested, its social function as a corporate validation of residents' individual strategies for managing life in residential care can be considered.

Its creation and instigation as material suitable for the Christmas concert rests upon the unique position of its originators. Whilst sharing a common experience of physical decline and loss of social roles, Arthur, Jack and other fit residents had retained the capacity to perceive and to articulate the paradoxes inherent within that common experience. Through their former status within the locality, their relative independence of staff's physical care, and their ability to assume prominent roles within the home, these residents represented a relatively desirable model of ageing. As an alternative interpretation of a present otherwise characterised by personal failure and a loss of hope, meaning and self-esteem, the power of the song rests upon its instigation by the one social group within the home who could offer a model of this kind. That its form corresponded to a familiar genre of inspirational writing, and its content contained allusions to the long-established values ascribed to Christianity and the world of nature, furthered the authenticity of the song to the ears of its potential singers.

As noted this last period of life is singular in its classificatory markers as compared with the various rites of transition through which individuals negotiated their passage during earlier years. The space between entry to and exit from the home is, in may ways, uncharted personal territory. It is within this territory that residents set their song. It is a symbolic statement which implicitly condenses the lost independence of the past, the pressing needs of the present and the imminent event of the future. In making this statement the singers orient themselves within the otherwise very disorienting concerns and pre-occupations of their past, present and future circumstances. Form, order and meaning are given to the otherwise unstructured descent into physical decline and death. Thus in the last verse, those who presently grope through the murk of the shadows are exhorted to remember and to hope, to look back and also to look forward.

In this way the song articulates the experiences and the needs of the insider, the member of a negatively percieved social category. Under the guidance of their more able and less circumscribed fellows, this interpretation is offered by residents to an outside audience.

Staff's responses to the offering of the song affirm its power as an alternative interpretation of ageing. Though they were asked to go to choir practices for 'support', they begrudged residents their presence in this form and offered little support. Behind the long rows of chairs, laid out school-room fashion for the residents, the staff sat clustered above them on table-tops. Making faces at one another, hoping for some fun, the staff did not sing. Though official and unofficial rest breaks are longed for throughout all working hours, the opportunity to sit down with residents for an hour or more was not welcomed by staff. One of them described Arthur's musical setting as 'tuneless' and drew attention to the residents' difficulty in singing it.

Staff's response indicates that the occasions of the choir practices were very much of the residents' own making. Required to associate themselves on an equal footing with residents, to express subservience to Arthur in his role as the haranguing school-teacher, staff were at pains to create what distance they could between residents and themselves. Sitting above and behind the ranked rows of elderly people, staff displayed their capacity for both physical agility and lively sociality by clustering together in informal, casually perched social groups.

Though rehearsals continued, Christmas came and went without a performance of the song. As Arthur put it in January:

'We weren't asked. We're giving it all up. We're vexed'

In the busy institutional schedule of the home, the wavering efforts of the residents to acknowledge and give form and meaning to their own physical deterioration and closeness to death, were quietly overlooked. Their difficulties in singing betrayed the aptness of its images for this context. It lent to residents the power of the weak and as such was quietly diffused and distanced by staff.

Arthur ended his short statement by saying:

'Well, we might try again next year'

True to the sentiments of the verses, Arthur had waited trustingly to be asked to perform his work. Being overlooked, he expressed his anger succinctly but, recognising his own impotence and the impossibility of satisfactory explanations, he substituted acceptance for anger and expressed his hopes for the following year. By June he was dead.

This chapter describes the strategies through which residents give shape to their passage through Highfield House. An institutional present lends new meanings to the life which is now lost to the past, and the increasingly tangible prospect of death. Whether through personal memorabilia, recurrent reminiscence, current social relationships, or new-found duties and performances, the past, present and future selves of each resident are brought together, and integration of some kind is attempted. The highly individualistic nature of these accounts can be contrasted with the next chapter's discussion of the more uniform institutional strategies through which a hospice seeks to create a sense of continuity and wholeness among those who come to die in its care.

Chapter Seven

The Hospice Alternative

To understand the development of the Hospice Movement in Great Britain during the last twenty years it must first be set within the context of the controlling world view which has predominated with the West since the scientific revolution of the sixteenth century. The institutional care of elderly people has been explored in detail, as one embodiment, or outcome, of this world view. It is a way of controlling and distancing physical deterioration which falls outside the powerful, curative scope of the medical model. The Hospice Movement is another way of managing dying, one which has a far longer history, but which has, until recently, been felt to be at odds with the dominant models of medical control and cure.

Through a detailed exploration of one specific hospice, the emergence of the Hospice Movement from the late 1960s onwards will be discussed. The Movement has taken as its focus the precisely defined separation between living and dying which is currently being maintained within Western society in general, and in institutions such as the residential home in particular. Through strategies to be exemplified in this chapter and the next, the Hospice Movement seeks to reintegrate the two categories of experience, 'life' and 'death', thereby highlighting the processual rather than oppositional nature of their relationship. Thus the cultural and social forms which go to make up Hospice care express, and elaborate upon, the idea that living and dying are a biological continuum.

The creation of buildings explicitly oriented towards the care of dying people has been the most overt manifestation of the concept of Hospice care. The first such building to emerge since the medieval period in Europe was St Joseph's Hospice in the east end of London in 1902. St Christopher's Hospice, the most influential of contemporary hospices, was founded in 1967 by Cicely Saunders. That there may appear to be a paradoxical dimension to the strategy of setting space apart for dying has been noted by its opponents. In earlier discussion I argued that the spatial separation of living and

dying in Western society reflects the predominance of a divisive
boundary between these two categories of experience. Thus, at a
public meeting in Newcastle in 1979, concerning proposals for a
new hospice, points were raised by those who felt such a venture
might threaten their own budgets. Using the example of an existing
Marie Curie Home for terminal cancer patients, it was argued that
separate spaces for dying raised patients' anxieties; that hospices
segregated the dying and placed death outside the experience of
most doctors and nurses; that a hospice made death more of a
mystery and a special case.

Anthropological accounts of ritual in more traditional societies
have demonstrated that 'making separations', 'setting apart' and
'the creation of the sacred' are closely interlinked cultural and social
strategies. They are all associated with those more fluid and unpredictable aspects of life which lie outside the carefully structured
categories through which human beings give order and coherence to
their environment and their own experience within it. In one way or
another, 'setting apart' is a strategy oriented towards the management of process – for example, transition from one social category to
another; from one calendrical period to another; from one area of
thought and experience to another. Movement may be between
conceptual categories – from the sacred to the secular; between
social categories – from adolescence to adulthood; or between
material categories – from summer to autumn, from life to death.
Movement of one kind rarely occurs without the ritual invocation of
all three.

Thus process or change is an area of experience which is often
managed through the cultural strategy of setting apart carefully
framed times and spaces. In our own society, where 'growth' means
accumulation rather than change, those processes which involve loss
and decline are often managed within separate spaces devoted
largely to the distancing and transforming of otherwise threatening
aspects of life. For example, in the residential home for elderly
people aspects of daily life outside institutional space are made use
of in metaphoric strategies which conceal rather than reveal the
'non-ordinary' processes framed within this space. As discussed
earlier, within more traditional societies, rituals associated with, for
example, healing, initiation or death can bring about a deepening of
the individual's awareness through exposure to the literal, material
substance of a society's root metaphors. By contrast, within an
institution such as a residential home for elderly people, the central
material experiences of adulthood, such as shared meals and a room

of one's own, are so re-produced as to create a fictive 'ordinariness' which diverts awareness from the biological processes which are taking place. Field material reveals that, even though it is given little explicit acknowledgement, deterioration nonetheless remains visible, and dying becomes conspicuous by virtue of its invisibility.

Entry into separate spaces of this kind indeed inspires fear, in that the biological processes of decay are so transformed as to represent a form of social death, a fate which effectively severs connections between an individual and their former social roles within the wider society. In this respect an institution such as a residential home must be seen as a special case, one which deviates markedly from the body of traditional ritual times and spaces through which process is elsewhere incorporated within the patterning of the social fabric.

The Hospice however can be seen to lie firmly within that wider body of ritual, or liminal, times and spaces. Its commitment to the reintegration of life and death is achieved precisely through a carefully framed encounter with death, one which becomes possible within the very deliberately structured environment of the Hospice.

The analogy of the stage has already been used to discuss the framing of ritual time and space. It was shown that certain factors pre-disposed the participant to respond to the inherent power of the symbolic forms contained within that space. These include an awareness or recognition of the special nature of that space, and a willingness to accept as authentic the authority which it embodies. When these dispositions exist within the participant, the apparently mundane objects, social roles and behaviours contained within spaces set apart for special (that is, religious, theatrical, healing) purposes begin to take on the power of symbols. In the case of the hospice, internal features such as the structuring of ward space, the organisation of timetables and the dress, bearing and style of staff, together evoke a set of meanings which effectively transcend the day-to-day immediacy of uncomfortable symptoms and strained family relationships.

The material to follow shows how traditional sources of power are appropriated – and fused – within a space set aside for dying. A distinguished visitor to St Christopher's Hospice in London is reported to have said to Cicely Saunders:

> You have here a very sophisticated approach to medicine; you have a very sophisticated approach to religion; and you have a very relaxed and homely atmosphere – and not one of those three goes together![1]

This complimentary remark highlights the fusion of traditional, but hitherto discrete sources of power within the Hospice. The readiness with which the contemporary Hospice Movement has been accepted within British society can, therefore, be made sense of in terms of its capacity to encapsulate a variety of traditional symbolic forms or sources of power. In so doing, it resonates, readily, within the experience of all who would fund it, work within it, or come to die in its care. I would identify the sources of power as follows:

(1) Christianity
(2) Traditional medical practice
(3) Heritage
(4) Traditional calendrical and life-cycle events

(1) As regards explicit Christian iconography, this is often confined to Hospice chapels. However many hospices describe themselves as 'Christian foundations'. When the isolation ward of a hospital in Sunderland was transformed into a hospice, it was renamed St Benedict's. In associated publicity, the Health Authority stated that they were:

> ... continuing a tradition set by St Benedict of Wearmouth who founded a monastery and hospice by the River Wear in AD 674.

Through the drawing of such a parallel, the body of Christian thought and feeling is being used to create a quite specific context for dying. Similarly the resonant, but non-specific associations of water within a society with a Christian tradition are drawn upon extensively within hospices. Blue uniforms, blue decorations, prints of sea-scapes, a logo incorporating a river valley, are all examples which show the use of water to suggest movement, passage, cleansing and purity.

(2) Framed within the quasi-Christian imagery of water, and identified in many cases by the name of a saint, the Hospice also retains key features of traditional medical practice. Doctor, Matron and nurse are all in evidence, as is the traditional medical hierarchy of sister, staff nurse and auxiliary. Though curative techniques have been foresworn for those whose death is inevitable, nerve blocking and the use of highly sophisticated drug 'cocktails' are medical remedies for the chronic pain which cancer patients may suffer.

(3) Links with a past tradition of service or devotion are often referred to within Hospice literature. It is this connection which is being made in the key reference to St Benedict's Hospice by the River Wear which endorses Sunderland Health Authority's publicity. A related strategy is the retaining of the trappings of an earlier wealth and respectability in properties to be transformed for Hospice use –

for example, the original wood panelling in the wards of Strathcarron Hospice. Similarly, in the case of Strathcarron Hospice, the
seventeenth century name of the region within which it is located,
'Strathcarron', has been reintroduced as part of the process of
transforming existing property, thereby rooting the present venture
firmly within the past.

(4) Fieldwork within Strathcarron revealed that birthdays,
Christmas, Burn's Night and all other calendrical events were
celebrated extensively through familiar forms such as fancy dress
and feasting. Indeed any event, such as a member of staff or even
short-term visitor leaving the hospice, was marked in some way,
often through gift-giving and the writing of comic poems to be
pinned up in the reception area. In this way an innovative approach
to dying was located within the wider, deeply familiar context of
family and community events.

In the specific case of the transformation of Randolph Hill, a
family mansion in Stirlingshire, and the resulting construction of
Strathcarron Hospice, a space has been created within which the
symbolising power of 'ordinary' cultural and social forms may be put
to new ends. In this context, traditional sources of power are
brought to bear upon a unique situation. The deaths which are now
occurring within Strathcarron Hospice might, until recently, have
taken place within the isolating context of intrusive, curative medical
technology. Inversions of the customary spatial and conceptual
separation of living and dying are therefore being continuously
introduced through the practice of Hospice care. The powerful
associations of medicine, of religion, and of death are being brought
together within this institution. Through the framework provided by
Hospice ideology, the power of each one is manipulated and made
use of in quite specific ways.

SETTING THE STAGE

Strathcarron Hospice is founded in a large family home formerly
known as Randolph Hill and, until 1978, the property of the family
of a local paper mill owner. Roadside gateposts mark the beginning
of a curving driveway which leads the visitor past lawns and rhododendrons to end in a broad flourish before double doors enclosed
in a pillared porch. The former family's high panelled reception
rooms at this public end of the mansion give way to smaller domestic
rooms, kitchens and outhouses, extending away downwards towards the River Carron which crosses the grounds behind further
banks of rhododendrons. The processes through which this family

mansion has been transformed into Strathcarron Hospice give insights into the particular cultural framing of death which it represents.[2]

As I will show, it is an institution where the idea and the event of death is acknowledged more openly than is customary in British society, and where its painful and frightening aspects are confronted, rather than distanced and avoided. The framing of space within and around Strathcarron Hospice, and the relationship with the surrounding community indicate the ways in which a particular kind of openness is being sought.

The primary material alterations to the original building include the extension of the back of the house to provide three small wards to accommodate up to thirteen patients, the setting up of a mortuary and the modification of cooking and laundry facilities. The original, extensive wood-panelling and an elaborate, intricately carved staircase darken the wards and the reception area – and require careful cleaning. Nonetheless, as an evocation of earlier wealth and respectability, their evocative power is retained in the creation of a dignified mode of dying.

The transformation, indeed inversion, of the name of the mansion gives an initial insight into the particular cultural elaboration of dying and death which takes shape in these modified spatial arrangements. The name of the river, 'Carron', little more than a stream, unobtrusive below the furthest domestic and outhouse buildings, is now displayed prominently in decorative blue lettering on a large white signboard at the entry gateposts. Replacing the former title, 'Randolph Hill', the word 'Carron' takes the prefix 'strath', meaning valley. In approaching the building, set on the rise of a hill, the patient, doctor or visitor is now entering a river valley. This image, evoked in the re-naming of the building, is echoed in an outline drawing of outstretched hands, wrists together, the heavier lines on the underside of the hands suggesting a valley. The word and the drawing, placed together on the signboard, affirm the image.

Through this signboard the presence of the hospice in the small Stirlingshire town, Denny, is made public and visible. In its form, the sign encompasses an allusion to nearby water in which the images of caring hands and a river valley are fused. In addition, the river valley, 'Strathcarron', is the seventeenth century name of the region. Now fallen into disuse, this name has been reintroduced, thereby stressing links between the present and the past, between contemporary hospices for the dying and medieval 'hospyces', or way stations, for pilgrims. Death and the care of dying people is thus being given prominence, in a very particular form.

The chosen imagery, of water, carries extensive associations, particularly with respect to Christianity. These range from its use as a specific Christian symbol of purification, baptism and re-birth – through to its extensive metaphoric use in giving form to such concepts as flow, tranquillity and peace. For those who enter the hospice, members of a society where a Christian ideology remains pervasive, water and its associated forms of the river and the valley retain powerful if non-specific meanings. In its broad yet very vague associations, water offers an effective fund of images through which the culture of care may be organised and articulated.

Entry to the hospice is now by way of new glass doors approximately halfway along the building. These have supplanted the original porched entrance door. To the left of these doors lie the three wards (two former reception rooms and an extension) which accommodate up to thirteen dying patients from any part of the central region of Scotland. These wards are named 'Avon', 'Endrick' and 'Devon', the three rivers which bound this region on the north, west and east sides. The patient's death will occur in one of these three wards, and their body will then be taken along the building, past the glass entry doors, the kitchen and the laundry, until it reaches the mortuary behind double doors at the far end of the building. In two parts, the mortuary comprises first a single, velvet-draped viewing room and then a simple storage room with pallets and a fridge for up to six bodies. This viewing room, the body's final destination, is named the 'Carron' room. Lifecourse and deathcourse are thus made continuous in the patient's transition from periphery to centre, from their life in the Central Region to their death by the River Carron.

Senior staff, the administrator and a consultant, responsible for naming the rooms, considered the possibility of using the names of mountains but finally chose rivers as 'living, symbols of life'. The administrator is aware that the Avon, Endrick and Devon bound the region to which the hospice's care is available.

An exploration of the relationship between the hospice and the surrounding communities reveals a further reflection of the choices made in the ordering, through naming, of the interior of the building. The image of a valley which both encloses and channels aptly represents the relationship between Strathcarron and the Central Region. Of the history of the hospice, the administrator told me that its present medical director floated the idea of a hospice in 1975. Despite the absence of deliberate fund-raising, repeated public meetings led to the accumulation of sixty thousand pounds within three years, and the name 'Strathcarron Hospice' became synonymous with terminal illness. Almost every aspect of the life of the hospice now involves a circular flow or movement, of people, money and gifts from all parts of the region in towards the focal point of the hospice and back out again.

The association of this open flow with the coming of death is indeed a transformation of prevailing practice which confines death to the isolation of hospital side-rooms and the seclusion of old people's homes. The openness begins with the communication, in some form, of a terminal diagnosis between consultant and patient, a strict pre-requisite for referral to Strathcarron. It is extended in the repeated visits of a hospice doctor, a Macmillan home-care nurse and a social worker to the home of the patient and their family. From this point onwards a volunteer may drive the patient and their family to the hospice for short-term admission, or for regular day-care visits. The latter comprise up to five hours spent in the day-care room where conversation, music and craft activities are available. Permanent admission occurs only if death is imminent and family can no longer support the patient at home.

After the patient's death their family, particularly spouses, may receive bereavement visits from their volunteer 'driver' or a volunteer bereavement visitor. They may also return at least once every month to the hospice to meet similarly bereaved people at an 'At Home' evening. Such visiting may continue well into the second year after the loss and as time passes the circle of bereaved people grows. While no charge whatsoever is made by the hospice to patients and their relatives, money and gifts are often donated 'in memoriam' by families. Similarly the daughters and wives of deceased patients often volunteer their domestic or nursing skills in the years following the death. Gift-giving is not restricted to bereaved people. Wedding bouquets and the middle tiers of wedding cakes are now being offered by those marrying within the region. Money flows into the hospice from many sources. These range from grants from Local Councils and the Health Board, to the contributions of Central Region Council employees who donate a small amount of their weekly wage.

Thus the relationship between Strathcarron and the surrounding communities can be described as an open channelling of resources which makes possible the provision of extensive and very flexible care of dying people. So sought after and respected has this kind of care become that, as local people admit, of the several collecting boxes on the pub bar, Strathcarron's always receives the small change. Staff at local hospitals are quick to provide seating and attention should a Strathcarron patient, openly 'terminal', require treatment such as an eye appointment.

Such a channelling of resources is made possible through the direct acknowledgement of death, one particular elaboration of the accurate medical diagnosing of illnesses such as cancer. This form of elaboration represents a deliberate choice. The carefully chosen imagery through which this choice is represented has multiple references. The linking together of the rivers at the periphery and at the centre of the hospice's sphere of operation, and the fusion of the valley with the caring hands are expressive on two levels.

The first, already discussed, is the flow or movement of money and people towards the hospice which is integral to its functioning. Patients and visitors are given a sheet with descriptions of exact routes to the hospice from seven different directions. Public signs to Strathcarron are prominent in the local town of Denny. In seeking to entertain patients and bring in further funds, staff jogged around the perimeter path of the hospice in preparation for a 'marathon' which involved relay teams of eight staff assembling at four points sixteen miles away from Strathcarron in each direction. Again the movement from periphery to centre was traced, this time through the runners and the sponsor money which they brought in as they raced back to the hospice.

The second way in which the imagery operates is through its explicit visibility, an inversion of the distancing of death which is elsewhere pervasive. The transformation of Randolph Hill has involved the placing of the name of the unobtrusive river Carron prominently at the entrance, the same name which is given to the mortuary. Thus in the deliberate choice to take up the possibility of knowledge about the future death of an individual and to amplify this possibility in an explicit system of purely palliative care, those who establish hospices are making a powerful statement. Death and the reality of human mortality are being placed boldly before the eye.

'Strathcarron', the river valley, can be seen as the organising metaphor through which this particular kind of openness is being created. The valley which leads towards their death, which steers awareness towards the inevitability of mortality, is subsumed within the hands which offer and support. With the powerful gesture of giving prominence to death comes the equally powerful promise of the relief of pain and suffering. Though the hospice has been able to accept all those referred to it within the Central Region, this acceptance is conditional upon the patient being told, in some form, the truth about their diagnosis. Those who seek pain relief become part of a movement towards Strathcarron Hospice, and ultimately towards the Carron Room within. This involves an extended exposure to death. Wards within the building open directly into the entrance area, a large stairwell to the left of the external glass doors. Dying people are thus made immediately visible.

Entry to this space can provoke fear. In seeking pain and symptom control patients confirm their diagnosis. An elderly patient, being helped back through the doors after a brief trip home to her cottage, said, 'I'll never get out of this place'. A younger couple, in their forties, were brought in for the dying husband to receive counselling, an attempt to help him cope better with pain. His wife's determined vitality, on show during the journey to the hospice, collapsed visibly on entry to the building. Similarly friends of patients sometimes have difficulty in referring directly to Strathcarron, and the word 'hospital' is used to mask the more unequivocal associations of the word 'hospice'.

In summary, the creation of Strathcarron Hospice, a culture of care, within Randolph Hill, can be seen as a way of bringing death to the fore by placing it at the centre.

Behind this powerful and sometimes fear-provoking gesture lie additional and different sources of power in the resources of narcotic drugs, extensive nursing care and a Christian foundation. Cicely Saunders pioneering research in pharmacology has resulted in the availability of highly sophisticated drug 'cocktails'. After an initially high prescription, such drugs can control pain through the regular administration of smaller doses which pre-empt its return. Nurse:patient ratios are high[3] and additional care is provided continuously by occupational therapists, Red Cross beauticians, and volunteers who offer patients companionship, outings, and practical help such as letter-writing. In Strathcarron the Chaplain's regular presence underscores a Christian emphasis. Phrases such as:

'... whether in this life or the next, she is in God's hands'

form part of his conversations with soon-to-be-bereaved relatives. Often conducted in public spaces within the hospice, such conversations make available a Christian perspective to a nearby listener. It is through the fusion of such resources that an open encounter with death is managed. It is the continuous task of all those associated with or encompassed by Strathcarron.

In the accompanying diagram each aspect of hospice care has been separated out in order to demonstrate the multi-dimensional

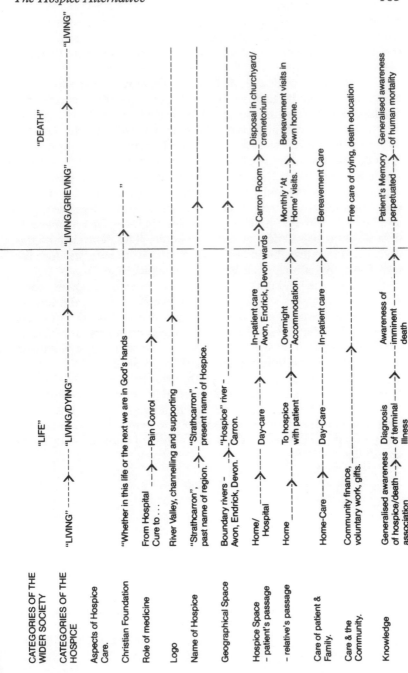

Figure 2: Hospice Care, the temporal, spatial and conceptual breaching of the prevailing life/death boundary.

The diagram shows Hospice care to be a cultural milieu within which the idea and the experience of transitions are imaged and expressed on multiple levels.

breaching of a prevailing life/death boundary. It is significant that while the role of medicine has been extended into the area of dying, it nonetheless remains limited to the control of bodily experience in life.

This chapter introduced the Hospice alternative to the strategies of separation and distancing though which the painful aspects of the ageing/dying process are managed in institutions such as the residential home. Earlier discussion of the residential home showed that its boundary served to sever connections between the process of growth and the process of decline – both temporally as well as spatially, both socially and conceptually as well as physically. Framed within this gulf, the bounding of institutional time and space figuratively re-creates the prevailing cultural categories, 'life' and 'death' and systematically imposes them upon an unevenly deteriorating population of elderly people. The centrality of this divisive, figurative boundary has become the focus for the transformative strategies embodied in Hospice care.

Spanning the boundary between life and death, hospices represent separate spaces within which the experience and the idea of transition is demonstrated and made possible. Thus the boundary between the hospice and the surrounding community is the site of maximal visible movement, a public space where the life/death continuum is powerfully suggested.

From an initial assertion that death is currently managed through a separation of living space and dying, discussion has now moved to the example of the Hospice. It exemplifies a set of innovative strategies which not only question but also actively re-structure the categories through which individuals in the West are currently living and dying.

Chapter Eight

Living With Death

Strathcarron Hospice has been shown to be a space within which the idea and the experience of transition is fostered. This chapter describes a day in the life of day-care patients, in-patients and relatives, giving insights into the ways in which a sense of movement or passage is gently brought home to them. As such, it represents an insider's view of the Hospice context. In contrast with the traditional, analytic form used to discuss the dislocating experience of ageing and dying in residential care, this account of the insider's view is presented in a more literary style in order that the holistic nature of patients' experience can be fully appreciated by the reader.

Many of Strathcarron's patients are drawn from working class communities to the south of Stirling. In accepting Hospice care they submit to a move out of their own cultural and social context and into a middle-class sphere, pervaded throughout by a Christian ambiance. Within this setting transformative processes of a cultural, social, emotional or medical nature may ensue – processes which encompass, and affect a new reintegration of former experiences. By noting in detail the varied sights, sounds, social encounters and pastimes, some novel, some deeply familiar to the incomer, a picture emerges of a very gentle yet inexorable encounter with the imminence of death.

STRATHCARRON HOSPICE: ENTRY TO EXIT

A larger crowd than usual gathers on a Friday morning in the sombre wood-panelled room at the end of the Strathcarron's central corridor. They have been brought from home to the foot of the outside steps by voluntary chauffeurs, homely, middle-class women and a few retired men. A wheelchair or a supporting arm steers them into the pine-scented hallway, wood-panelled too and dimly-lit. Some have come from grey brown council houses on desolate Falkirk estates, out of the shabby, damp-smelling glamour of densely patterned furnishings and outsize, plastic three-piece suites. Others leave behind modest stone-built cottages in the scattering of villages at the foot of the Ochils, untidy double-beds set up behind net-curtained bay-windows in front rooms. Commodes, potties and morphine-laden bedside tables reveal current pre-occupations.

Among these passengers many have cancer and most are expected to die within months. Through their consultant or their GP they have been referred to the country mansion, the local 'big house', set half-way between Stirling and Falkirk. The change in their bodies has precipitated regular journeys out of a modest and now constrained workaday domesticity, and away into the more imposing dimensions of the former mansion of the owner of a local paper-mill.

In late middle-age some passengers have learned quickly of their condition, struggled at night times with the knowledge. Wigs and headscarves are a telling mask for their hair-loss by chemotherapy, the fear-provoking procedure which certifies the condition. Older passengers, long-retired, perhaps resident in old people's homes, are less sure. Referral to the destination known as Strathcarron Hospice, signifies little more than a tiresome and seemingly pointless change in routine.

In states of mind and body such as these, all are brought, alone or with a relative, between the stone gate-posts at the top of Randolph Hill. Beyond lie three and a half acres of carefully cultivated park-land, through which a curving driveway leads the patient to the double glass doors of the hospice. Concrete steps, plus ramp, plus extensive handrails suggest the particularity of its function. Ascent accomplished, a waiting stretcher trolley, and a distinctively scented atmosphere confirm speculation. Prints of waves breaking, of Impressionist yachts at sunset, ease the passage into a hallway/stairwell reception area. Here a mosaic impression of handcraft and medicine confronts the patient.

The carefully sustained, seemingly limitless warmth of their voluntary chauffeur is now mirrored in the greeting of a voluntary receptionist. Embroidering or knitting patch blankets, the receptionist is framed within a scene of 'Guess-my-Birthday' baby dolls; a glimpsed sluice room; inert, crochet-blanketed bodies; and collapsed, waiting wheelchairs. Rarely empty, this space is a meeting point. Four doorways and the staircase provide entry for sombre-suited doctors, administrators, undertakers and the chaplain; for white and blue uniformed female nurses and domestics; and for less readily-identifiable female home-care nurses, voluntary helpers and the social worker. Loudly humourous greetings and a quieter and more urgent exchange of messages merge in an atmosphere of heady seriousness. Threading their way through this public space towards toilets and lounge, in-patients may sometimes be identified by dressing-gown or by hand-held catheter bag. In other cases slippers and a slow tread are the only indication.

Moving into this space, greeted by the receptionist, the cancer-bearing visitor is appropriated by those around them, drawn into role as a member of the social category 'day-care patient'. Double doors beyond open to reveal the destination of the day, the meeting place of Friday's larger crowd than usual. Entry to this room confers membership of the day-care category. Faltering or refusal is not uncommon. The music, the cigarette smoke and the noise and bustle of activity can overwhelm the timid and the very weak. They seek a return to the peacefully predictable routines of previous months' isolation in sick room or residential home. Those who persist are edged by relative or chauffeur into large armchairs among a group of up to a dozen people. Again greetings are readily offered; again the handwork. In armchairs, wheelchairs or on a settee, the group is assembled around a coffee table at the lighter end of this panelled room. To their left and right, corner windows give onto the entrance driveway. Between the tomato plants they have been helped to grow, they glimpse the hospice traffic of cars, delivery vans and hearses.

Fred Challis is a regular member of this group. He is brought in throughout the week, yet appears reassuringly bronzed and full-cheeked. In 1982 his face appeared in the medical director's publication, 'Terminal Care'. In 1983 the hospice bulletin reports Fred, 'the doyen of our patients', being photographed with the day-care sister for a poster advertising the hospice. The first arrival every morning, he establishes his solid presence on the settee beneath the window, spreading his rugwork across his knees. Fred is indeed the 'doyen' or senior member among this transitory group of dying people. Visually prominent, featured in hospice publicity, Fred is not about to die. His tumour has been removed, but for more than a year he has continued to pass his days in these familiar surroundings while his daughter is at work nearby. Fred is chronically deaf. Though a greeting for new arrivals often comes first from Fred, there is little by way of further conversation. He remains as a silent and reassuringly whole representative of the category of terminally ill people into which the newcomer has been introduced.

Those who cluster about Fred, and those who sit apart in the darker end of the room are similarly difficult to identify with any precision. Most are in their sixties, many appear resigned, withdrawn or weary. Fiona McIntyre sits in an armchair near Fred. She is composed, alert, ready to respond or to argue, though her eyes may be closed when conversation begins. Her immaculate, stylish suits, her jewellery and her hairdo suggest a business woman, tired now but still ready to correct the ill-informed or reproach a complainer. Many assume she is a visitor, but Fiona is growing smaller, greyer and more lined as the weeks pass. Her external elegance conceals the catheter bag strapped to her leg. Little remains of her bladder now. For months the hospice had been Fiona's country hotel, the refuge which she booked in and out of, apologising when her need arose. Now she leaves the hospice only occasionally. She has labelled all the possessions in her flat, given away jewellery and electrical goods where she saw a need. With the menu for her funeral tea drawn up, the outfit she will wear in her coffin selected, she passes her days as best she can, knitting little string dishclothes and threading together plastic purses.

Mr Farr has been brought in by a volunteer from his austere council house in Stirling. He is older than Fiona or Fred, wiry and thin with a pinched, wistful face. Long years of independent bachelorhood and a highly successful career in gardening lie behind him. Around his house a garden flourishes still, carefully tended. Corms recovered from the cellar bloom extravagantly in the kitchen and an old wireless and a dependable wind-up clock sustain him through evenings in the sparsely-furnished living-room. Mr Farr's speech is spare, delivered in a husky, fading voice. The day-care sister has squeezed him into the centre of the group, tucked in beside Fred and his rug on the settee. He frets quietly. He doesn't want to come all this way just to sit about all day. He expected some kind of treatment and wonders why they can't discover what is wrong with him.

At Fiona's suggestion Mr Farr selects a thriller from the bookcase opposite, but his restlessness persists. The Council have recently renovated his house, taken down the picture rails he used to hang his 'good mirrors', replaced his locks with ill-fitting aluminium substitutes, trampled some of his plants. He needs to get home, he needs to place his bets for the 3.30, he needs to see some improvement in his condition.

Morag Watson has taken the place beside Fiona. In her eighties she fills her armchair amply. She is a little breathless and large dark eyes beneath fluffy, white hair betray a controlled sense of anxiety. She and Fiona recognise one another as pals. When Morag was brought into the hospice from an 'Eventide Home' she was desperate for companionship and found it in Fiona. She is expansively warm, talking repeatedly of how marvellous Fiona was to her when she arrived, what a wonderful person she is. Ever-impressed by Fiona's stoicism, Morag feels put to shame by her, horrified by an unexpected glimpse of Fiona's wound. Morag's symptoms have been effectively brought under control since her admission. Like Fred she has no further urgent need for care but dreads a return to the 'Eventide Home'. The vitality of her friendship with Fiona, her own openness, echoed in the warmth of her children and grand-children who visit daily, are all felt throughout the hospice. Declared 'good for morale', she is allowed to stay on, enjoying both days and nights at Fiona's side.

Other day-care visitors crowd in around this foursome. A small, swarthy man edges his wheelchair close to the table. Iain is in his forties, suffering from multiple sclerosis. He hammers small wooden stools together, dispensing a strong undercurrent of camaraderie. Ada Waters and Vera Duffy respond, talking with urgency about rent increases. Ada visits occasionally, with some difficulty. Last year she was a constant figure in this room, strong and supportive towards Eddie, her husband who was to die on New Year's Eve. She gave little thought to the emptiness which lay ahead and braves an overwhelming sense of loss as she walks alone now, up the hill to the hospice seeking sympathetic company. Vera Duffy's deep and force-ful voice sustains the conversation, joking and challenging. She is reconciled to her cancer now and brings a home-made dumpling for Michael Dunn, a young, motherless victim of Friedrich's Ataxia, the motor-neurone disease more dreaded within the hospice than can-cer itself.

Across the room another man in his sixties sits alone, squarely and placidly. When approached he is responsive and welcoming, but grey-faced, hair harshly shorn. His gait is slow and awkward, but he shows pleasure in movement and talks animatedly of the hip replace-ment operations he has just undergone. In the ward behind him, May, his wife, is deteriorating rapidly. They came from Ireland together, years and years before, childless, devoted to one another, staunch Roman Catholics. She lived in the hospice while his hips were replaced, taking small plastic bags of her own fruit across when she visited him in Falkirk. On his recovery she went home delight-edly, 'to be with my man'. Determinedly asserting her 'improve-ment', she refused to go back 'over there' and he agonised in a silent attempt to 'keep it from her'. Now he and his unemployed friend, Paddy, keep glum vigil at her bedside. The statuette of the Virgin

Mary beside her on the locker has been brought expressly from Italy by the home-help. He intends it to be placed alongside her in the coffin.

In the darkest corner of the day-care room, under another print of waves breaking, a younger couple smoke together in silence. Boredom and strain mix in their thin features. The care they commit themselves to giving to the elderly man in the ward nearby is barely received. The woman's father has extensive brain secondaries and his rambling, incoherent speech and his blindness confound all who would nurse or comfort him.

Though this Friday crowd is large it is not atypical. In-patients, day-patients, relatives and the bereaved all take their places alongside one another. For much of the day they may be left somewhat to their own devices. Pain, grief, boredom and fatigue can easily stifle fluent conversation. All are careful to defer to the possible suffering of another. Though the vitality of patients such as Fred, Fiona and Morag reassures, the motionless, emaciated bodies in the wards beyond can sober the impulse towards a too-buoyant humour or a too-bitter complaint.

Day-care is intended by staff as a gentle introduction to the hospice. It represents an offer to patients of company, an ample meal, handwork and medical supervision. The more that trust and familiarity can be established within the patient, the less severe their suffering is predicted to become.

In the confines of the dark-panelled room at the end of the building, encounters with illness, dying and bereavement are inevitable. The transition from first diagnosis to final bereavement, with each and every slow stage in between, all find some expression in such very mixed groups. As time passes day-care patients may prune the frequency of their visits. Shared lifts and long hours in adjoining armchairs facilitate an intimacy which is inevitably vulnerable to the uneven progress of different tumours. Violet Charlton isn't there this Friday. She's already pointed out how hard it is making friends with 'ladies' and then they die.

> 'Its alright for the nurses', she says, 'its their job. Its no so good when you're one of the passengers.'

The existing hospice is to be extended over the next few years.[1] Priority is being given to new, subdivided day-care facilities to the east of the present room, nearer still to the main road. Additional wards are to come later. They will extend southwards, away towards farmland at the back of the hospice. A covered corridor will link this south-facing extension with the morgue at the western extremity of the building, thus providing an external and quite separate route for the passage of bodies.

Plans such as these extend and enhance the offer of day-care, the gentle introduction to a company of the dying. In addition, design choices have been made which will serve to create separations between the various social categories to whose members the hospice offers care. In today's context such distinctions blur, giving rise to ambiguities and uncertainties. In the offer of a space for patients such as Fred Challis and Morag Watson, certain ambiguities are fostered. Their presence, together with a proliferation of the voluntary, the homely and the hand-stitched, soften the anticipation of a final and ultimate transition to the small mortuary rooms at the far end of the building. The anticipation itself is nonetheless inevitable. In the present circumstances, juxtapositions of physical pain, grief, fatigue and fear are encountered frequently.

Mr Farr is taken outside by a volunteer to ease his restlessness. The stocking of the flower beds around the hospice interests him, provoking long reminiscence of even grander gardens he has tended. Newly-laid flags draw him among the beds, leading him up the pathway which skirts the large windows of the main ward. He pulls only a token weed, his gaze drawn away inside the building. 'Are these the wards then ?' he asks. He pauses, seeming to want to say or hear more, but remains silent.

Mr Farr is spending his Friday in this way because he has chosen to accept an offer. Though the day-care sister extends the offer welcomingly, she is an NHS-trained nurse and a little bemused by her responsibility for a service which is entirely optional, yet deemed highly valuable for patients. Patients' difficulty in interpreting and responding to signs of ill-health or distress among fellow visitors is matched by staff's uncertainty in the fostering of an appropriate atmosphere among day-care patients. Notions of a suitable mode of caring vary among staff. In conscious opposition to the routinisation of hospital practices, they have made an explicit commitment to very flexible caring, determined by the needs and wishes of the individual. Inevitably it is an ethos which is subject to a circumstance in which many individuals, the unwell, the dying, the soon-to-be-bereaved and the grieving, share a confined space.

Mary Saunders, the hospice social worker, is a single woman in her early forties, a committed Christian, who expresses a personal preference for solitude. Her response to those individuals who withdraw, overwhelmed by public exposure in the crowded day-care room, is powerful. Her offers of rescue are prompt. Mary states

openly that the lack of privacy and peace in the hospice sometimes
alarms her, and she strives to stifle the noise of excessive laughter
and the thud of footsteps.

Margaret Owen, day-care sister, approaches such issues from a
different perspective. Together in their small, shared office, she self-
mockingly mimics her 'big sell' for day-care. With a few dance steps,
she announces crafts, parties and an outing to the Edinburgh Tatoo.
As a nurse, she is indeed bemused by her role as hostess to the newly-
diagnosed. She has developed an approach in which the element of
choice is elaborated. Margaret initiates activities or events. Their
outcome is unpredictable, a matter of choice among patients. She
interprets potentially distressing encounters or separations according to current ideologies which stress the therapeutic value of
honesty and frankness.

Those who cluster at the coffee table this Friday are offered the
possibility of a slide show by Margaret. For an hour or so they have
been helped by an ex-handicraft teacher to stitch fluffy toy animals.
Fiona and Morag have worked in silent concentration at one another's sides, responsive to this brief respite from dish-cloths and plastic
purses. The day-care sister's initial suggestion of slides has been
accepted and the question of including the bed-ridden arises. Un-
daunted by the fact that the men in the adjoining ward are too ill to
come through, Margaret enlists support to re-establish the day-care
group (plus screen and projector) in among them. The upheaval is
enormous. Meal trolleys are folded away, pot plants stacked up on
the window sill and the ward coffee table is pushed out into the
garden. Curtains are drawn, leads trail and all access to the adjoining
nurses' station is blocked by a tight bunching of chairs. The day-care
group move through slowly, in ones and twos. With care they take
seats, concerned not to obscure a neighbour's view or disturb the
four men lying in this ward. The men's beds, set among a busy
clutter of lockers and wardrobes, take up most of the space in this
further, high-panelled room.

In moving through, at Margaret's suggestion, the orientation has
shifted away from the comings and goings of the entrance thorough-
fare towards a view of sunlit, stone-walled lawns, screened by a long
clustering of well-established trees. Sunlight floods through large
ward windows. Tom Renshaw, on the right, lies motionless, yellow-
ing and emaciated. So conspicuously ill is he that only a close
inspection reveals signs of life. His eyes lie half-open, as in death, but
their remote, thoughtful gaze is directed towards the light, suggesting a passenger on watch as a shoreline recedes. He is dying very

slowly and his wife's large, handsome face is crumbling with the alcohol necessary for yet more visiting. Watching the new and growing dissimilarity between the faces of Tom and his brother, she makes loud, brash remarks:

> 'They're all the same, these bloody Renshaws. I really fancy you in that state Tom'

The warm and gentle style of fifty hospice staff jolts in the face of her defiance.

Billy Charlton's wife is no longer a visitor but now a quasi-staff member. In a hospice apron she tends him throughout the day, a critical substitute for his body's lost mobility. Humour, vitality and expressiveness are now crowded exclusively upon his large well-made head. Below, a naked conglomeration of torso, twisted lifeless arms and a remaining, soon-to-be-amputated leg all lie ill-concealed beneath crochet blankets on an aluminium bed cradle. The healthy, almost joyful, cast of his features contrasts noticeably with an unsmiling weariness in the face of the wife beside him.

Roger Harmer sprawls across a bed to the back of the room. Florid and plump, he shows no external signs of disease. Dressed still, in thick blue cardigan and belted, crimplene trousers, he appears angrily discontent. His admission to the hospice is the staff's attempt to give his family a break. He promised to have no contact with them for a fortnight but already he has phoned here and there, always with a different and more worrying account of his plans. Staff tire rapidly of his complaints about food, smoking and television.

On the bed opposite, sightless Tommy Farquar mumbles, shifting from side to side, always disturbingly close to the next stumbling foray into the room.

Margaret erects the screen, curtains are drawn and the unfocussed slide show begins. The material for this August morning's event is drawn from two earlier occasions, a Burns Night hotel supper and a Christmas-time hospice party. Slides show staff in unfamiliar evening-wear, elaborate, formal and glamourous, clustered together at candle-lit tables. With dry humour, Margaret establishes a sense of benign voyeurism among the day-care audience, pointing out large jugs of orange juice when alcohol is clearly more central to the occasion. Playing upon an atmosphere of mock titillation, she also introduces shots of the hospice Christmas party with a comment, 'Lots of money has been offered for us to suppress some of these pictures'. They show staff in other, more bizarre guises. Santa, the Pied Piper, two large fairies, Worzel Gummidge, a giant baby, and Buttons are all seen to cavort in the same, familiar setting as the morning's slide-show.

The day-care audience laughs afresh as they witness the surprise juxtapositions of this revealing masquerade. On the slides another audience is seen to witness the carnival. They too are familiar members of the in-patient/day-patient categories and today's audience calls out their names in school-room unison. On her bed a woman is seen to indulge in the 'good things' of life, cigarette hanging from her lips, beer bottle lying in her hand and huge pants strung from the bedrail with a note asking Santa to fill them. Only a chill, an inaudible sigh, acknowledges the transience of the dead audience, frozen on the translucent plastic of the slides.

Tom Renshaw has now fallen asleep and Roger Harmer ceases to pretend any interest. Fred Challis complains that at least fifteen slides were omitted, the ones in which he appeared. Margaret offers to retrieve them but the others are tiring, they have seen enough. She notes that Tom is asleep, 'Well, that shows it was a nice soothing show'. Slowly the ward is restored to its original order. 'Well that was a nice little morning interlude', she concludes.

For those who visited the hospice for day-care, the anticipation of a frightening future has been gently advanced in the few slow paces from day-care room to ward. The interlude to which they were entertained drew them still further forward in a shared retrieval of the familiar names of those who have preceded them. Drawing on the value attributed to honesty in current ideologies of terminal care, Margaret defines the interlude as 'good grief therapy'. And then begins to speculate about the effect on Fred Challis and Fiona of being party to so very many deaths. Theory tempts her again and she raises the possibility of 'measuring the effect'.

In this, as in all such day-care 'interludes', a lively entertainment involves an encounter with death. A party on the previous Friday afternoon had led day-care patients to seats outside in the garden and 'Chateau Strathcarron', the wine they had been helped to make. As quiche and fresh-cream strawberry tarts were handed round, beds were trundled heavily from wards and out over flagstones. Each one bore the immobile body of a dying patient, their condition made pitifully evident in the strong, early afternoon sunshine. Seeking to overcome the slightly nervous formality common to the early stages of parties everywhere, Margaret asked if anyone could sing. Though most staff were already retiring to the periphery of the group, a few visiting relatives, a volunteer driver and two volunteer/students remained among patients. Johnny Bell, the driver, was swift to accept this further opportunity to volunteer himself. In a resonant and determinedly vibrato voice, Johnny worked his way through each verse of a series of sentimental Scots ballads. The introduction of yodelling in the third song brought the company to the brink of mild, stifled hysteria. Billy Gordon, a former psychiatric patient now seated at the bedside of his child-like, dying wife, rose in spiky blonde wig to offer a similar if more restrained rendering of yet another Scots ballad. Michael Dunn, the young man whose control of his vocal chords had been largely eroded by motor-neurone disease, was then pressed to attempt 'Michael Row the Boat Ashore'. As he struggled to produce some appropriate sounds, the balance of the entire event hovered delicately between the wildly farcical and the desperately tragic.

The group who had clustered in bright sunshine, exposed for a brief, intense hour to the extraordinary frailty of the human condition, retained their places. The sun moved lower in the sky and they sat on in the gentler light, relaxed and mellowing. Making no move, they were approached by volunteers for their orders for tea, and mixed grills, chips and roasted cheese were all carried out to them. In ones and twos they eventually made a chauffeur-driven return to cottages and council houses.

Fridays are the high-spot of the day-care week. Events such as the two described, proliferate on this day. Those visitors who persist, who accept membership of the day-care category, are party to incidents and events which invariably further the anticipation of increasing deterioration and death. In a rich variety of guises, staff draw them, in whatever comfort may be possible, from the east to the west end of the building. As they step out from front doorsteps into the cars of ready volunteers, they become passengers whose transience is to be very gently and carefully brought home to them.

Chapter Nine

Ageing and Death: The Continuing Challenge

Entry to Strathcarron Hospice introduces the interested outsider to an informal, carefully structured social context where relationships are quite evidently characterised by warmth and openness. Participant observation draws the researcher closer, into individual lives and deaths of the kind described in the last chapter. It sensitises her to underlying issues, such as the difficulties of managing a pervasive awareness of imminent death.

Earlier methodological discussion identified the relationship between researcher and informant as the source of anthropological knowledge. Insights into the way in which a particular quality of experience is generated stem from that relationship. In the course of fieldwork I entered both a hospice and a residential home for elderly people as a member of the dominant category of younger adults for whom death is not felt to be an imminent likelihood. In so doing I took on relationships with those who, through their closeness to death, are customarily hidden and kept at a distance in British society. By crossing this social and spatial boundary I was made aware of the transient nature of both my social identity and my physical self. As the last chapter showed, it is an awareness which, even in the practised care of a hospice, can be embraced only gradually and in a piecemeal, often painful fashion.

What I gained, therefore, is an understanding of the carefully differentiated nature of the relationship between members of the two social categories, 'the living' and 'the dying' – and the paradoxical fragility of individual membership of either of these two categories. The continuing challenge of ageing and death concerns the way in which that relationship is conceptualised and made manifest. As my field material shows, there prevails within contemporary British society an implicit commitment on the part of 'the living' to not only controlling but also giving care to 'the dying'.

This chapter explores the tension between these two dimensions of their relationship, showing the sometimes uneasy negotiation of power which prevails between them. The institutional structuring of social categories within the residential home provides an initial example of how individuals encountering death seek both to stress and to transgress the social categories, 'living' and 'dying', which distinguish them from one another.

Winnie Elliott, a resident of Highfield House, had been in sickbay for more than four months, categorised by staff as 'frail', 'likely to pop off soon'. When Jan, a care assistant of about twenty, entered the room Winnie said, 'I'm fed up'. 'Well, I am too, Winnie', replied Jan. 'Well, you took the job on, I didn't', answered Winnie. Sue held a clenched fist to Winnie's face and Winnie laughed.

This simple exchange of joke and counter-joke exemplifies a gentle wrangling over power which goes on continuously within Highfield House. Bedbound and alone Winnie, predictably, is fed up. Jan can do little to alleviate the situation. Jan jokingly claims to share Winnie's boredom, figuratively setting herself up as Winnie's equal – which in reality she is not. Yet implicitly the same fate may await her. Winnie jokingly blames Jan for taking on the job of caring for her, care upon which Winnie quite evidently depends. And yet Winnie suffers in her confinement behind bed bars. Finally Jan, powerless to terminate Winnie's suffering, offers a clenched fist, mockingly asserting a physical power which she has and yet cannot use, in the face of Winnie's joking rudeness. And Winnie laughs in the face of the mock aggression just as the dependent child laughs when tickled by its more powerful mother. At the end nothing has changed. They have played with the forms which constitute their situation and their relationship, but the episode has altered neither the constraints of Winnie's physical helplessness nor the limitations of the institution. Winnie has been able to claim a little attention and Jan has been able to make her laugh. By being rude to each other they have asserted the sense of closeness and intimacy which they have developed in the course of their extended relationship.

Condensed within this fleeting incident are many of the issues and paradoxes which lie unreconciled beneath the surface of institutional life. In unravelling this 'gentle wrangling over power' a tension between the concepts of care and of control becomes apparent. As I have suggested, this tension can be seen to permeate the wider society within which the residential home is set – and to materialise in the jokes, rationalisations and dilemmas which pattern everyday encounters between the carers of Highfield House and their dependent charges.

The example of Winnie Elliott shows one very elderly woman seeking to manage her own frailty within a social context where she finds herself dependent upon, and vulnerable to, the power of a controlling institution. She encounters the paradox of a system of care which has arisen out of a view of the world as being amenable to human control, and yet which addresses itself to uncontrollable, incurable forms of human deterioration.

It is this paradox which the Hospice Movement seeks to overcome. Its work represents a commitment to care which questions the hegemony of a curative medical model. And indeed, in seeking to transcend the boundaries through which death is kept at a distance from life, it also transcends many of the social boundaries, or hierarchies, through which power is organised within Western society. Nonetheless, while individual patients may be allowed maximal freedom, and indeed are referred to as the 'team leader' among a team of experts,[1] their care is administered through hierarchical channels of power which reflect the inherent inequalities of the wider social structures within which the Hospice is embedded.

Thus both Hospice and residential home share a common historical context within which the natural or material world has increasingly been seen as amenable to human control and dominance from the beginning of the sixteenth century onwards. It is within this context that medical skills, knowledge and technology have come to assume a powerful curative role vis a vis the human body. By the same token bodily or emotional suffering which proves resistant to medical control, in assuming an uncontrollable disordering aspect itself becomes powerful.

Bereavement counselling provides an example of the responses evoked by suffering within British society. While the notion that 'it helps to talk over problems with someone else' is commonly held to be true, bereaved individuals who approach Cruse-Bereavement Care are often very desperate to alleviate the painfulness of their own circumstances through some more immediate means.

Thus whilst there is an acknowledgement that talking and emotional expression such as crying may help, there is also the contrasting notion that problems have solutions which can be pursued in a linear fashion through the engaging of a strong will. To dwell repetitively upon apparently irresolvable despair is frequently given cultural and social discouragement. Similarly the detailed recounting and expression of painful emotional experience to its ultimate limits is not perceived as a forward-looking approach to problem solving. It is thus often only with time that the bereaved person recognises that the counsellor will listen, both intensively and extensively, to such talking – and that they will stay present throughout prolonged and powerful expressions of grief or anger. Doubts nonetheless often remain within the bereaved person as to the efficacy of such a process and the meandering back and forth between a figurative 'normality' and a literal despair tends to prevail.

In addition, these doubts are not confined to the individual suffering a bereavement. The training of counsellors involves challenging the idea that 'help' means resolving or removing problematic emotional pain. In place of this assumption, an awareness of the spiral path into and through suffering is cultivated. The counsellor is seen as one who accompanies rather than acts upon the bereaved person. Nonetheless, despite training, the idea that 'helping' means solving or removing suffering can be deeply embedded, and the counsellor's more passive accompanying role often brings with it a feeling of discomfort or uneasiness. Thus counsellors can discover themselves diverting their energies towards more practical problems such as health or housing. Fieldnotes reveal my own experience of these feelings when first making a visit in the role of Cruse counsellor:

Mrs Crawford looked solemn, puffy-faced and slightly wet-eyed. She sat me on the end of her sofa, taking a chair close by herself. Perching on the corner of her chair she leant forwards towards me. Very quickly she told me that her husband had died in November. She'd spent time with her daughter in Sussex but when she was at home she felt very lonely and depressed. She thought I might be able to help her. She told me this hastily and urgently, large wet eyes close to mine. I felt somewhat overcome by this directness. Much as I had feared, here was someone desparate for a lifeline – one I felt both obligated to offer yet very aware of not being able to produce. I had to struggle against my nervousness and self-consciousness in these new surroundings - and to guard particularly against just not taking in what she was saying.

After Mrs Crawford's initial description of events and emotions, I began to feel anxious that my passive and self-consciously sympathetic listening was proving a disappointment to Mrs Crawford. I felt I had to hold back my few pieces of advice and comfort for later and not plough into her grief too fast. She leant back in her chair, talking in an apparently deflated and less urgent style. I felt I must seem so much younger than she was – and so evidently not in possession of any profound resolution to her misery.

The idea that 'problem solving' is a cultural concept specific to the West is echoed in an example used by Lakoff and Johnson in their discussion of metaphor (1980:143-144). In the statement 'the solution of my problems' the word 'solution' was (mis)understood by an English-speaking Iranian student to refer metaphorically to the chemical process of temporarily dissolving substances (problems) in liquid, out of which other substances (problems) would be precipitated. Viewed from such a (non-Western) perspective Lakoff and Johnson argue that 'Problems would be part of the natural order of things rather than disorders to be 'cured'.

Using the term 'culture' in a limited sense, to refer only to traditional societies, Illich too makes a distinction between Western and more traditional responses to pain. He writes 'Culture makes pain tolerable by integrating it into a meaningful system, cosmopolitan civilization detaches pain from any subjective or intersubjective context in order to annihilate it'(1975:93).

THE COMMITMENT TO CARE

While both the Hospice and the residential home for elderly people have emerged within the context of the Western view of a controllable natural world, there stands alongside this world view a concept of care which can be traced to early Christian origins. In opposition to the analytic, rule-bound mode of thought through which scientific knowledge and, ultimately, dominance of the material world was developed, the Christian doctrine of all-encompassing love takes as its pre-condition the transgressing of rules, divisions or categories. As we saw, when Fabiola, the Roman matron, became a Christian disciple of St Jerrome she extended the boundaries of Roman hospital provision to include not just warriors, gladiators and slaves, but also beggars, orphans, pilgrims, and sick and dying people. In the spirit of Christian love, she transgressed both social and political boundaries, and created one of the earliest hospices. The New Testament Gospels offer repeated examples of the expression of such a concept of love. Indeed they are grounded in the belief that:

> God so loved the world that he gave his only begotten Son to the end that all who believe in him should not perish but have everlasting life.[2]

In earthly form his son Jesus Christ fosters the concept of unconditional love through the parables of the Good Shepherd who cares for the frailest of his flock[3], the Good Samaritan who leaves his chosen path to care for the sick[4], and the father who extends unconditional love to his undeserving prodigal son.[5] This theme is echoed throughout the gospels, both in the teachings and in the life of Christ.

Within contemporary Western culture 'care', grounded in a Christian concept of love, and 'control', grounded in a post-medieval scientific view of the natural world, co-exist in uneasy proximity. In a secular, state-run institution such as the residential home, 'care' is offered within and through structured channels of control. Just as religious belief and practice are regarded in this context as matters of individual choice, so 'care' is offered in the form of individual acts of humour, generosity or ingenuity. Remaining always in tension with one another, control, as a limiting, dehumanising practice, readily evokes the cultural requirement for care – and care, a form of love which brooks no discriminations or constraints, rapidly brings exposure to 'problems' and the cultural requirement that they be controlled.

THE POWER OF THE WEAK

As I will show, ageing in residential care is managed not only in the face of, but also by means of the tension between these two modes of thought and practice, 'care' and 'control'. Thus Winnie and Jan manage their respective experiences of ageing through a gentle wrangling which brings care and control together in quietly humourous ways. Confined behind bedbars Winnie is committed to care; uniformed in institutional space Jan is committed to caring for her. Both individuals are subject to the limitations of the human body and the controlling structures of the residential home. While Winnie's figurative 'rudeness' and Jan's figurative 'violence' readily evoke the literal disorder which might ensue if individual feelings were given free rein, the sense of daring is confined, quite safely, to the realm of the imagination. It is a matter of laughter rather than subversion. Their finely tuned balancing of care and control can be contrasted with the disorder precipitated by Annie Crosby, an individual whose choices, while minimal, were less restricted than Winnie's. Her case study, which follows, illustrates the need for care at a time in life when disability cannot be eradicated by medical control. Though admission to 'care' might have distanced the disordering manifestations of Annie's dependency, she was resistant to the forms of control which the residential home represents. Her temporary presence within the home therefore proved to be a powerful and disruptive force.

Annie Crosby, a wealthy woman in her eighties, had recently

returned to her birthplace in the North East to be near her sisters. Supported by the home help service, she lived alone in a modern flat, one which she found much to her liking. As one of the first five women to graduate from a University in this region in 1918, Annie had many treasured associations with the area. Her education remained a useful resource as fairly serious reading kept her occupied and alert. Nonetheless, despite her assets, Annie found herself in a socially marginal and isolated position. She was widowed and childless, a hysterectomy having followed the stillbirth of her one baby. She told me:

> 'Once you lose your partner, if you have no family, the world drops around you, drops completely.'

Her widowhood she described as 'seven lost years'. Grief marred her visits to old friends in Lancashire, her former married home. Arthritis curtailed her outings to old University haunts in the North East. As she explained:

> 'I'm very proud. I don't like to be an exhibition.'

In addition the ties with her sisters which drew her back to the North East were no longer viable to the extent she would have liked.

Annie was offered 'care' in Highfield House between 10 a.m. and 4 p.m. on several days of the week with a view to her eventual admission as a permanent resident. Both the authorities and Annie herself had perceived the difficulties of her marginal social situation. In her possible admission to residential care, to a space which is physically, socially and structurally marginal to the rest of society, lay an acknowledgement of her situation.

Being sufficiently independent to retain her freedom Annie, the 'day-care', viewed the implications of admission with scepticism. She said:

> 'I've discovered that I could never live in this. I would get so I was sitting about doing nothing, or I would go potty... some of the residents drive me mad. They never have a book or a paper... if I couldn't read I would die.'

It was a case of 'Abandon Hope all Ye who enter Here', she'd told a friend. Such vehemence was rare from settled residents. Lacking choices or alternatives, they were more veiled in their allusions to the systems of control through which their 'care' was administered.

In clinging to a social role which she could no longer sustain Annie, and the care staff, became forcibly aware of the uncontrolled processes of her physical deterioration. As loneliness and physical handicap dogged her attempts at independence Annie became increasingly low-spirited. In caring, intermittently, for Annie, care staff were exposed to an unpleasant smell, the product of her mild incontinence and her restricted washing habits. This they resented strongly. Had Annie been admitted to permanent care the deterioration of her body would have been brought under control.

Annie hesitated. She was bathed rather precipitately one afternoon, her soiled clothes removed for cleaning and, as another resident said:

'... they put other people's clothes on her after her bath.'

Bathing Annie brought staff forcibly into contact with uncontrolled physical deterioration. The personal smell of permanent residents is controlled through regular baths, each one carefully logged into a record book. Annie's uncontrolled smell offended – not only on a physical but also a cultural level which is specific to parts of the North East. As members of mining communities with an economic base involving unavoidable contact with dirt, many care staff perceive personal hygiene as a sign of highly valued respectability. They stress that right up until death, their mothers:

'... kept themselves spotlessly clean, spotlessly clean.'

Annie's smell confronted staff with the literal reality of old age. Only by drawing on their knowledge of her wealth could they dispel the power of uncontrolled physical deterioration. In implicit contrast with their poor but spotlessly clean mothers, they described Annie's 'dirtiness' in class-based terms. Thus:

'That's always the way. You find its the rich people that are the dirtiest. I can see Annie just sitting by the fire all day, eating – like a little pig'.

Annie, for her part, finding herself both offered and given a bath on the same afternoon, was also forcibly confronted with her own physical frailties and the dependency which she tried indefinitely to postpone. In a similar vein to the staff, Annie too invoked a cultural perspective, transforming a threat to her personal independence and power into a question of bad manners. In an implicit allusion to the staff's working class origins she described the rapid offering and then giving of the bath on the same afternoon as 'not etiquette'. As the baths continued to be given, she preserved her lady-like status by treating the Matron's apparent bad manners as an eccentricity:

'I'm tickled to death about these baths', she said. 'I wash down every day at home'.

Avoiding outright rudeness, she told me guardedly that she:

'... didn't care for the Matron.'

Annie's class-based statements are a powerful affirmation of her own past independence. 'Bad manners' is the cultural concept through which she refers to the systems of control which threaten that independence. The distance which she places between her own social background and that of the staff can be seen as a metaphoric strategy which obliquely allows her to resist the threatening systems of control through which her dependencies might be cared for.

Annie was never admitted to Highfield House and remained uneasily peripheral to both the outside world and the institution itself. To her, permanent residence in 'care' represented a yielding of control which prefigured an ultimate loss of personal control at death. Yet in remaining uncared for Annie's position in the wider society became increasingly tenuous. As she was aware, her growing physical deterioration made her prominent, 'an exhibition', whenever she went out into the town.

While both Winnie and Annie represented challenges to the controlling care of institution, Annie's more effective attempts were made at greater personal cost. In resisting control she remained uncared for. Uncared for she was vulnerable to suffering which might get rapidly out of control. Already under control, Winnie's gentler challenge provoked care in the form of figurative violence – the clenched fist. Remaining at the periphery of the system, an involuntary embodiment of uncontrolled physical frailty, Annie provoked literal, if oblique, verbal violence from the staff. With respect to the institution, much of Annie's remaining power resided in her weakening body, one which lay disturbingly beyond the limits of curative medical techniques and could now only be cared for.

POWERHOLDERS

The cases of Winnie Elliott and Annie Crosby show individual residents seeking to manage their own ageing process in a context where care is offered within and through structured channels of control. Within this secular, state-run institution caring itself is manifested in individual acts of kindness or humour. It is in this way that a balance is brought about between the limiting, dehumanising practice of control, and unconditional, loving care which brooks no discriminations or constraints. In the person of Mrs Chapman, the Matron of Highfield House, the juxtaposition of caring individuality and membership of a controlling category is marked. Structurally powerful, she manipulates the relationship between these two possibilities in order to exercise control. Structurally powerless residents struggle to retain individual control by resisting institutional categorisation – whilst at the same time avoiding the prominence accorded to disordered and deteriorating individuals and, additionally, the final individualising of death.

My own 'admission' to Highfield House was the point at which my contact with Mrs Chapman was most extensive. The following extracts from fieldnotes illustrate the powerful way in which she is able to move between the roles of 'Matron' and 'the Matron', from a caring individual to the representative of a controlling category:

> Mrs Chapman seemed very open to my interests and spoke of 'really getting to know the residents' – working with the care assistants was the only way. I would get attached to the residents by bathing, dressing and caring for them – they would talk to me, tell me all their secrets, all their problems. I could also sit with the staff and find out how things were for them. She said she had a very good staff – it would be strange for me at first but it was the only way. She said I would really enjoy working in the home. (Highfield House fieldnotes. Day one).

> Mrs Chapman eventually appeared in blue mules and a peasant- style blue crimplene dress. She spoke to me in her office in a self-revealing, forceful and yet chatty style. She showed a very real love and fascination for old people. She gave me her views on the lack of discipline in young people, on the battles she'd had with families, on character in the young – she said she could tell within a month if a Job Creation youngster would make something of their lives. In her story-telling she stared at me, re-enacting the aggressive parts she'd taken before with me as her new victim. Yet she threw in confidences about the state of her health, her need to unwind, her sensation of coldness despite the sun. She told anecdote after anecdote about her residents. One old lady had refused an operation, wanting to be left to die. Mrs Chapman had taken her in a wheel-chair on a tour of the home on Christmas Eve and had promised her a visit to 'somewhere special' (Mrs Chapman's flat in the home). There they had drunk sherry together – got tipsy – and old Molly was happy. She died in January after only one day in bed.

> There was the story of a fight with a resident's daughter-in-law. Mrs Chapman had suggested that residents have only one plant in their rooms and have the rest out in the public areas of the home (owing to rotting of the window sills). The daughter-in-law had put in a complaint to County Hall without telling Mrs Chapman. Mrs Chapman had her in her office, told her off, and refused to allow her to visit the old man in his bedroom

again. A similar battle had occurred over a china cabinet and Mrs Chapman had threatened to put it out into the grounds. Betty May, a resident, was meanwhile hovering at the office door and Mrs Chapman got her in and, with much hugging, hand-holding, touching of clothes and hair, she joked with Betty May, refusing to seriously discuss ninety-four year old Betty's complaints, keeping her face very close to Betty's the whole time. Mrs Chapman had made much of hygiene and cleanliness, talking of the dirty marks on residents' clothes as they passed her door. She said old people had dirty habits and had to be encouraged to be clean and tidy. She also complained about poor treatment in the local hospital, residents returning from there with bedsores etc. She felt that standards had declined seriously in the hospital -she had even seen a ward sister wearing Jesus sandals. Mrs Chapman had been a nurse herself at one time. She said that she had done every job there was in the home – right down to cleaning out the toilets. (Highfield House fieldnotes. Day two).

These two encounters with Mrs Chapman reveal almost every dimension of her power. What I was offered on first admission promised to fulfill all my hopes for extensive access to what went on in the home. What is significant is the prescriptive manner of the telling – how I was going to feel about residents; how they were going to respond to me; the nature of the strangeness and of the enjoyment I was going to experience.

On second entry Mrs Chapman met me at her desk, her official, powerful position within the home, whilst dressed in the most informal manner. I was made to wait and then informed of her views on discipline in young people, dirty habits in old people and assertiveness in middle-aged people – her residents' relatives. Anecdotal material lends substance to what is essentially a declaration of her intent and suggests that she speaks from a great breadth of personal experience. Similarly, the verbal declaration I was given was complemented by a performance or demonstration of how to control and how to care – as in her management of Betty May's complaints. Finally, she fragments her entire conversation with confidences and asides about current difficulties in her personal state of health and well-being.

Barthes in *The Blue Blood Cruse* shows how press revelations of the 'human' face of royalty underscore their elitist status:

> ...if one is amused by a contradiction, it is because one supposes its terms to be very far apart. In other words, kings

have a superhuman essence, and when they temporarily bor-
row certain forms of democratic life, it can only be through an
incarnation which goes against nature, made possible through
condescension alone. To flaunt the fact that kings are capable
of prosaic actions is to recognize that this status is no more
natural to them than angelism to common mortals, it is to
acknowledge that the king is still king by divine right.
(1973:32-33)

In her role as 'the Matron', Mrs Chapman could reduce a
domestic to an entire lunch-time's weeping, and could inspire care
staff to pull me bodily out of her sight when I smoked a visible but
illicit cigarette in the staff room. I would argue that just as the
'prosaic actions' of kings underscores their divinity, so the human
weaknesses revealed by Mrs Chapman rendered her authority yet
more impenetrable. One further example from fieldnotes illustrates
the approach which she deployed so frequently. On this occasion she
was speaking to me in the foyer after approximately two months
fieldwork:

Matron pursued her usual themes of how 'canny' the residents
were and what a good staff she has – she relies on their close
contact with residents to give her feed-back on how everyone
is doing. She went on to talk about her own state, how she
wasn't feeling herself – she thought she was going through the
change – her hormones were unbalanced and she takes a long
time to pull herself round in the mornings. She feels she has the
support of her staff – she can 'bawl them out' and they still
support her. She says she tries to be understanding with the
residents when they are being difficult – they do have a lot of
problems. She said that a resident's house was up for sale and
the contents scattered just recently – the resident had had all
her parent's possessions in the house and was very emotional
about it afterwards. Matron said she felt really upset for her
and went up and had a good cry about it in the evening. This
chat – so sudden and so compelling – seems a classic example
of a particular kind of exercise of power. The coolness at other
times is suddenly dispelled and a sense of a 'special' intimacy
is given as a lot of personal information is revealed.

Throughout my entire period of fieldwork Mrs Chapman continued to move back and forth between the roles of 'Matron' and 'the
Matron'. Seemingly aloof and inaccessible when in her office, she
would go and come at random within the rigidly structured times
and spaces of bed-sitting rooms, dining-room and kitchen. Her

starched, all-white uniform dress contrasted with care staffs' more informal blue-checked dresses or overalls. It also contrasted strongly with her appearances in elegant and often close-fitting dresses worn together with mules or carpet slippers. Again her choice of clothing, like her appearance, was unpredictable. Furthermore, in its apparently very idiosyncratic mix of official, formal and informal categories of style, the Matron's dress accurately reflects her ambiguous position within the institution. As she moves within the home – her domestic and her work place – she embodies not only the informal, domestic task of caring but also the official, hierarchised processes of control. Unlike care staff who came into the home to work according to a rigid rota of shifts, Mrs Chapman, like the residents, lived in the home and her on and off duty periods were not easily distinguishable. By contrast, my own less than rigid comings and goings were often a topic of conversation with staff. While my working presence represented nothing more than an extra, often superfluous, pair of hands, any deviations I made from a roughly formulated personal timetable always invited enquiry.

In summary the Matron is so located as to exercise indirect yet maximal control over the processes of ageing/dying both through her access to medical resources and through her control of care staff continuously involved in the management of these processes. Through the personal style of Mrs Chapman, the authority vested in the role of 'Matron' is articulated in particular ways. The tense ambiguous relationship between caring and controlling, which care staff experience, is clarified and indeed made use of by Mrs Chapman in her continuous and unpredictable transition between a caring and a scaring mode of behaviour, from the role of 'Matron' to the other role of 'the Matron'.

IMPLICIT STRUCTURES OF CONTROL: STRATHCARRON'S REVEALING MASQUERADE

The creation of hospices, such as Strathcarron, can be seen as an attempt to confront the tension between the conflicting concepts of care and control. Whilst the controlling, rule-bound regime of Highfield House serves to maintain an ever-crumbling separation between 'life' and 'death', Strathcarron offers care to those who are making a quite explicit transition from life to death. As shown, this endeavour is pursued through the creation of a symbolic 'life'/'death' continuum. In that the boundary between 'life' and 'death' continues to prevail within the wider society, the transforming or muting of established categories/boundaries requires that they be raised as a conscious focus for attention. Thus the Hospice, in seeking to transcend such boundaries must formulate deliberate strategies. By seeking to blur the divisive boundaries which structure gender relations, professional and social class systems, and religious affiliations in British society, an attempt is being made to create a sense of movement or flow at all levels, and thereby symbolically incorporate and reintegrate each aspect of the past, present and future of the dying individual. In this way, the relationship between 'the living' and 'the dying' can be more easily be understood as not only caring, but also as fluid and less rigidly defined.

The following fieldmaterial exemplifies the implementation of such strategies. Closer analysis highlights some of the difficulties which can inhibit this approach. Individuals, such as Annie Crosby, who contemplate a life 'in care' at Highfield House, will receive that care through implicit, structured channels of control. Individuals diagnosed as terminally ill who are encountering death in Strathcarron Hospice, are given an explicit offer – of care and of control. That control is not, however, an aspect an asymetrical distribution of power as in the social hierarchy of Highfield House. Rather, it is one aspect selected from the controlling power of medical technology – that is to say, pain control. Technological control and Christian care are thus drawn upon simultaneously, but in careful distinction from one another.

The discussion of field material to follow takes a second look at the August morning's slide show which was screened to patients on one of Strathcarron's wards. Displaying themselves in humourous, and less than dignified guises, the staff stage a performance which allows patients to witness the transcending of divisions of status in the course of the Christmas party. Closer examination also reveals this hospice event to be an implicit play upon its internal professional, religious and gender divisions – and the dynamics of power which link them. When Strathcarron's 'caring team' let their hair down, their normally hidden, hierarchical relationships with one another become evident in a humourously overdramatised performance. This example reveals the complexities and ambiguities of managing a caring team, who offer unconditional support to the patient as a whole being, within a wider society where care and control are more commonly encountered in often deliberately blurred conjunction. As already argued, the ease with which Hospice care has been assimilated into British society rests upon its appropriation of traditional forms or sources of power. Familiar professional, social and gender-based hierarchies must be seen as an important dimension of this readily accepted cultural constellation.

The slide show offered to hospice patients who come into and out of the building for day-care was staged in one of the hospice wards, thereby providing entertainment for the bedbound – and a gentle introduction to the context of dying for the more fit. Its content is a figurative representation of a team of doctors, nurses, administrators and domestic staff who seek to care for dying people outside more traditional, hierarchical structures of power. They appeared in the Christmas party guises of Santa, the Pied Piper, two large fairies, Worzel Gummidge, a giant baby, and Buttons.

In this small institution where patients of all categories share a single day-care room, the staff – doctors, domestics, nurses and volunteers – also work together in close proximity. Address is invariably by Christian name and a joking, caring intimacy prevails. Flowery collars and aprons provide an attractive relief to the clinical white of nurses' uniforms. In their varying colours they also distinguish rank or category. Although such distinctions reveal a division of labour, the concept of a 'caring team' predominates. The informal scattering of furniture in the one staff lounge and dining-room is seen to mitigate against an hierarchical distribution of status. Nonetheless hints emerge of an implicit structure, entirely in keeping with the hierarchical system of social class and gender division in the wider society. Thus, in what one of the doctors described as the 'high nonsense' of Christmas-time, implicit systems and hidden tensions come to light.

For example, Sally, in a blue dress with white daisy-chain collar, is Matron. Tall, slim and girlish, she possesses a soft-voiced, intelligent sensitivity, very much in contrast with images of large-bosomed, officious Matrons. When nurses and volunteers adopted 'Sally' as their term of address for her, the Matron chose to stress her position of dominance in the 'caring team' and insisted on the use of her title in the public spaces of the hospice. Sally of the private morning meetings with doctors, home-care sisters and social worker, moves out into the public space of nursing and domestic staff as 'the Matron'.

Similarly an implicit social organisation of space reveals the continuous emergence of the social hierarchies of the outside world. Thus the private spaces of the nursing and domestic staff are a bathroom and a backstep, away at the west end of the building, tucked behind the white board fence which conceals a revolving washing-line and the external entry to the mortuary. Snatched smoking and illicit snacking on hospice food takes place here. On her

break from hoovering and washing-up, one of the domestic staff
squatted on the backstep and observed:

> 'Its like Upstairs Downstairs. The elite upstairs in the lounge
> and us down here.'

An explicit welcome awaits her in the staff lounge upstairs at the east
end of the building. Like all domestic staff, she accepts this welcome
only occasionally and with diffidence, preferring a hard-backed
chair away behind the upholstered furniture in the centre of the
room. Her grudging deference to an 'elite' finds an echo in the very
respectful deference of volunteers to medical staff. Voluntary recep-
tionists at the stairwell switchboard swop schoolgirl shock/horror
stories of cutting off senior staff's phone calls and give hand-over-
mouth accounts of their appearances on the balcony above their
heads.

Conformity to such a distribution of status remains implicit as an
aspect of the 'staff' role within the hospice. Made visible only in the
use of private spaces or through transgression, the hierarchical
structuring of power is scarcely perceptible in the gentle banter
which pervades a public space such as the reception area.

Conformity to the doctrines of Christianity is another somewhat
ambiguous aspect of the 'staff' role within the hospice. Though the
institution grew primarily out of five years work by members of a
Baptist church in Stirling, care is taken not to impose its Christian
foundation inappropriately among patients. There is little by way of
prominent Christian iconography in the public spaces of the building and the short morning service, held in the day-care room before
visitors arrive, is attended voluntarily by staff. Patients in the wards
can listen in on headsets but only if they choose to do so. Like the
hierarchical structuring of status, the assumption of a commitment
to Christian belief among staff remains an implicit aspect of relationships within the hospice. The day-care sister had taken up her
post somewhat later than other staff members. Though her relationships with other staff are close and easy, she sometimes voices
reservations about the predominance of a Christian 'emphasis' in
many areas of hospice life. As a non-Christian she feels the lack of
scope for expressing adherence to other belief systems.

As an additional undercurrent to issues of professional/social
status and religious affiliation, there also prevails the asymmetric
distribution of power and status between men and women which is
common to the wider society. Those who fill the roles of doctor,
administrator, Chaplain and chef are men. With few exceptions,
those filling the roles of Matron, social worker, home- and day-care

sister, nurse, clerical worker, domestic and volunteer are all women. While single women in their thirties or early forties fill the higher status positions of Matron, social worker and day-care sister, it is married women with children who predominate. The skills they have acquired in child-care and domestic management are put to use in their role as the institution's 'Front Women'. Downstairs, in wards and reception, their unassuming, empathetic patience and warmth prefaces the more high-powered medical and administrative resources of the male staff above.

Issues and conflicts of this kind remain carefully submerged within the much-discussed and highly-valued concept of the 'caring team'.

'They're a great bunch'
said the Administrator as he threw a pebble up against the lounge window where most staff take lunch-time coffee. The 'high non-sense' of occasions such as the Burns Night supper and Christmas party is seen as an explicit representation of an egalitarian community. A doctor described how a whole range of individuals have 'gelled' in this community where humour 'bubbles up all the time' and all must be prepared to 'have their leg pulled'.

The occasion of the slide-show was an invitation for patients whose current fear and suffering is managed through the skills of the caring team, to laugh for a second time at the antics of a staff upon whom they depend. What was exposed to them as a titillating behind-the-scenes glimpse of the staff at play, can be seen as a representation of a quite different kind.

In making their choices of costume, staff drew on the associations of a range of stock characters in a larger-than-life re-creation of their implicit relationships with one another. That the medical director should play Santa would seem to go without saying. He is both the head of the medical team whose skills are accorded greatest status, and also the primary worker in establishing the hospice. Cloaked and bearded in the guise of Santa, this rather reserved man moved into a prominent, central space as the airborne deliverer of magical goods from another realm. In the depths of winter, close to the end of the year, he is the Father who brings the child its longed-for toy and condemns any bad behaviour.

Many aspects of the Director's relationship with those who come to die in the hospice find overt expression in the role of Santa. These include his benign and fatherly power to discuss, decide and to dispense drugs on their behalf; the respect and gratitude which patients feel towards him; the implicit moral and religious framework through which he advises and orders a patient's care. In comparison with nurses, he is relatively elusive as far as patients are concerned. In private, and at times in public, he is ready to offer not only a drug regime and medical care but also frank criticism. Always addressed as 'Dr ...', his presence is sought after and his advice heeded. Slightly incredulous laughter was provoked by one very ill and confused patient who summoned him by the title 'Uncle ...'.

Santa entered the party in the wake of Sally, the Matron, dressed as the Pied Piper. Again the associations of this piebald, villainous hero are expressive. Sally/Matron manages an ambiguous role as a sweet-voiced, daisy-chained carer who is also known to give 'rows' to all nursing and domestic staff for small transgressions such as working bare-legged.

Two other characters, much to the fore in all slides, were a pair of fairies. They were vast in black stockings, garish makeup and camisole tops. Unlike the Medical Director, physically concealed behind beard and cloak, a doctor and the administrator chose to reveal themselves very much in the flesh. Their stalwart masculinity was thus heavily emphasised in this earthily sexual parody of ethereal, whimsical feminine forms.

Female members of staff were seen in guises which reflected a lower status or less central position within the implicit hierarchy of the hospice. The home-care sister plays an independent and very responsible role in her more solitary work in the community. Nonetheless in 'team' meetings she is deferent to the medical staff, pursuing her own ends through persuasion. Though she too inverted her own gender, it was as Buttons, the low-status boy page. The very tall domestic who was reluctant to take up her place in the lounge entered as the giant helpless baby with dummy and nappy, crying for her 'Mammy' throughout the party. Margaret Owen, the non-Christian newcomer, ever slightly at odds with the peace and order of the hospice, appeared as Worzel Gummidge, the audacious outsider, the straw man-of-the-fields who wreaks havoc by moving into the flesh-and-blood world of human beings.

Thus in Christmas-time fancy dress the dissonant presence of hierarchichal structures of power is made evident in an over-determined, heavily-dramatised form – then to be transformed into a further, summer morning's diversion for yet more patients. When staff choose to 'let their hair down' by way of entertainment for patients, they are creating one more opportunity for patients to experience the transcending of category. And in their choice of disguise staff also, implicitly, re-affirm those structures through which a necessary sense of cultural continuity between the hospice and its wider social context is maintained.

The revealing masquerade is a powerful performance within which the tensions between care/equality and control/hierarchy are both heightened and transcended. Separating boundaries are both dramatically overstated and also humourously transcended or subverted.

In summary, the four examples selected from field material – Winnie Elliott, Annie Crosby, Mrs Chapman, and the hospice slide show, are alike in their densely patterned character, one which encompasses both the evocation and the disguise of the conflicting issues, care and control. Those empowered to care for both the weakening bodies and the needy selves of ageing and dying people find themselves in an uneasy encounter with the powerful evidence of physical deterioration and decay, conditions largely resistant to medical control. For all caring staff, self control and the control of others are complex and challenging issues. In both the residential home and the hospice controlled caring and careful control must be continuously maintained – lest they be transformed into uncontrolled, unmanageable caring or careless, callous control.

This chapter shows ageing and death to be a continuing challenge, one which is currently encountered through a sometimes uneasy tension between two modes of thought which have come to predominate within the West in the course of the last two thousand years. Accounts of insiders' experiences reveal the tension between these two grand themes being encountered, managed, and in part overcome, on a day-to-day level.

La Rochefoucauld's statement that 'neither the sun nor death can be looked at with a steady eye' is borne out repeatedly in these accounts (orig. 1678; 1967:13). Whether in the context of residential care, hospice care or bereavement, we have discovered individuals seeking both to make sense of, and to avoid, an inevitable exposure to human mortality. In seeking to foster an awareness of approaching death, institutions such as the Hospice take on a demanding task which requires both delicacy and courage, depending upon the varying needs of different individuals.

As the limitations of post-Cartesian rationality are acknowledged, so the demands placed upon health care workers become more onerous. Economic necessity has limited the growth of Hospice building, shifting emphasis increasingly towards the implementation of home-care services which carry its ideology even further into the community. Those who work in this more isolated setting, like those who take on the care of a dying relative at home, lack the protection afforded to individuals encompassed within the highly structured social categories of an institution such as Highfield House. Unconditional love, as manifested in concepts such as Hospice care of the whole person, brings with it exposure to human suffering and loss on bodily, spiritual and social levels. In a society where distancing and controlling boundaries remain pervasive, the needs of those willing to transcend such boundaries in either their professional or personal lives can remain unmet. If the growing status attributed to doctors during the eighteenth century lent the emergent middle classes a sense of control over their own mortality, that control has subsequently engendered the need to recreate a more accepting response to death during the second half of the twentieth century. The continuing challenge of death today demands that those willing to offer unconditional love in the form of caring accceptance must find acknowledgement of their own needs for care, both within and beyond professional and institutional boundaries. It is thus that death comes to challenge not only the way in which we age and die, but also the way in which we live.

In summary, the varied experiences of death which are here juxtaposed represent an account of the currently fluid, transitional nature of both practice and philosophy associated with the management of death. It is an account which not only documents the care of terminally ill people in two very different institutions, but which also seeks to elucidate the quality of experience associated with death in settings of this kind. The book itself is therefore both a commentary on and a contribution to the changes in practice and philosophy which it charts. Working within the context of a growing critique of strategies which ensure that death keeps its distance, the use of insider-oriented anthropological field methods represents a parallel challenge to the hegemony of a scientific, control-oriented approach to human experience. Thus the voices which speak both directly and indirectly through these pages have found their way via a methodological framework which transgresses the boundaries customarily required between the categories, 'researcher' and 'informant'.

Chapter One discusses ageist jokes, a form of humour echoed in the sexist and racist jokes which consolidate the distances and inequalities separating members of the dominant social categories, male, white, heterosexual, middle class, from members of subordinate social categories, female, black, homosexual, working class. Yet in reinforcing the distinctions between the social categories 'adult' and 'elderly', ageist humour also acknowledges a disturbing but inevitable fusion of these two categories, one which is possible only rarely in the areas of gender or race. Ultimately 'adulthood' and 'old age' are separable only temporally. Their social separation is a cultural construction of the flimsiest kind.

Just as the process of ageing challenges the culturally and socially constructed boundary between the categories 'adult' and 'elderly', so death renders the customary separation of 'researcher' and 'researched' untenable. As a focus for research, death can in no way be confined to, or contained within the experience of the informant alone. As the one certainty in the life of the researcher it represents a powerful link between her experience and that of the informant. It is a link which not only raises serious questions about the boundary between the researcher and their informants, but also one which challenges the traditional Western separation of the intellect and the emotions. As Fairhurst asserts, 'unpleasant aspects of doing research on the elderly, particularly those in hospitals, are inextricably linked with the notion of personal experience' (1981:97). Thus research among ageing, dying and bereaved people not only educates in a traditional intellectual sense, it also distresses, giving the researcher a taste of painful experiences which her future probably holds.

Social anthropology emerged in the last century as the study of the exotic 'other'. Whilst the cultural shock induced by participant observation in faraway settings can still be relied upon to provide a sense of 'otherness', the sustained process of interpreting field material involves the deeper insertion the researcher within their culturally and socially specific self. Reflexivity, the indivisibility of subject and object, is the hallmark of the anthropological approach. From the early 1970s fieldwork has moved closer to home for many Western anthropologists. There has been a shift of focus from tribe to category. With this shift has come an increasingly explicit discussion of the emergence of anthropological knowledge from out of the relationship between researcher and informant. Thus the reflexivity engendered through the anthropological study of the exotic Other is now raising broad methodological questions for research within the social sciences generally. This book makes a connection between the post-Cartesian scientific world view, which informs the cure-oriented medical model of human life, and the continuing value attached to the notion of 'objectivity' in social science research, where the connection between self and other is rigorously controlled. Changes in the way in which death is being managed have focussed on the need to reinstate the currently severed connections between life and death, in order that death shall regain its human dimension. In charting these changes, the present study has used methods which similarly stress rather than repress the connections between researcher and informant. The resulting knowledge of the quality of experience associated with death must therefore be understood to have arisen out of an intersubjective dialogue between members of these two categories.

If the relationship between researcher and informant provides the primary source of subsequent anthropological knowledge, the question of how that final knowledge is actually produced must also be addressed. The present volume comprises two complementary halves, the first being of a broad ranging, theoretical nature, the second offering very detailed ethnography. The meaning of material gathered through participant observation becomes apparent only as a result of a movement back and forth between the two; in Geertz's words, a 'tacking back and forth' between everyday immediacies and the over-arching concepts which frame them (1977:482). While intimate involvement with experiences associated with death is a necessary dimension of fieldwork, that involvement does not, of itself, provide an understanding of how those experiences came into being. As Geertz asserts, 'The ethnographer does not, and in my opinion, largely cannot, perceive what his informants perceive' (1977:482). Ethnographic material illuminates only when set within the context of larger bodies of theory, that theory being in part the symbolic capital of the insider, in part the property of the Western anthropologist.

Thus the first half of this book comprises accounts of the management of death in contemporary, historical and cross-cultural settings, ranging from healing and funerary ritual, through to media representations and bereavement counselling. Through each of these accounts key debates concerning the question of meaning were raised. Central is the profound challenge to the existence of meaning itself which any death represents. The body of anthropological work addressed to ritual allows insights into the ways in which human beings have sought to incorporate death within the broader spectrum of meanings through which their experience gains coherence. Using a range of cross-cultural examples, the circular relationship between death ritual and other key areas of life within any particular society is revealed. Thus the relationship between life and death implicit within any one example of death ritual can be seen to reflect other cultural and social relationships, such as those to do with marriage arrangements, ethnicity, and outsiderhood. These primary cultural and social concerns are themselves re-stated in dramatised, ritual forms at the time of a death. For an anthropologist a funeral can be a decisive moment in their unravelling of the beliefs and values of a particular society.

Having explored the structural and thematic congruence between death ritual and other aspects of cultural and social life, the question of how meaning is apprehended still remains. As Moore and Myerhoff (1977) assert, the essentially constructed nature of any ritual is something which must be most strenuously masked in its unfolding. That which is created must be experienced as that which is given. Ritual knowledge is intrinsically holistic, entirely beyond verification, and usually presented in the form of postulates. A careful appraisal of the work of Geertz, Turner, and Ricoeur allowed for a more detailed account of the process through which power accrues to ritual forms such as black ribbons, wreaths, candles, crosses. As was shown, ritual forms can be seen as concrete embodiments of a society's key organising metaphors, the images which in poetry might be used metaphorically, but in ritual are presented literally.

The second half of the book provides an account of how such processes take place. It takes the reader into two of the non-ordinary spaces within which death is framed in contemporary Western society. What we encounter there is suffering which falls outside the controlling cure-oriented medical model. In the residential home for elderly people, space and time are manipulated in such a way that the approaches of death are masked and the illusion of homely independence is fostered. Thus the limitations of the medical model, its inability to grant immortality or even prolonged vitality, are disguised. Within this framing of institutional time and space, residents offer resonant verbal and bodily resistance in the form of apparently gentle yet barbed reminders of the imminence of their deaths.

In a similar fashion the ethnographic account of Strathcarron Hospice carries forward the earlier discussion of the grounding of the Hospice Movement in the early Christian offer of unconditional love, a form of hospitality which predates the rigorously controlled admissions procedures of contemporary hospitals. An exploration of the construction of time and space within a contemporary hospice reveals the complex social and symbolic processes through which the existing boundary between life and death is gradually being dismantled.

This book stems from extensive reflection upon three personal bereavements. In each case any profound awareness of death was inhibited by excluding hospital regulations, parental protectiveness, and unfamiliar ritual practices. I carried a sense of puzzlement about a personally remote event into the research for this book. I carry out of it a deepening sense of the intimate relationship between death and life, an awareness of the vulnerability which this relationship bestows upon every individual, and a commitment to acknowledging that vulnerability in the face of a still frightening and mysterious dimension of human existence.

Notes

Preface

1. Anthropology developed as a separate discipline in Great Britain towards the end of the nineteenth century. While both Edward Burnett Tylor and Sir James Frazer contributed significantly to its development (See Tylor, 1871 and Frazer, 1890), they drew on the accounts of travellers and colonial administrators, theorising about more traditional, non-European societies largely from a social evolutionary perspective. Only with the work of R. Radcliffe-Brown (1881-1955) and B. Malinowski (1884-1942) at the beginning of this century did the value of empirical study of living societies come to be understood. Thus Tylor and Frazer, in generating social theories on the strength of existing accounts of other societies, came to be known as 'armchair' anthropologists.
2. See the private field diary kept by Malinowski, published only posthumously (Malinowski, 1967).

Chapter One An Approach to the Field

1. See The Order for the Burial of the Dead. In *The Book of Common Prayer and Administration of the Sacraments ... according to the use of the Church of England.* (A.R. Mowbray), London. p.216.
2. Hertz makes this point, saying '... primitive peoples do not see death as a natural phenomenon: it is always due to the action of spiritual powers, either because the deceased has brought disaster upon himself by violating some taboo, or because an enemy has 'killed' him by means of spells or magical practices' (orig.1907; 1960:77).
3. See Bloch and Parry (1982).
4. 'Work and Organisation in Geriatric Wards'. Talk given in Newcastle Health Research Unit, October 1982.
5. See Thane (1983).
6. With the exception of 'Strathcarron Hospice', the names of all individuals and institutions have been changed in order to maintain confidentiality.

Chapter Two Boundaries between Life and Death

1. For example, mutual aggression persists between those of differing religious identities in Northern Ireland. In this context, the possibility, even probability, of a violent death is a known dimension of promoting one's own affiliation. Similarly, in South Africa, vulnerable black communities seek determinedly to subvert harshly imposed, and limited, white definitions of the meaning of being black. Again the high risk of violent death is seen to be part of the process of change.
2. Mortality Statistics: Review of the Registrar General on Deaths in England and Wales, 1985. DH1 No.17, p. 14. OPCS, HMSO, 1987.

3. Durham Advertiser. 27.10.78

4. Turner (1967: 93-111) uses the example of Ndembu rituals of initiation to point out that the symbolic use of aspects of the human body, blood and nakedness, connote not only growth as in menstruation and birth, but also death as in killing and the corpse.

5. 'Old People's Attitudes to Death in the Twentieth Century'. Paper given at the Society for the Social History of Medicine's spring day conference, 'Old Age'. Oxford, 12.5.84.

6. Newcastle Evening Chronicle. 29.9.79

7. Durham Advertiser. 5.10.78

8. Newcastle Evening Chronicle. 17.9.79

9. Newcastle Evening Chronicle. 1979

10. 'Bereavement in Childhood'. Talk given in the Fleming Hospital, Newcastle. Spring 1979.

Chapter Three Death Past and Present

1. 1959 - Cruse-Bereavement Care. 1969 - The Society of the Compassionate Friends.

2. Annual Abstract of Statistics. No.124. HMSO: London, 1988. p.35.

3. The Times Health Supplement. 13.11.81, p.4.

4. The Times Health Supplement. 13.11.81, p.4.

5. Nichols, K. 'Since Nobody's Perfect'. Guardian, Society Tomorrow. 4.5.83, p.13.

6. Bristol Cancer Help Centre, Grove House, Cornwallis Grove, Clifton, Bristol. The Centre's approach includes intensive counselling to promote positive thinking; relaxation; and a strict diet. Imagery techniques are used, involving the patient's capacity to fantasise that their own defence mechanisms are eating away a tumour.

7. See Chapter 1, note 2.

8. The Order for the Burial of the Dead. In *The Book of Common Prayer and Administration of the Sacraments ... according to the use of the Church of England.*(A.R. Mowbray: London), pp.213-216.

9. See Grossarth-Maticek (1980) whose longitudinal studies of cancer patients show that certain personality traits, such as rationality and anti-emotionality, greatly increase the risk associated with physical variables such as high blood pressure and smoking. Similarly Thomas (1976) found that people who die from cancer differed from their peers in retrospective analyses of personality. Samuel Epstein, Professor of Occupational and Environmental Medicine at the University of Illinois argues that between twenty and forty per cent of cancers are work-related. Industrial pollution and chemicals used in consumer products are additional sources of risk (Epstein 1979).

10. Occupational Mortality: Registrar General's Decennial Supplement, 1970-72, series DS no.1, OPCS, 1978.

11. Thus, for example, Strathcarron Hospice nurses working continuously with cancer patients were nonetheless startled to see the words 'Cancer Center' writ large on the side of an American hospital in a training video they were watching. (In America where the patient is also the customer, doctors give fuller information to avoid malpractice suits).
    Similarly, in the North East of England, 'Twilight Nurses' (district nurses who give terminal care in the home), report extreme reluctance on the part of relatives and some general practitioners to utter either the word 'cancer' or the word 'morphine'. So firmly is morphine associated with cancer pain that the husband of a cancer patient shredded the tell-tale medicine boxes, disposing of them in

plastic bags lest the dustman should make out the labels and gossip.

12. Terminal Care: report of a working group of the standing sub-committee on cancer of the standing medical advisory committee of the Central Health Services Council. Unpublished document presented to the Department of Health and Social Security in March, 1980.
13. C. Saunders, *Care of the Dying.* (Macmillan Journals Ltd.: London, 1976), p.6.
14. Mortality Statistics. Cause. DH2, No.12. HMSO.: London, 1985, pp. 6-7.

Chapter Four Setting the Stage for Death

1. See Ricoeur (orig.1975;1978), (1981).
2. See David Jenkins, 'Fairy-tales and the Church'. The Observer, 23.12.84, p.8.
3. 'Highfield House', a guide for residents. Durham County Council Social Services Department. Appendix C. While the guide's cover refers specifically to Highfield House, its eight enclosed pages are sent out, in appropriate covers, to all the homes in the city. Thus we see the pervasiveness of the strategy through which problematic, individual deterioration is subsumed within membership of a single, depersonalising category, 'resident'.

Chapter Five Keeping them Going: The Work of Care Staff

1. This chapter includes an abbreviated and amended version of my 'Cultural and social interpretations of 'dying' and 'death' in a residential home for elderly people in the North East of England' in Curare, 1985.

Chapter Six One Way Journeys: Residents' Experiences

1. This chapter includes abbreviated and amended versions of my 'Residential Care and the Maintenance of Social Identity' in Jefferys, 1988, and my 'Just a Song at Twilight' in Jerrome, 1983.
2. For example:
   The brightest star in the sky tonight
   Is our darling Mother saying goodnight.
   (Durham Advertiser, 2.12.78)

   A ray of sunshine came and went
   A precious gift was only lent.
   (Durham Advertiser, 2.2.79)

   If heaven is full of roses, pick a bunch for us
   Take them to our mother, Lord, and tell her they're from us.
   (Durham Advertiser, 5.10.78)

   You potter no more in your garden
   Down the path you no longer walk
   Because you are sleeping peacefully
   In the most beautiful garden of all.
   (Durham Advertiser, 2.2.79)

3. The National Assistance Act, 1948, Pt.III, Section 21, requires that residential care shall be provided 'for those in need of care and attention not otherwise available'.

Chapter Seven The Hospice Alternative

1. Carey, J. The Gentle Art of Dying. The Times Health Supplement, 4.12.81, p.12.
2. Field material describes the hospice as it was in 1983. Further changes have subsequently been carried out, the plans for which are discussed in Chapter

Eight.
3. There is one nurse to every 2.8 patients at any given time. See Strathcarron Hospice. Annual Report and Accounts for the year ending 31 December, 1981.

Chapter Eight Living with Death
1. In 1985 new sub-divided day care facilities were completed, and the hospice currently offers sixteen beds, two in single rooms, seven in one large room, four in another, and three in another.

Chapter Nine Ageing and Death: the Continuing Challenge
1. J. Carey, The gentle art of dying. The Times Health Supplement, 4.12.81, p.12.
2. The Gospel of St John, 3.16.
3. The Gospel of St John, 10.1f.
4. The Gospel of St Luke, 10,30f.
5. The Gospel of St Luke, 15.11f.

References

ARDENER, E., Introductory Essay. In E. Ardener (ed), *Social Anthropology and Language*: ASA Monographs 10. Tavistock: London, 1971.

ARIES, P., *Western Attitudes to Death from the Middle Ages to the Present*. Johns Hopkins University Press: Baltimore, 1974.

ARIES, P., *The Hour of our Death*. (Originally published in French by Knopf: Paris, 1978). Allen Lane, Penguin Books: Harmondsworth, 1981.

BARTHES, R., *Mythologies*. (Originally published in French by Editions du Seuil: Paris, 1957). Granada Publishing Ltd: London, 1973.

BERGER, J., *About Looking*. Writers and Readers Publishing Cooperative Ltd: London, 1980.

BERGER, J. and MOHR, J., *A Fortunate Man*. Writers and Readers Publishing Cooperative Ltd: London, 1976.

BLOCH, M. and PARRY, J. (eds). *Death and the Regeneration of Life*. Cambridge University Press: Cambridge, 1982.

BOAS, F. *The Mind of Primitive Man*. (Originally published 1911). Free Press Paperback: New York, 1965.

BOURDIEU, P., *Outline of a Theory of Practise*. (Originally published in French by Librairie Droz: Switzerland, 1972). Cambridge University Press, 1977.

BOURNE, S., *The Psychological Effects of Stillbirths on Women and Their Doctors*. Journal of the Royal College of General Practitioners, 16, 103-112.

CAPRA, F., *The Turning Point*. Wildwood House: London, 1982.

CANNADINE, D., 'War and Death, Grief and Mourning in Modern Britain'. In J. Whaley (ed), *Mirrors of Mortality*. Europa Publications Ltd: London, 1981.

CAREY, J., 'A Suitable Case for Treatment'. *The Times Health Supplement*, 13-11-81, p.14.

CLOUGH, R., *Old Age Homes*. Allen & Unwin: London, 1981.

DU BOULAY, J., 'The Greek vampire: a study of cyclic symbolism in marriage and death'. *Man*, XVII, 1982, 219-238.

ESSLIN, M., 'The Stage: Reality, Symbol, Metaphor'. In J. Redmond (ed), *Themes in Drama 4, Drama and Symbolism*. Cambridge University Press, 1982.

EPSTEIN, S.S., *The Politics of Cancer*. Anchor/Doubleday: New York, 1979.

EVERS, H., 'Care or custody ? The Experiences of Women Patients in Long-Stay Geriatric Wards'. In B. Hutter & G. Williams (eds), *Controlling Women*. Croom Helm: London, 1981.

FAIRHURST, E., 'A Sociological Study of the Rehabilitation of Elderly Patients in an Urban Hospital'. Unpublished doctoral thesis, University of Leeds, 1981.

FARIS, J.C., 'Occasions and "non-occasions"'. In M. Douglas (ed), *Rules and Meanings*. Penguin Books: Harmondsworth, 1973.

FEIFEL, H., (ed) *The Meaning of Death*. McGraw-Hill: New York, 1959.

FERNANDEZ, J.W., 'The Performance of Ritual Metaphors'. In J.D. Sapir & J.C. Crocker (eds), *The Social Use of Metaphor*. University of Pennsylvania Press: Philadelphia, 1977.

FORD, C., 'Dissecting the elderly: forging a sociological tool'. Synopsis of paper presented at British Society of Gerontology Annual Conference, Exeter, September, 1982.

FRAZER, J.G., *The Golden Bough*. (Originally published in 1890). Macmillan: New York, 1963.

FRISCH, M., *Tagebuch 1946-1949*. Suhrkamp Verlag: Frankfurt am Main, 1950.

GEERTZ, C., 'Religion as a cultural system'. In M. Banton (ed), *Anthropological Approaches to the Study of Religion*. ASA Monographs 3. Social Science Paperback: London, 1968a.

GEERTZ, C.,*Islam Observed. Religious Development in Morocco and Indonesia*. Yale University Press: New Haven,Conn., 1968b.

GEERTZ, C., *The Interpretation of Culture*. Hutchinson: London, 1975.

GEERTZ, C., 'From the Native's Point of View'. In J.L. Dolgin, D.S. Kemnitzer & D.M. Schneider (eds), *Symbolic Anthropology*. Columbia University Press: New York, 1977.

GILLIE, O., 'The 69-hour life of John Pearson'. *The Times Health Supplement*, 13-11-81, p.4.

GILLIE, O., 'Cash Shortages Limits Heart Transplants'. *The Sunday Times*, 30-9-84.

GLASER, B.G. and STRAUSS, A.L., *Awareness of Dying*. Aldine: Chicago, 1965.

GLASER, B.G. and STRAUSS, A.L., *Time for Dying*. Aldine: Chicago, 1968.

GORER, G., *Death, Grief and Mourning in Contemporary Britain*. Cresset Press: London, 1965.

GROSSARTH-MATICEK, R., 'Synergistic effects of cigarette smoking, systolic blood pressure and psychosocial risk factors for lung cancer, cardiac infarct and apoplexy cerebri'. *Psychotherapy and Psychosomatics*, 1980, 34, 267-272.

HAZAN, H., *The Limbo People. A Study of the Constitution of the Time Universe among the Aged*. Routledge, Kegan & Paul: London, 1980.

HERTZ, R., *Death and the Right Hand*. (Originally published in French in l'Annee Sociologique, 1907). Free Press: New York, 1960.

HINTON, J., 'The physical and mental distress of the dying'. *The Quarterly Journal of Medicine* (NS), 1963, 32, 1-21.

HINTON, J., *Dying*. Penguin Books Ltd: London, 1967.

HOBMAN, D., *The Social Challenge of Ageing*. Croom Helm: London, 1978.

HOCKEY, J., 'Death and Society'. Unpublished BA dissertation, University of Durham, 1978.

HOCKEY, J., 'Just a Song at Twilight: Residents' coping strategies expressed in musical form'. In D. Jerrome (ed), *Ageing in Modern Society*. Croom Helm: London, 1983.

HOCKEY, J., 'Cultural and Social Interpretations of "dying" and "death" in a residential home for elderly people in the North East of England'. *Curare*, Sonderband 4, 1985. (Sterben und Tod. Verhandlungen der 7. Int. Fachkonferenz Ethnomedizin; April, 1984)

HOCKEY, J., 'Residential Care and the Maintenance of Social Identity: Negotiating the Transition to Institutional Life'. In M. Jefferys (ed), *Growing Old in the Twentieth Century*. Routledge: London, 1989.

HUMM, M., 'Autobiography and Bellpins'. In V. Griffiths et al., *Feminist Biography 2: Using Life Histories*. Studies in Sexual Politics, University of Manchester: Manchester, 1987.

ILLICH, I., *Medical Nemesis: The Expropriation of Health*. Caldar & Boyars Ltd: London, 1975.

ISAACS, B. and NEVILLE, Y., *The Measure of Need in Old People*. Scottish Home & Health Department, HMSO: London, 1976.

JUST, R., 'Some problems for Mediterranean Anthropology'. *Journal of the Anthropology Society of Oxford*, 1978, 2, 81-97.

KAPFERER, B., 'First class to Maradana: secular drama in Sinhalese healing rites'. In S.F. Moore and B.G. Myerhoff (eds), *Secular Ritual*. Van Gorcum: Assen, 1977.

KUBLER-ROSS, E., *On Death and Dying*. Tavistock: London, 1970.

KUBLER-ROSS, E., *Death - the Final Stage of Growth*. Prentice Hall: New York. 1975.

LAKOFF, G. and JOHNSON, M., *Metaphors We Live By*. University of Chicago Press, 1980.

LA ROCHEFOUCAULD, F., *Maximes*. (Originally published in 1678 under the title *Reflexions Morales*). Editions Garnier Frères: Paris, 1967.

LEVI-STRAUSS, C., *Tristes Tropiques*. (Originally published in French by Plon: Paris, 1971). Jonathan Cape: London, 1973.

LEWIS, E., 'Mourning by the family after a stillbirth or neonatal birth'. *Archives of Disease in Childhood*, 1979, 54, 4, 303.

MacDONALD, B. with RICH, C., *Look Me in the Eye: Old Women, Ageing & Ageism*. The Women's Press: London, 1984.

MALINOWSKI, B., *A Diary in the Strict Sense of the Term*. Routledge and Kegan Paul: London, 1967.

MARTINS, H., 'Introduction Tristes Durées'. *Journal of the Anthropological Society of Oxford*, November, 1983.

MEULENBELT, A., *For Ourselves: Our Bodies & Sexuality from Women's Point of View*. Sheba Feminist Publishers: London, 1981.

MOONEY, B., 'Issues of life and death'. *The Sunday Times*. 13-2-83, p.38.

MOORE, S.F. and MYERHOFF, B.G. (eds)., *Secular Ritual*. Van Gorcum: Assen, 1977.

MURRAY PARKES, C., 'Recent Bereavement as a cause of mental illness'. *British Journal of Psychiatry*, 1964, 110, 198.

MURRAY PARKES, C., 'The effects of bereavement on physical and mental health: a study of the case records of widows'. *British Medical Journal*, 1964, 2, 274.

MURRAY PARKES, C.M., *Bereavement. Studies of Grief in Adult Life*. Tavistock: London, 1972.

MYERHOFF, B.G., *Number Our Days*. Dutton: New York, 1978.

NICHOLS, K., 'Since Nobody's Perfect'. The Guardian. 4-5-83, p.13.

OKELY, J., 'The Self and Scientism'. *Journal of the Anthropological Society of Oxford*, 1975, 2, 171-188.

OKELY, J., *The Traveller-Gypsies*. Cambridge University Press, 1983.

RICHARD HILLIER, E., 'Terminal care in the United Kingdom'. In C.A. Corr & D.M. Corr (eds), *Hospice Care: Principles and Practice*. Faber & Faber: London, 1983.

RICOEUR, P., *The Rule of Metaphor*. (Originally published in French by Editions du Seuil: Paris, 1975). Routledge, Kegan & Paul: London, 1978.

RICOEUR, P., *Hermeneutics and the Human Sciences*. Cambridge University Press, 1981.

ROBB, B., *Sans Everything*. Nelson: Walton-on-Thames, 1967.

ROTH, J.A., '"Management Bias" in Social Science Study of Medical Treatment'. *Human Organization*, 1962, 21(1), 47-50.

SAUNDERS, C., *Care of the Dying*. (Originally published by Macmillan: London, 1959). Macmillan Journals: London, 1976.

SAUNDERS, C., 'The last stages of life'. *American Journal of Nursing*, 1965, 65, 1-3.

SAUNDERS, C., *The management of terminal illness*. London Hospital Medicine Publications, 1967.

SCARISBRICK, J.J., *What's Wrong with Abortion ?* Life: Leamington Spa, 1980.

SHELDON, J.H., *The Social Medicine of Old Age*. The Nuffield Foundation: London, 1948.

SMITH BOWEN, E., *Return to Laughter*. Gollanz: London, 1954.

SONTAG, S., *Illness as Metaphor*. Penguin Books: Harmondsworth, 1983.

STANNARD, D., *The Puritan Way of Death: a Study in Religion, Culture and Social Change*. Oxford University Press: New York, 1977.

STEVENSON, T.H.C., 'The vital statistics of wealth and poverty'. *Journal of the Royal Statistical Society*, 1928, 91.

SUDNOW, D., *Passing On: The Social Organization of Dying*. Prentice-Hall: New Jersey, 1967.

TAMBIAH, S.J., *Culture, Thought and Social Action*. Harvard University Press: Cambridge, Mass, 1985.

THANE, P., 'The history of provision for the elderly to 1929'. In D. Jerrome (ed), *Ageing in Modern Society*. Croom Helm: London, 1983.

THOMAS, C.B., 'Pre-cursors of premature death and disease'. *Annals of Internal Medicine*, 1976, 85, 653-658.

TINKER, A., *The Elderly in Modern Society*. Longman: Harlow, 1981.

TOWNSEND, P., *The Last Refuge*. Routledge, Kegan & Paul: London, 1964.

TOWNSEND, P., *Poverty in the United Kingdom*. Allen Lane: London, 1979.

TOWNSEND, P. and DAVIDSON, N., *Inequalities in Health: the Black Report*. Penguin Books: Harmondsworth, 1982.

TOWNSEND, P., FILLEMORE, P. and BEATTIE, A., *Health and Deprivation: Inequality and the North*. Croom Helm: London, 1987.

TOYNBEE, P., 'What Arthur Koestler could do with dignity, the law forced James Haig to do brutishly and cruelly'. *The Guardian*, 25-4-83, p.10.

TUNSTALL, J., *Old and Alone*. Routledge, Kegan & Paul: London, 1966.

TURNER, V., *The Forest of Symbols*. Cornell University Press: New York, 1967.

TWYCROSS, R.G., *The Dying Patient*. Christian Medical Publications: London, 1975.

TYLOR, E.B., *Primitive Culture*. Murray: London, 1871.

WENGER, C., 'Loneliness: a problem of measurement'. In D. Jerrome (ed), *Ageing in Modern Society*. Croom Helm: London, 1983.

WHALEY, J., (ed) *Mirrors of Mortality*. Europa Publications Ltd: London, 1981.

WICKS, M., *Old and Cold*. Heinemann: London, 1978.

WILLCOCKS, D., 'Evaluating the consumer view of residential care'. Synopsis of paper presented to the British Society of Gerontology Annual Conference; Hull, September, 1981.

WILLIAMS, I., *The Care of the Elderly in the Community*. Croom Helm: London, 1979.

Index

abortion, 40, 66
accidents, 22, 23, 25-6, 119, 120, 138
afterlife, belief in, 33
ageist jokes, 10, 14, 197-8
AIDS, 74, 75
America, 47, 76n
Americans, native, 86-7
Angela (worker at Highfield House), 115
anthropology, 2-3, 5, 16-17, 21-2, 28, 81, 198
Archer, Hannah (resident in Highfield House), 136-7
Ardener, E., 17
Aries, P., 28, 35, 46, 56
Armstrong, Lily (resident in Highfield House), 138
Arthur, Dr Leonard, 41

Bacon, Francis, 60, 61
Baldwin, Nellie (resident in Highfield House), 124-5, 138
Barthes, R., 188-9
Beattie, A., 73
behaviour and health, 64, 73, 75n, 76
Bell, Johnny (volunteer at Strathcarron Hospice), 176-7
bereavement, 1-5, 38, 44-9, 201
and understanding of death, 64
counselling/support in, 3, 4, 49-54, 162, 180-1
see also Cruse
Highfield House residents' experiences of, 134-5, 136-7, 151-2
stigmatisation of, 38, 47
Berger, J., 27, 56, 72-3, 80
birthdays, 96, 141, 146, 159
Black, Dora, 49
Black Report, 73
black, symbolism/ritual use of, 33, 34, 35, 44, 46, 87

Bloch, M., 10n, 65
blood, ritual and, 29-30, 31
Boas, F., 86-7
bodies, dead, see corpses
Bororo, 89
Bourdieu, P., 17, 20, 71-2, 84, 88
Bourne, S., 40
Brandon, Ethel (resident in Highfield House), 120
Bristol Cancer Help Centre, 69
British Medical Association, 66
Brooks, David, 6-7
Brown, Ada (resident in Highfield House), 139, 140

cancer, 69, 73-9, 113, 168
concealment of diagnoses of, 1, 76, 78
treatment of, 78, 158
candles, 29, 30, 31, 87
Cannadine, D., 28, 44-5
Capra, F., 56, 58, 60, 62, 70
care/caring work, 18-20, 111-13, 194, 197
and control, 24-5, 183-6, 191, 196
Carey, J., 41, 157n, 180n
Carey, Mabel (resident in Highfield House), 136
Carr, Ethel (resident in Highfield House), 128-30, 131, 132, 135, 140-1, 146, 149
Carstairs, Albert (resident in Highfield House), 126
Carstairs, Mabel (resident in Highfield House), 118-19
Carstairs, Maggie (resident in Highfield House), 125-6
Cartwright, Hannah (resident in Highfield House), 126
Cat Harbour, death ritual in, 33-4, 35
Challis, Fred (patient at Strathcarron

Hospice), 169-70, 172, 173, 176
chaos, 25-6
Chapman, Mrs (Matron at Highfield
    House), 93-8, 106, 107, 108,
    109, 186-90, 196
Charlton, Billy (patient at Strathcarron
    Hospice), 175
Charlton, Violet (patient at Strathcarron
    Hospice), 172
Christianity, *see* religion
class, *see* social class
cleanliness, 185, 188
Clough, R., 12-13, 20
'common sense', 17, 18, 57
control
    care and, 24-5, 183-6, 191, 196
    see also power
corpses, 46, 96, 117, 119
counselling, 4, 76, 80, 164
    see also under bereavement
Crawford, Elsie (resident in Highfield
    House), 151-2
Crawford, Mary (resident in Highfield
    House), 115
Crawford, Mrs (widow), 50, 52, 54, 181
Crosby, Annie (resident in Highfield
    House), 137, 183-6, 191, 196
Crowther, Sissy (resident in Highfield
    House), 139-40, 146, 149
Cruse, 4, 7, 55, 63n, 180-1
    history of, 49-50
crying, 1, 32-3
cultural style, 22-6
curses, 10

dance, 31, 81, 89
    imagery of death as, 70
Davidson, N., 73
Dawlish, Mr (widower), 50-1, 53, 54
death
    'acceptable', 3, 37, 109
    age at, 78, 109 as blow to society, 28,
        35
    as transition, 88
    attitudes to, 16, 90, 98, 124-6, 197
    'bad', 74
    causes of, 64, 73, 76, 78
    desire for, 67-8, 118, 187
    dignity in, 70-1
    experience of among different age
        groups, 45
    expression of conceptions of, 8
    history of attitudes to, 44-5, 46-7, 56-
        62

history of treatment of, 28, 29, 35-6
hospices and, 163, 166
imagery of, 70-1, 72
in Highfield House, *see under*
    Highfield House
in Strathcarron Hospice, *see under*
    Strathcarron Hospice
initiation and, 39, 64-5
maintenance of boundary with life,
    see life/death boundary
meaning, 9-10, 82-3
medicine and, 8, 27, 166
    see also medicalisation
'natural/unnatural', 70-1, 72, 74
need for social help over, 27
place of, 27, 36
professional appropriation of, 36, 37-
    8, 45-6
    see also medicalisation
publications about, 3, 4, 49, 82
rituals, *see* ritual
social, 115, 116, 157
social invisibility of, 27-8
stigmatisation of work concerned
    with, 37, 38
understanding of, and understanding
    of health, 58
validation and, 81-2
violent, and change, 32n
death-bed scenes, idealisation of, 35, 46
dependency, 11, 12, 15, 92, 143
    and style of care workers, 24
    global, 62
depression, 49, 68
Descartes, René, 60-1, 62
deterioration, measuring of, 111-12
deviance, sanctioned, 34
disability, 64, 65
    attitudes to, 40, 41, 66, 67, 68
distancing, 24
Dixon, Alice (resident in Highfield
    House), 118-19
doctors, 72
    work in hospices, 79-80
dressing up, 175-6, 191-2, 194-6
drugs, 164
Du Boulay, J., 29-31, 81, 84
Duffy, Vera (patient at Strathcarron
    Hospice), 171
Dunn, Michael (patient at Strathcarron
    Hospice), 177
dying, categorisation as, 92, 93, 178

ecology, 62
economics, 11-12, 14-15, 76, 162-3, 196
Edgar, Ian, 7
Edgar, Mabel (resident in Highfield House), 114
Elliott, Winnie (resident in Highfield House), 22-5, 179, 180, 183, 186, 196
emotions
    and cancer, 75
    displaying, 32-4, 38
    Hospice Movement and, 76-7
environment, 62, 75, 76
Epstein, Samuel S., 75n
Esslin, M., 86
euphemisms, 38-9, 119, 120
euthanasia, 43, 45, 66, 67-8
Evers, H., 12, 134, 143
EXIT, 43, 67-8
experientialism, 82, 83
    see also metaphors

Fabiola, 59, 60, 182
Fairhurst, E., 14, 198
families, 46-7, 50
fancy dress, 175-6, 191-2, 194-6
Faris, J.C., 33, 34
Farquar, Tommy (patient at Strathcarron Hospice), 175
Farr, Mr (patient at Strathcarron Hospice), 170, 173
fear, 157, 164
Feifel, H., 3
Fernandez, J.W., 86-7
Fillemore, Peter, 7, 73
finance, *see* economics
Firth, Janey (resident in Highfield House), 137-8
folk wisdom, 147, 148
Ford, C., 14
Foster, 'Granny' (resident in Highfield House), 114
Frazer, James, 5n
Frisch, M., 86
funeral parlours, stigmatisation of, 37
funerals, 2, 28, 46
    and privacy, 48
    Christian, liturgy, 10n, 71
    for stillborn babies, 41
    Hindu, 65
    in Cat Harbour, 34
    of Highfield House residents, 93, 141

Galileo Galilei, 60
Gandhi, Indira, 65
Garrow, Dr, 68
Geertz, C., 21-2, 57, 69, 85, 88, 199, 200
gender
and caring work, 18-19, 194
    and division of labour, 108, 193-4
    and experience of bereavement, 38
    and experience of old people's homes, 132, 134, 135, 140, 141-3
    and power within Highfield House, 108
    and views of own life history, 132-3, 134, 135
General Medical Council, 66
gerontological research, 11-14, 198
Gillie, O., 41-2
Glaser, B.G., 3
Goffman, E., 47
Gordon, Billy (patient at Strathcarron Hospice), 177
Gorer, G., 27, 44, 50
Grant, Arthur (resident in Highfield House), 128-9, 130-2, 133, 134, 136, 141, 142, 148, 150, 152, 153-4
    song set by, 141, 142-50, 151, 152-3
Greece, death ritual in, 29-31, 35, 81
Green Party, 62
grief, 49
    and ritual, 89
    expectations of, 34
    public expression of, 44, 45, 47-8
    unacceptability, 38
Grossarth-Maticek, R., 75n
gypsy culture, 31-3, 35, 81

Hall, Elsie (resident in Highfield House), 140
Halliwell, Ethel (resident in Highfield House), 149
handicap, *see* disability
Harmer, Roger (patient at Strathcarron Hospice), 175, 176
Hazan, H., 145-6
Headley, Bill (resident in Highfield House), 149
health
    expectations of, 65-6, 71
    politics of, 71, 72, 73, 80
    understanding of, 58-62, 63-4
Hepple, Alice (resident in Highfield House), 121-2, 140-1

Hertz, R., 10n, 28, 35
Heslop, Grace (resident in Highfield House), 136, 141, 150
Hicknott, Michael, 67
Highfield House, 18-19, 91-106, 183-90, 191
    Christmas concerts, 142
    daycare in, 184-6
    death within, 92, 93, 96, 101, 110, 117
    Friends of, 101, 104, 105, 134
    Guide Book, 101-3
    Matron, *see* Chapman, Mrs
    metaphor, *see under* metaphor
    mortuary, 96, 101, 117, 123
    naming of, 101-2, 103-4
    nicknaming of residents, 100
    Open Days, 101-2, 105, 141
    power within, *see under* power
    report book, 100-1, 113-15, 119
    residents' attitudes, 124-6
    residents' experiences of, 118, 121-2, 131, 138, 139-54, 179-80
    residents' previous experiences, 127-38, 140
    workers, 93-4, 107-9, 122-3, 179
    workers' attitudes, 125-6, 153
    see also old people's homes
Hillier, Richard, 3
Hindu metaphors, 64-5
Hinton, J., 3, 4, 82
Hobman, D., 11
'Hope' (poem), 143-50, 151, 152-3
hospice movement, 63, 69, 155-6, 158
    attitudes to death, 8, 16, 180
    background to, 3, 59, 77, 182
    ideology, 73, 76-7, 158, 182-3
    opposition to, 156
hospices, 4-5, 157-9
    finances, 76, 162-3, 196
    honesty in, 69-70
    naming of, 158, 159, 160-2, 163
    see also Strathcarron Hospice
Humm, M., 132-3
humour, *see* jokes

Iain (patient at Strathcarron Hospice), 171
identity
    and residence in old people's homes, 110-11, 112, 113-15, 126-8, 135, 138-9, 153
    ethnic, and death, 31-2, 81
    insider/outsider, 32, 33

Illich, I., 27, 56, 57, 58, 69, 70-1, 72-3, 74, 79, 80, 182
illusion, 86
imagery, *see* metaphor
'In Memoriam' columns, 47-8, 147
incontinence, 119-21, 185
individuality, *see* identity
inequality, 71, 72, 73, 77
infants, handicapped, 40, 41, 64, 65, 67, 68
information, *see* knowledge
initiation, death and, 39, 64-5
Isaacs, B., 11

Jackson, Mrs (widow), 51, 53-4
James, Allison, 7
Jan (worker at Highfield House), 24-5, 179, 183 Janet (worker at Highfield House), 122-3
Jenkins, David, Bishop, 87
Jenkins, Patrick, 73
Johnson, Alice (resident in Highfield House), 137
Johnson, M., 9, 15, 82, 83-4, 87, 106, 182
Johnson, Marie, 7
jokes, 10, 14, 113, 197-8
    as means of mentioning death, 125, 126
Just, R., 16-17

Kabyle, 71-2
Kapferer, B., 56
Kathy (worker at Highfield House), 123
killing, 41, 68
King, Mrs (resident in Highfield House), 114
Kirby, Mrs (widow), 51
knowledge
    fragmentation of, 56
    self and, *see* self and knowledge
    withholding of, 1, 76, 78
    withholding of, *see* information, withholding of
Knowles, Joan, 7
Koch, Robert, 74
Kübler-Ross, E., 49, 76

La Rochefoucauld, F., 82, 83, 196
Lakoff, G., 9, 15, 82, 83-4, 87, 106, 182
language, 16, 38-9, 58-9, 85, 88, 105
    in Highfield House, 100, 114, 118-19, 120-1, 122, 123
    in naming of homes, 103-4

nicknames, 100
see also metaphor
laying out of bodies, 46, 96
Lévi-Strauss, C., 89
Lewis, E., 40-1
life
    defining, 40-1, 64, 65
    definitions excluding old age/dying, 92, 93, 115, 178
    see also life/death boundary *and* life/death continuum
    morality of maintaining, 41-4
    quality of, 42-4, 65-8, 80
life/death boundary, 36-40, 54-5, 65-7, 156, 166
    and metaphor, 84
    maintenance of within Highfield House, 116-19, 121-3
life/death continuum, 155, 161, 166, 190-1, 201
life expectancy, 65, 73, 76, 197
'life satisfaction' tests, 12-14
liturgy, 10n, 71
Locke, John, 61
loneliness, 13
Lorraine (worker at Highfield House), 107
Lumsden, Charlie (resident in Highfield House), 123
Lyons, Albert (resident in Highfield House), 133-5, 141, 149
Lyons, Mark, 43

McDonald, B., 92-3, 125
McIntyre, Fiona (patient at Strathcarron Hospice), 170-1, 172, 174, 176
McIntyre, Jack (resident in Highfield House), 134, 141, 142, 152
Malinowski, B., 5
Malley, John, 7
marriage, Greek death ritual and, 30, 31, 81
Martins, H., 27-8
Mary (worker at Highfield House), 108
Maureen (worker at Highfield House), 122-3
May, Betty (resident in Highfield House), 188
meaning, 10, 82, 85-6, 88
    culture and, 57-8
    death and, 9-10, 35, 82-3
    hospices and, 157
    pain/suffering and, 57, 79, 182

ritual and, 28, 29
theatre and, 86
see also metaphor
media, 27, 39
medical infallibility, myth of, 68-9, 72, 73, 74, 77, 78
medical treatment, 41-4, 57, 66
    holistic, 62, 80
    limitations, 74
    military metaphors of, 78
medicalisation, 8, 36, 57
    and understanding, 37-8
    ethics and, 66-7
    history of, 57-62, 70-3
metaphor, 9-10, 11, 16, 21-2, 25, 26, 54-5, 82-8
    arbitrariness, 87
    death in, 39, 64-5, 88
    from nature, 37, 147, 148
    illness and, 69, 74-6, 78
    in Highfield House, 94, 97-106, 110, 116-17, 118, 123
    in Strathcarron Hospice, 163
    of caring/controlling, 24, 25
    power and, 15, 106
    thought and, 82
    used by Highfield House residents, 125
    see also language, meaning and symbolism
methodology, 6, 8-9, 10-21
Meulenbelt, A., 40
mobility, 111
Molly (resident in Highfield House), 187
Mooney, Bel, 67
Moore, S.F., 58, 87, 89, 200
murder charges, 41
Murray Parkes, Colin M., 3, 4, 49
Myerhoff, B.G., 58, 87, 89, 151, 200
myths, 9, 72, 82
    see also medical infallibility

naming, 100, 103-4, 158, 159, 160-2, 163
nature
    attitudes to, 60-2
    metaphors of, 37, 147, 148
Ndembu, 39n
Nellie (resident in Highfield House), 124-5, 138
Neville, Y., 11
Newfoundland, 33-4, 35
newspapers, 'In Memoriam' columns, 47-8, 147

Newton, Isaac, 61
Nichols, K., 68-70
Norman (worker at Highfield House), 107, 108
nuclear holocaust, threat of, 45

objectivity, 9, 14
    see also self and knowledge
occasions, 159, 175-7, 191-2, 194-6
Okely, Judith, 7, 14, 31, 32-3, 81, 84
old age
    attitudes to, 10, 11, 15, 197-8
    history of categorisation, 11-12, 13, 15
    physical experience of, 11, 14, 20, 22-6, 92-3, 111-12, 125, 146
    and imagery of 'Hope', 144-5, 146
old people
    outliving own generation, 109-10
    social marginality, 109-11, 115
old people's homes, 3, 12-13
    attitudes to death in, 81
    criteria for admission to, 116, 148
    fiction of ordinariness, 156-7
    historical background, 180
    meaning of, 25
    naming of, 103-4
    purpose, 115-16
    reasons for entering, 131, 138, 139
    residents attending hospices, 168, 169, 170-1
    residents' resistance to interviews, 19
    work in, 18-20
    workers' style, 22-5, 109, 111, 112-13, 186
    see also Highfield House
Owen, Margaret (worker at Strathcarron Hospice), 174, 175, 176, 195

pain, 57, 78-9, 80, 182
'pampering', 90, 98
Parry, J., 10n, 65
participant observation, 15, 17-21
Patterson, Mrs (bereaved mother), 51
Pearson, John, 41
physical experience, 83, 84
    see also under old age
poems, 47-8, 143-50, 151, 152-3, 159
pollution, 29-30, 32, 33, 36, 185
Porter, Mrs (resident in Highfield House), 137, 146
postulates, 87, 89
potlatch, 87
power, 14-15, 106

and research, 15-16
    hospices and, 158, 180
    meaning and, 85-6
    weakness and, 20, 125, 153, 179, 186
    within Highfield House, 96, 99, 102, 107-9, 113-15, 153-4, 189-90
    within Strathcarron Hospice, 191-6
privacy, 24, 46-7, 48, 50, 174
problem solving, 180-2

Radcliffe-Brown, R., 5
Randolph Hill Mansion, *see* Strath-carron Hospice
Reed, 8
regeneration, 10
religion, 29, 46, 56-9, 85-6
    and imagery of death, 70-1
    and medical treatment, 57
    changes in, 66, 87
    fundamentalist, 62
    hospices and, 158, 161, 164, 167, 182-3, 193
    imagery of, 144, 145, 147, 148-50, 152-3
Renshaw, Tom (patient at Strathcarron Hospice), 174-5, 176
research methods, *see* methodology
residential care, *see* hospices *and* old people's homes
retirement, 11-12
Richardson, 45
Ricoeur, P., 82, 84-5, 87, 200
ritual, 8, 28-35, 39, 54, 84, 156, 199-200
    and power, 85, 86, 87-90
    and privacy, 48
    and transition, 156
    and war, 44-5
    danger in, 58, 87
    framing in, 85, 86, 87, 89
    healing, 56
    idealisation of, 28-9, 45
    legal requirement, 58
    old people's homes and, 98
    separation and, 156
Robb, B., 11
Robson, Ethel (resident in Highfield House), 123
Robson, 'Gran' (resident in Highfield House), 140, 141
role play, 17
romantic love, 104-5
Roth, J.A., 14
rubbish, 125

St Benedict's Hospice, 158
St Christopher's Hospice, 155, 157-8
St Joseph's Hospice, 59, 155
Sally (Matron at Strathcarron Hospice), 192, 195
Samwell, Inge, 7
'satisfaction' tests, 12-14
Saunders, Cicely, 3, 49, 76n, 155, 157, 164
Saunders, Mary (worker at Strathcarron Hospice), 173-4
Scarisbrick, J.J., 40
Scott, Tom, 7
secrecy, 1, 76, 78
    see also silencing
self and knowledge, 5, 8-9, 14-16, 26, 198, 199
sexuality, 93, 105
Sheldon, J.H., 11
silencing, 92, 93, 113, 125
    see also secrecy
Simpson, Bob, 7
skills, caring, 18-20, 194
Smith Bowen, E., 5
Smith, George (resident in Highfield House), 133, 134, 141
social class, 71
    and cancer, 76, 77
    and caring work, 19, 23-4, 26
    and cleanliness, 185
    and experience of old people's homes, 140, 143, 185-6
    and life expectancy, 73, 197
    hospice care and, 167
social events/'occasions', 33, 34
Society of the Compassionate Friends, The, 63n
Sontag, S., 56, 69, 74-5, 76, 78, 80
spirals, 30, 31
Sri Lanka, 56
Stannard, D., 28
status, death and, 71
Stevenson, Dr T.H.C., 73
stigmatisation, 125
    of bereaved people, 38, 47
    of people with AIDS, 75
    of people with cancer, 75, 76-7
    of work concerned with death, 37, 38
stillbirth, 40-1, 66
Strathcarron Hospice, 7, 22n, 77, 79-80, 159-66, 168, 190-6
    chaplain, 164
    criteria for admission to, 162, 164
    daycare in, 79, 162, 169-77, 191-2

death in, 161, 162, 164
Matron, 192, 195
mortuary, 161
naming, 159, 160-2, 163
'occasions' in, 175-6, 191-2, 194-6
patients' experience of, 164, 167-72, 174-7
power within, 191-6
workers, 173-4, 192-6
voluntary, 19, 162, 164, 167, 176-7, 193
Strauss, A.L., 3
stress, 113
subjectivity, 9
    see also self and knowledge
Sudnow, D., 47
suffering, 57
    see also pain
Susan (worker at Highfield House), 107
Swinburn, Gertie (resident in Highfield House), 114
symbolism
    hospices and, 157, 158, 160-1
    water, 158, 160-1, 163
    see also metaphor

Tambiah, S.J., 10
Thane, P., 11, 15n
theatre, 86, 157
Thomas, C.B., 75n
Thomas, Dr Michael, 66
Thompson, Mrs (widow), 51
time, 9, 70
    framing, 156, 157
    organisation within Highfield House, 110-12
Tinker, A., 12
Torrie, Margaret, 49-50
Townsend, P., 11, 73
Toynbee, P., 42, 43-4
tradition, 158, 160-1
transplants, 41-2, 64, 65, 66
tuberculosis, 69, 74
Tunstall, J., 11
Turner, V., 39n, 87-8, 200
Twilight Nurses, 38, 76n
Twycross, R.G., 78
Tylor, Edward Burnett, 5n

understanding, 21-2, 57, 58
    medicalisation and, 37-8
    see also meaning
USA, 47, 76n

Valentine's cards, 101-2, 104-5
vampires, 30, 31
verse, *see* poems
victim-blaming, 64, 73, 74-5

war, 44-5, 130-1, 136
Ward, Isabella, 43
water, symbolism of, 158, 160-1, 163
Waters, Ada (patient at Strathcarron Hospice), 171
Watson, Morag (patient at Strathcarron Hospice), 170-1, 172, 173, 174
Watson, Mrs (resident in Highfield House), 121, 122
weakness and power, *see under* power
Wenger, C., 13

West, Molly (resident in Highfield House), 121, 122
Wicks, M., 11
widows, 38, 44
  see also bereavement
Willcocks, D., 13
Williams, I., 11
Wilson, Bel, 7
Winnie (resident in Highfield House), 22-5, 179, 180, 183, 186, 196
Women's Movement, the, 62
Worden, ?, 49
world views, 58-63, 155, 182, 198-9

Young, Malcolm, 7